Kentucky Innovators

FAMOUS (AND INFAMOUS) KENTUCKIANS WHO LED THE WAY IN THEIR FIELD

Kentucky Innovators

FAMOUS (AND INFAMOUS) KENTUCKIANS WHO LED THE WAY IN THEIR FIELD

PAUL W. BASS

Acclaim Press
MORLEY, MISSOURI

Acclaim Press
— Your Next Great Book —
P.O. Box 238
Morley, MO 63767
(573) 472-9800
www.acclaimpress.com

Book & Cover Design: Frene Melton

ISBN: 978-1-956027-21-1 | 1-956027-21-1
Library of Congress Control Number: 2022931430

First Printing: 2022
Printed in the United States of America
10 9 8 7 6 5 4 3 2 1

Contents

Chapter Six: **Politics** *(Legislative and Judicial)*

Chapter Seven: **Sports**

Chapter Eight: **Others**

Acknowledgments

Two individuals provided the inspiration and motivation for this book. Dr. Jerry Plunkett, from Dixon, Missouri, gave me the initial concept for a book of Missouri Innovators. His original idea of examining scientific and industrial innovators was expanded to include other areas of personal achievements. Doug Sikes, publisher of Acclaim Press in Sikeston, Missouri, encouraged me to consider a second book of innovators from the neighboring state of Kentucky. He challenged me to continue the initial concept for books of innovators from other neighboring states: Oklahoma, Kansas, and Arkansas. These are future projects under consideration.

My wife of forty-nine years, Jan, has patiently provided the very necessary proofreading of the first draft for this book. She still has hopes that I might learn from my past writing mistakes.

Randy Baumgardner, from Acclaim Press, has provided his usual great service as a careful designer and editor. His attention to guiding the book from final draft to completed product has been an interesting journey for this author.

To these and others who have assisted in proofreading, I extend my true thanks and appreciation.

Author's Notes

For many writers, the author must persuade the publisher of the author's great idea for a book. In the case of this book, the publisher had to persuade the author to write the book. In 2018, I completed my twelfth book, *Missouri Innovators*. It was written at the suggestion of Dr. Jerry Plunkett, who was an inventor from Dixon, Missouri. He also encouraged me to consider a series of books on innovators from other states.

Missouri Innovators was one of the most enjoyable books in my researching history. I learned many new, fascinating facts about distinguished Missourians. Some Missourians were well known and others were new discoveries for me. I am proud to be a Missourian and was honored to have discovered the great accomplishments of these fellow citizens.

My publisher, Doug Sikes, was very encouraged by the *Missouri Innovators* project. He saw the potential of statewide appeal for the book and the word-of-mouth promotion for the book. I had done many book signings and presentations in the preceding years with my book on *The History of Fort Leonard Wood* (2016). Those experiences caused me to look forward to the same promotional events across the state with this new book.

Doug travels and does a lot of book sales in the state of Kentucky. He asked me to consider writing a book about Kentucky innovators. He was confident that he could sell a lot of books there. After some preliminary research, I discovered a number of individuals from Kentucky who fit the criteria of being an innovator. Doug and I began to consider the possibility of a continuing series from other neighboring states. Preliminary research has also convinced me of the feasibility of such a project. That brought me back to Dr. Jerry Plunkett's original suggestion. Other states now being considered for the immediate future are Oklahoma, Kansas, and Arkansas.

Introduction

Kentucky is known as the "Bluegrass State." It is a nickname based on the bluegrass found in many of Kentucky pastures due to the fertile soil. The state has also provided the fertile soil for the growth of the individual spirit that produces innovations to add to the quality of life for people around the world. This book attempts to examine a number of those individuals in the state's history who are innovators.

What is the difference between an innovator and an inventor? Defining terms may offer some insight. An "inventor" is defined as one who "originates or creates as a product of one's own ingenuity, experimentation, or contrivance." An innovator is one who "introduces something new; makes changes in anything established." An inventor may create a product, but an innovator may make it better.

There are a few books written about famous Kentuckians, which are written on an older children's level by talented elementary school teachers. It is also necessary to consider the difference between a "famous Kentuckian" and a "Kentucky innovator." Famous Kentuckians may not be innovators, and Kentucky innovators may not be famous. An attempt will be made to consider those famous Kentuckians who were or are innovators.

The use of the word "innovator" in this book is used to describe individuals who have made significant contributions in various fields of life. These individuals all have some connection with Kentucky. They were either born in Kentucky or chose to live in Kentucky. They are recognized as sources of great pride for the state. Many of them, sadly, had to leave the state to find implementation of their innovations. Regrettably, those making their way into actual production of innovative technology usually found outlets outside of the state.

It was necessary to limit the number of Kentuckians considered for this book. In the individual fields, there are others who could have been included in detailed examination. A listing of other notables in each field is also included, acknowledging their contributions and perhaps inspiring a reader's additional research. The selection of the individuals in the book is purely the choice of the author. There are others that could have been included.

The internet continues to expand and make many resources available for quick research. There is still a cautionary note about the credibility of some websites. At least five or more websites have been compiled for each subject to determine information that is accurate and as current as possible.

This book has several purposes. First is to educate Kentuckians about their proud individual heritage and accomplishments. Second is to encourage our state leaders to provide more business and economic incentives in helping the innovators to remain in Kentucky for research and production purposes. Third is to inspire our youth to be challenged by their fellow Kentuckians who have succeeded in personal innovations.

It would be great to see this listing of respected Kentucky innovators grow exponentially statewide because of increased awareness of the importance of education, research, and industry. With the advances of technology and communication, Kentuckians have every opportunity to continue to accomplish importance progressive innovations.

Kentucky Innovators

FAMOUS (AND INFAMOUS) KENTUCKIANS WHO LED THE WAY IN THEIR FIELD

Chapter One

Entertainers

(television, movies)

George Clooney

Lexington

Actor/Director/Producer

Many of the innovators in the state series have passed on. Only a few are recognized for their accomplishments while they are still active among us. Kentucky is fortunate to have a number of such current innovators, especially in the field of entertainment. One of the more recognizable names is that of George Clooney. He has excelled in several areas of entertainment and social activitivism

He is an actor, director, producer, screenwriter, activist, businessman, and philanthropist. He came from a very public and famous family. He is a very familiar face and presence among American audiences today. He is a product of Kentucky.

George Timothy Clooney was born May 6, 1961, in Lexington, Kentucky. He was born to Nina Bruce (Warren) and Nick Clooney. Nina was a former beauty pageant queen, and Nick was a former anchorman and television host. Nick's sister, Rosemary, was also a famous singer. George was born into a family of mixed European ancestry. He is very distantly related to the mother of Abraham Lincoln.

He spent most of his childhood and youth in Ohio and Kentucky. He was raised in a strict Catholic family but later left the faith. He began his early education at the Blessed Sacrament School in Fort

Mitchell, Kentucky. When his family briefly moved to Ohio, he attended St. Michael's School in Columbus before going on to Western Row Elementary Public School in Mason, Ohio. He transferred to St. Susanna School in Mason. The Clooneys left Ohio in 1974 when George was in seventh grade and returned to Augusta, Kentucky. In middle school George developed Bell's palsy, which left part of his face paralyzed. It lasted for nearly a year.

George attended Augusta High School, where he was a good student. He developed an interest in baseball and basketball. After high school he even tried out for the Cincinnati Reds baseball team with unsuccessful results. He went on to attend Northern Kentucky University for several years and transferred to the University of Cincinnati, majoring in broadcast journalism. He never received a degree.

He found his real life's education in the business world. He sold women's shoes, sold door-to-door insurance, stocked store shelves, did construction work, and even cut tobacco. His break in the acting world came when his cousin, Miguel Ferrer, got him a small part in a feature film. That experience led to his big break in television in 1979, playing the handyman on *Facts of Life*. In 1984, he played Dr. Doug Ross on the popular sitcom, *E/R*. He had other roles in television on *Golden Girls*, *Roseanne* (1988), *Baby Talk*, *Bodies of Evidence*, and *Sisters* (1991). His real notoriety came with the renewed role of Dr. Doug Ross on the award-winning drama series, *ER* (1994–1999). He received two Primetime Emmy Award nominations in 1995 and 1996 for Best Actor in a Television Series. He also received three Golden Globe nominations in 1995, 1996, and 1997 for the same category. In 1997 he was voted "Sexiest Man Alive" by *People Magazine*. In 2003 he was ranked #3 of the "Top Sexiest Men." In 2006, he was again voted "Sexiest Man Alive."

The popular and professional performances on television led him to a number of important roles in significant films: *From Dusk Till Dawn* (1996), *One Fine Day* (1996), *Batman and Robin* (1997), *Out of Sight* (1998), *The Thin Red Line* (1998), and *Three Kings* (1999). Although he was not pleased with his role in *Batman and Robin*, the other appearances won him acclaim.

The year 2000 found Clooney starring in two very popular movies: *The Perfect Storm* and *O Brother, Where Art Thou?*. These two movies increased the public's awareness of his name and talent. The next year he starred in the very successful movie *Ocean's Eleven*. The movie's success prompted two sequels in 2004 and 2007.

In 2001, Clooney teamed with Steven Soderbergh to found a new production company, Section Eight Productions. This allowed Clooney to have his directorial debut in 2002 with the movie *Confessions of A Dangerous Mind*. His movie *Syriana* (2005) earned him his first Oscar for Best Supporting Actor. His movie *Good Night and Good Luck* (2006) earned Clooney two Academy Award Nominations for Best Director and Best Original Screenplay. Section Eight Production closed in 2006.

That same year Clooney teamed up with Grant Heslov to form Smokehouse Productions. He was able to give more attention to his directing and producing while still finding acting opportunities. The movie *Michael Clayton* (2007) earned him a Best Actor nomination. Other movies from Smokehouse Productions were *Leatherheads* (2008), *The Men Who Stare at Goats* (2009), *Burn After Reading* (2008), *Fantastic Mr. Fox* (2009), and *Up In the Air* (2009). Although he was nominated for several awards, it was not until his performance in *The Descendants* (2011) that he won the Golden Globe Best Actor Award. 2013 was a major milestone for Clooney with his film *Argo*. It won the Best Picture Award from the Golden Globes, BAFTA, and the Academy Award. Other film projects in 2013 were *The Ides of March*, *Gravity*, *The Monuments Men*, and *August: Osage County*. Other films of Clooney were *Tomorrowland* (2015), *Money Monster* (2016) and *Suburbicon* (2017).

Clooney is also very active in political and humanitarian causes. He has sought funds and attention for the crises in Darfur and Haiti. He was appointed a United Nations "Messenger for Peace" in January 2008. In 2017, Clooney and his wife Amal donated $1 million to the Southern Poverty Law Center to help fight hate groups.

He has long supported national Democratic candidates. He is a supporter of gay rights. When he was attacked in the 2016 presidential campaign by Donald Trump and Trump's supporters as being a "Hollywood Elite," he replied:

> Here's the thing: I grew up in Kentucky. I sold insurance door-to-door. I sold ladies' shoes. I worked at an all-night liquor store. I would buy suits that were too big and too long and cut the bottoms off to make ties so I'd have a tie to go on job interviews. I grew up understanding what it was like to

> not have health insurance for eight years. So this idea that I'm somehow the 'Hollywood Elite' and this guy [Trump] who takes a s--- in a gold toilet is somehow the man of the people is laughable. People in Hollywood, for the most part, are people from the Midwest who moved to Hollywood to have a career....

Regarding his social life. Clooney has had a number of relationships with various women of notoriety. He was married in December 1989 to Talia Balsam, a marriage that lasted for four years. After that he continued relationships with other famous women. In September 2014 he married his current wife, the human rights lawyer Amal Alamuddin. On June 6, 2017, Amal gave birth to a daughter, Ella, and a son, Alexander. They currently live in Los Angeles, California, and own several other international homes.

Clooney is a very private person and struggles to remain so. He expresses his thoughts on the subject very clearly: "I'd rather have a rectal exam on live TV by a fellow with cold hands than have a Facebook page!" Regarding his career, he stated, "Directing is really exciting. In the end, it's more fun to be the painter than the paint." When asked in an interview about any desire to run for office, he replied, "No, I've slept with too many women, I've done too many drugs, and I've been to too many parties."

George Clooney continues to be an innovator in various fields of the entertainment industry. He has earned his significant monetary rewards and has a desire to make this a better country and a better world. All of this began early in his life in the nourishing soil of Kentucky.

Johnny Depp

Owensboro

Actor

Another currently popular actor with great acclaim has early Kentucky roots. He has continued some important Kentucky traditions in his value of hard work and his love for horses. He found recognition and notoriety beyond the borders of Kentucky. Johnny Depp has been described as one of the most versatile actors in Hollywood.

John Christopher Depp II was born on June 9, 1963, in Owensboro, Kentucky. His parents were Betty Sue Wells and John Christopher Depp. He was the youngest of four children. His mother was a waitress, and his father was a civil engineer. His family origins can be traced back to Elizabeth Key Grinstead, the first slave to sue for her freedom in 1655.

The family moved numerous times in his early childhood. He lived in over twenty different locations until settling with the family in Miramar, Florida, in 1970. When he was twelve years old, his mother bought him a guitar. Although schooling was not a high priority due to all the family moves, he did enjoy learning to play the guitar. He found his identity and social acceptance playing in garage bands. He achieved moderate success with a band called The Kids.

He was close to his grandfather, who died when Depp was seven years old. His parents divorced when Depp was fifteen. That same year he dropped out of school. He would later recall, "I'd been in high school three years, and I may have just walked in yesterday. I had, like, eight credits. I was in my third year of high school and I didn't want to be there. I was bored out of my mind and I hated it."

The band headed west for Los Angeles with hopes of signing a recording contract. The band changed their name to Six Gun Method, but was unsuccessful in finding a record deal. The band split up, and Depp joined with a band called Rock City Angels. He and the band achieved moderate success with the album *Young Man's Blues.*

The band's bass player and singer had a sister who attracted Depp's attention. On December 20, 1983, Depp married Lori Anne Allison. To make financial ends meet, the pair found employment in other areas of work. Lori worked as a makeup artist, and Depp worked as a telemarketer for ballpoint pens. During their time in Los Angeles, Lori introduced Depp to her friend, actor Nicolas Cage. Cage encouraged Depp to consider a career in acting. Depp made his film debut in 1984 in a low-budget but very successful movie, *A Nightmare on Elm Street.* The marriage ended in divorce in 1985.

In 1987, Depp's big hit came when he starred in the popular television series *21 Jump Street.* His role lasted for four seasons of the series. In 1990, he found great success teaming up with director Tim Burton. They would begin a long relationship together in producing widely acclaimed films. The first was the very successful *Edward Scissorhands* in 1990. The decade of the 1990s saw Depp's popularity rise as a result of his appearing in a number of very good films. In 1994, he teamed with Burton to star in the lead role of *Ed Wood.* Depp was nominated for the Golden Globe Award for Best Actor. In 1997, he played a major role in *Donnie Brasco.* In 1998, he appeared in the film *Fear and Loathing in Las Vegas.* That same year he also appeared in *The Astronaut's Wife.* In 1999, Depp found a winning team effort with Burton in the film *Sleepy Hollow.* The 1990s proved Depp capable of playing a variety of different roles very successfully. That would provide increased opportunities for unique roles in the next decade.

In 2001, Depp starred as Abberline in *From Hell.* In 2003, he starred in *Once Upon a Time in Mexico.* That same year he was introduced as Captain Jack Sparrow in *Pirates of the Caribbean: The Curse of the Black Pearl.* The family film was an enormous success, only adding to Depp's character roles. The film would lead to later sequels. In 2003, he was voted *People* Magazine's "Sexiest Man Alive" and *E!* "Entertainer of the Year." In 2004, he starred in *Secret Window* and in *Finding Neverland.* Another collaboration with Burton took place in 2005 with the film *Charlie and the Chocolate Factory.* He was again nominated for a Golden Globe Award for Best Actor. In 2007, he starred in *Sweeney Todd: The Demon Barber of Fleet Street.* In 2009, he was again voted *People* Magazine's "Sexiest Man Alive." In 2010, Depp starred in *Alice in Wonderland.* In 2012, he starred in *Dark Shadows.* There were many other films throughout the two decades mentioned above. Since 2012, Depp has made many other films with future projects under consideration. In June 2012, Depp won the MTV Generation Award.

Depp's expanded his professional life by establishing his own production company, Infinitum Nihil ("Nothing is Forever"), in 2004. The company was able to produce several of the successful films mentioned above. Depp continued his early interest in music, especially the guitar. He has played accompaniment to several successful singers and in 2015 formed a supergroup with Alice Cooper and Joe Perry called Hollywood Vampires. He also became a winemaker and co-owned a French restaurant in Paris. In 2017, his $3,000,000 Kentucky horse failed to sell at auction.

His personal relationships were not as successful as his films. After the divorce in 1985, Depp had a series of short-termed relationships with some famous costars in his films. Among these were Jennifer Grey, Sherilyn Fenn, Winona Ryder, and Kate Moss. While filming in France in 1998, Depp met French Acres sans singer, Vanessa Paradis. They have two children. They separated in June 2012. He dated and in May 2016 married actor and model Amber Heard. Within a week, Heard got a restraining order against Depp claiming "verbal and physical abuse." After a long and very public airing of grievances, a settlement was reached in December 2016. A divorce was granted one month later.

Depp has an unfortunate record of civil complaints against him in his world travels and business dealings. He has also filed claims against some past business associates who purportedly cheated him. He has found some stability in his relationships with his two children. He confessed that "Anything I've done up till May 27, 1999, was kind of an illusion, existing without living. My daughter, the birth of my daughter, gave me life." He also stated, "The only creatures that are evolved enough to convey pure love are dogs and infants."

Depp has appeared in over fifty-nine films and made twenty-six music recordings. Many of the roles Depp played involved scenes with horses. His love and great respect for horses was generated because of his upbringing around these creatures in Kentucky.

Irene Dunne

Louisville

Actress

She is named the most successful actress to never have won an Academy Award. Although she was nominated five times, the prize eluded her. She found her voice and talent and was trained in Kentucky. Her fondest family experiences happened in her home state. She was widely respected by her colleagues for her variety of acting genres. She is also recognized for her great philanthropic heart and fundraising efforts. She was able to avoid the sensationalism and negative aspects of life in Hollywood.

Irene Marie Dunn (an "e" would be added to her surname later in her career) was born on December 20, 1898, in Louisville, Kentucky. Her parents were Adelaide Antoinette Henry Dunn and Joseph John Dunn. Her father was steamboat inspector for the federal government, and her mother was an accomplished pianist. Irene was the oldest of two children, having a younger brother named Charles. The home was filled with music, and Irene was trained at early age with piano and voice lessons. She had fond memories of her early family experiences in Kentucky. Her first production performance was in Louisville at the age of five. She appeared in a production of *A Midsummer Night's Dream*. She stated, "No triumph of either my stage or screen career has ever matched the excitement of the trips down the Mississippi on the river boats with my father." Sadly her father died in 1909. The family moved to St. Louis, Missouri, and then moved back to her mother's hometown of Madison, Illinois.

The family was raised in a strict but happy Catholic home. Irene performed in church and middle and high school plays. She graduated from Madison High School in 1916. After graduation, she attended the Oliver Willard Pierce Academy of Fine Arts in Indianapolis, Indiana, for one year with a scholarship. There she perfected her singing talent. The next year she moved to St. Louis and earned her teaching certificate from Webster College. Turning down a teaching opportunity in Indiana, she accepted a scholarship to study music at the Chicago Musical College.

In 1920, she moved to New York in hopes of finding opportunities to perform in professional musicals. At that time she changed her last name by adding an "e" to the end—Dunne. Although she was unable to find acceptance in the Metropolitan Opera Company, she was able to find work with a traveling theater company. She made her Broadway debut in 1922 in the production of *The Clinging Vine*. She found continual work in other musicals. Her big break came in 1929 with her performance in *Show Boat*. That role led to the signing of a contract with RKO movie production Company.

Dunne found film success with her debut in the 1930 movie *Leathernecking*. Her role in the 1931 movie *Cimarron* earned her an Academy Award nomination for Best Actress. She played roles in *Back Street* (1932), *Magnificent Obsession* (1935), *Sweet Adeline* (1935), *Roberta* (1935), and the movie version of *Show Boat* (1936). Her acting and singing were highly recognized and rewarded with then significant payrolls for her performances—$150,000 per movie.

Dunne added to her successful recognized talents when she began to appear in comedic roles. At first uncomfortable with the new roles, she soon found herself enjoying the change of performances. She appeared in *Theodora Goes Wild* (1936), *The Awful Truth* (1937), *Love Affair* (1939), and *My Favorite Wife* (1940). She was again nominated for a Best Actress Academy Award for her roles in *Theodora Goes Wild* and *The Awful Truth*.

The 1940s were very good for Dunne. She found excellent roles and gave memorable performances in movies such as *Penny Serenade* (1940), *The White Cliffs of Dover* (1944), *Anna and the King of Siam* (1946), *Life with Father* (1947), *I Remember Mama* (1948), and *The Mudlark* (1950). She received another Academy Award Nomination for Best Actress in her role in *The Mudlark*. Dunne continued with one other film, *It Grows on Trees*, before her retirement in 1952. She said, "I drifted into acting and drifted out. Acting is not everything. Living is."

Dunne remained aloof from the traditional Hollywood image of bizarre behavior and lifestyle. She found her stability in her own family. In 1928, she married Francis Dennis Griffith, a dentist from New York. They had a long-distance marriage before he gave up his practice to join her in Hollywood several years later. They were both members of the Knights of Malta and members of the Church of the Good Shepherd. In 1936, they adopted a four-year-old girl, Mary Frances Griffith, from the New York Founding Hospital. The family settled in a new home in Beverly Hills. They would later have two grandchildren. They remained together until his death in 1965. It is certain that the happiness in the marriage and family was influenced by the early childhood memories of Irene.

Upon Dunne's retirement from films, she found time and opportunity to participate in television performances on *Ford's Theatre*, *General Electric Theater*, and the *Schlitz Playhouse of Stars*. More personally satisfying for Dunne was her participation in charitable concerns. Her affiliation with the Roman Catholic Church was very important. In 1949, Notre Dame University bestowed on her the Laetare Medal. She was called "an example of talented Christian Womanhood." Her work as a fundraiser for various Catholic organizations was widely recognized.

Dunne also worked as a fundraiser for the American Red Cross, American Cancer Society, Boy Scouts of America, and the Republican National Party. In 1955, she was asked by Walt Disney to christen the Mark Twain River Boat on Dedication Day at Disneyworld. It is certain that thoughts of father were very present at that ceremony. In 1957, President Eisenhower honored her by his appointment of her as one of five alternate delegates to the United Nations. She received numerous honorary degrees, which included those from Chicago Musical College, Loyola University, and Mt. St. Mary's College. Regarding her educational experiences, she said, "No education is ever wasted and everything you learn is helpful in acting."

Dunne's last public appearance was in April 1985 at the dedication of a bust in her honor at St. John's (Roman Catholic) Hospital. Her foundation had raised over $20,000,000 for the organization. She was too ill to attend the Kennedy Center Honors program for her in 1985. She died in her home on September 4, 1990, as a result of heart failure. She was buried at Calvary Cemetery in East Los Angeles. Her personal papers were given to the University of Southern California. Upon her death, President Ronald Reagan stated, "Losing her is like losing a member of the family. She's a special lady who will live in our hearts forever."

Dunne performed in many stage productions, made over forty-one movies, and appeared in numerous television appearances. She was remembered as maintaining a sense of normalcy in Hollywood. She once stated, "There seems to be a general impression that to be known as normal in Hollywood is akin to being labeled as a rare animal in a zoo."

Dunne's "normalcy" is attributed to her happy family beginnings in Kentucky. Deep family values and an environment for development of talent certain qualify Irene Dunne as a Kentucky innovator.

D. W. Griffith

La Grange

Filmmaker

Before there were talking films, before there were full-length motion pictures, before there was the booming city of Hollywood, a Kentucky innovator used his early life experiences and family heritage to become one of the most prolific and creative film producers in history. He was a product of post-Civil War prejudices and the effective use of the American Industrial Revolution creations for the common man.

David Llewelyn Wark Griffith was born on January 22, 1875, in LaGrange, Kentucky, on farmland. He was one of seven children born to the family. His mother was Mary Perkins Oglesby. His father was Jacob Wark "Roaring Jake" Griffith. He had served as a lieutenant colonel during the Civil War in the Confederate Army. He served in the Kentucky Orphan Brigade under the leadership of General John C. Calhoun. Jake was wounded several times during the war. The children were entertained by the stories of their father's war stories and influenced by his racial prejudice, evidenced by many of the Confederate supporters. Jake would go on to serve as a Kentucky state legislator. The family was raised as Methodists.

Young Griffith occasionally attended a one-room schoolhouse, where he was taught by his older sister. He also spent much time in a library and enjoyed reading. When Griffith was ten years old, his father died of stomach ailments, caused by war injury. The family was left destitute and struggled to survive for several years.

When Griffith was fourteen years old, the farm was abandoned, and the family moved to Louisville, Kentucky. An unsuccessful attempt was made to operate a boarding house. Griffith left high school to find work and help support the family. He worked in a dry goods store and later in a bookstore.

Even with little education, Griffith developed an interest in playwriting. He left home to pursue that career but with little success. He was offered the opportunity to act in several minor stage and early film productions. His appearances were mostly as an extra. He traveled around the country learning the techniques of storytelling, getting it on film.

In 1908, Griffith was a stage extra in a production of *Professional Jealousy* for the Biograph Company. Through a series of illnesses and production failure, the Biograph director position came open. Biograph co-founder Henry "Harry" Marvin offered the job to Griffith. He made his first short movie for Biograph entitled The *Adventures of Dollie*. He would go on to direct another forty-eight shorts for the company in that year. Between 1908 and 1913, Griffith would produce 450 short films. He began experimentation with unique film production techniques.

In 1910, Griffith made his first trip to California, seeking a site for his film *In Old California*. He found a small village called Hollywood. He was the first person with the first company to produce a film in Hollywood. In 1914, Griffith produced his first feature film, *Judith of Bethulia*. Biograph was opposed to the longer film formats, claiming "a movie that long hurt the [audience's] eyes." With Biograph's opposition and the ensuing production cost overruns, Griffith parted ways with Biograph. With a committed company of actors, they joined the Mutual Studio, later to be formed with Harry Aitken as the Reliance-Majestic Studio.

In 1915, Griffith produced *The Clansman*, which would become known as *The Birth of a Nation*. Set during and after the Civil War, it offered common Confederate racial prejudices and glorification of the Ku Klux Klan. It was recognized as the first feature-length American film. It achieved notoriety on many scales. It used effective and innovative filming techniques. It broke all previous box office records. It was very controversial. It was even challenged by the National Association for the Advancement of Colored People. It was actually banned in several

American cities. In spite of the controversy, several prominent leaders in the film industry invested in the film and made huge profits. One such person was Louis B. Mayer, who made use of the profits in later establishing the Metro-Goldwyn-Mayer studios.

Personally, Griffith was deeply hurt by the criticism. In 1916, Griffith tried to answer his critics with a new film, *Intolerance*. The two-and-a-half-hour film was released depicting scenes of the wrongs of racial prejudice and encouraging brotherhood and understanding of all people. The film did not match the success of *The Birth of a Nation* but did help to ease some of the national tensions. The costs for production with the unusually large sets and exotic costumes were not covered by the total box office profits. Griffith had invested most of his own finances in the film's production. The financial loss experienced followed him through most of his life.

In 1917, Griffith's production company dissolved. He would later join with Charlie Chaplin, Mary Pickford, and Douglas Fairbanks to form United Artists studios. He produced a number of feature films at United Artists. Among them were *Broken Blossoms* (1919), *Way Down East* (1920), *Orphans of the Storm* (1921), *One Exciting Night* (1922), *America* (1924), and *Isn't Life Wonderful* (1924). With only a few of the films finding success at the box office, Griffith was forced to leave United Artists.

Griffith was strongly opposed to talking movies, feeling that music alone was the only needed sound. He was eventually persuaded to direct a part-talkie movie, *Lady of the Pavements* (1929). He would later direct two full-sound movies, *Abraham Lincoln* (1930) and *The Struggle* (1931). Those would be his last directed films. He was asked by later director Hal Roach to assist on the production of *Of Mice and Men* (1939) and *One Million B.C.* (1940).

Griffith's personal life during his professional career was very troubled. He lived a hermit's life at the Knickerbocker Hotel in Los Angeles. He lived off of the income from an annuity he had purchased in the height of his professional career. On July 23, 1948, he was found unconscious in the hotel's lobby. In transportation to the hospital, he died of a cerebral hemorrhage. A public service was held in his honor at the Hollywood Masonic Temple. There was a large crowd in attendance but with few stars present. That is disappointing as it was Griffith who began the movie industry in Hollywood and lived to see its growth into huge industry it would become. He was buried at Mount Tabor Methodist Church Graveyard in Centerfield, Kentucky.

The great actor Orson Welles commented, "I have never really hated Hollywood except for its treatment of D. W. Griffith. No town, no industry, no profession, no art form owes so much to a single man." Charlie Chaplin called Griffith "[t]he teacher of us all." Legendary actress Lillian Gish called him "the father of film." In 1938, the Directors Guild of America named the Best Lifetime Achievement award in his honor. He is credited with being the first person to state "Lights, camera, action" in 1910.

He would produce over 450 short films and 80 feature-length films in his career. He rather egotistically stated, "Actors should never be important. Only directors should have power and place." D.W. Griffith began his life's journey on a Kentucky farm. He received his early education in a Kentucky schoolhouse. He developed his interest in books and stories in Kentucky. He would find his final resting place in a Kentucky church graveyard. He is a unique Kentucky innovator.

Florence Henderson

Owensboro

Actress

She was known as "America's Mom." She had a distinguished career that spanned sixty-five years on stage, in film, and on television. She received her early education and honed her performance talents in Kentucky. She was well respected by the entertainment industry leaders and performers for her multi-faceted abilities.

Florence Agnes Henderson was born on Valentine's Day, 1934 in Dale, Indiana. Her parents were Elizabeth Elder Henderson, a homemaker, and Joseph Henderson, a tobacco sharecropper. She was the youngest of ten children. The family was poor, and the times after during the Great Depression were very difficult for the large family.

Soon after her birth, the family moved to a tobacco farm near Owensboro, Kentucky. There Florence developed talents at an early age in singing and performance. By the age of two, she had a broad repertoire of fifty songs. At the age of eight, while at the local grocery store, the workers would require her to sing before they gave her the groceries. She improved her musical education and talent in the local school and churches. At the age of sixteen, she earned money singing for the local civic organizations.

In 1951, Henderson graduated from St. Francis Academy in Owensboro, Kentucky. She never forgot the valuable life lessons she learned from the Catholic sisters and would contribute financially to their causes after her successful career. After graduation from high school, Henderson traveled to New York City to go the American Academy of Dramatic Arts to study singing and acting. While in New York City, she had the opportunity to join several touring companies and be a chorus member on Broadway.

In 1952, composer Richard Rogers chose her for the lead role in a touring production of the hit musical, *Oklahoma!* She had also performed in *South Pacific* at Lincoln Center. She made her Broadway debut in 1952 in the musical *Wish You Were Here*. In 1953, Henderson starred in the Broadway revival of *Oklahoma!* Two years later, she starred in the longest-running 1954 musical, *Fanny*. That year she also appeared on television with Gordon McRae in the *General Foods 25th Anniversary Show: A Salute to Rodgers and Hammerstein*. She again appeared on television in 1957 on two episodes of the *United States Steel Hour* and in 1958 on the CBS-TV musical adaptation of *Little Women*.

In 1962, Henderson received the Sarah Siddons Award for her work in Chicago theater. That same year, she became the first woman to guest host *The Tonight Show* between permanent hosts Jack Paar and Johnny Carson. Also that year, Henderson became a regular feature on *The Today Show*. She also was a regular guest on popular variety and talk shows hosted by Ed Sullivan, Merv Griffin, Steve Allen, and Dean Martin. Henderson also performed in 1963 on the broadcast of *The Voice of Firestone*. She began an active career having produced record albums under RCA Victor.

In 1969, Henderson was working in her first feature film, *The Song of Norway*. Toward the end of the film production, Henderson was given the opportunity to join the cast of a new television sitcom series, *The Brady Bunch*. She played the role of the family mother, Carol Brady, for five seasons until 1974. Her name recognition and popularity allowed her to become known as "America's Mom." After the show reached the minimum number necessary for syndication, it was cancelled. Henderson had wanted Carol Brady to get a job, but the producers objected.

Henderson's success allowed her to appear in commercials. She had promoted Oldsmobile and was a spokeswoman for Wesson Oil (for thirty years) and Polident (despite her personal need for it). She also enjoyed television game shows. She was a frequent panelist on the numerous popular game shows throughout the late 1970s and continued up to the early 2000s.

In 2007, Henderson hosted the *Florence Henderson Show*. In 2008, at the 33rd Gracie Awards Gala, Henderson won an Individual Achievement Award and an Outstanding Host Award for the *Florence Henderson Show*. The variety and talk show was nominated for an Emmy Award in 2010. She continued to make cameos on a variety of television shows. In 2010, Henderson competed in *Dancing with the Stars* show. She wrote a memoir in 2011, *Life is Not a Stage: From Broadway Baby to a Lovely Lady and Beyond.*

Henderson's personal life is one of interest. In 1956, she married Ira Bernstein, a theater producer. They had four children. Their marriage ended in divorce in 1985. Two years later, Henderson married Dr. John George Kappas. He was a noted hypnotherapist who had helped her overcome stage fright and the fear of flying. Henderson would eventually become a licensed hypnotherapist. Their marriage ended with his death in 2002. Throughout the 2000s, Henderson was an active fundraiser for the Sisters of St. Benedict in Ferdinand, Indiana. They were among the early educators and encouragers of Henderson.

Henderson remained active hosting shows and making special guest appearances. In 2015, Matt Lauer, host of *The Today Show*, told Henderson, "There are just some things we can't do at 81." She replied, "I didn't get that memo." She continued to work.

On November 23, 2016, Henderson was admitted to the Cedars-Sinai Medical Center in Los Angeles. She died the next day of heart failure. Her death came as a shock as there had been no evidence of any physical problems. Henderson was cremated and interred at Westwood Village Memorial Park Cemetery in Los Angeles.

In Henderson's career, she had appeared in thirteen films, ten stage productions, and over fifty-five television shows. She was a singer, an actress, a charming television host, and a very considerate and well-respected person. Her initial talent was nurtured and encouraged in her early life in Kentucky.

Ashley Judd

Ashland

Actress

She is a well-known actress and national/international political activist. Although she was not born in Kentucky, she was raised and educated in the state and still maintains allegiance to the University of Kentucky sports programs. She has had a successful career in films and television roles. She has even considered a run for the U.S. Senate seat in Kentucky.

Born Ashley Tyler Ciminella, Ashley Judd was born on April 19, 1968, in Granada Hills, California. Her father was Michael Charles Ciminella, a marketing analyst for the horseracing industry. Her mother was Naomi Judd, at that time a homemaker, much later to become a popular singer. There was an older sister, Wynonna, who would also gain success as a singer. The couple divorced in 1972.

Naomi, Wynonna, and Ashley moved to Kentucky, Naomi's home state. The family moved numerous times within the state, and Ashley attended thirteen schools before she arrived at college. Among those schools were the Sayre School in Lexington, Kentucky, and the Paul G. Blazer High School in Ashland, Kentucky. In the late 1980s, Ashley attended the University of Kentucky. She majored in French and minored in anthropology, art history, theater, and women's studies.

She completed her B.A. requirement but did not graduate with her class. She considered assignment to the Peace Corps but did not follow through.

After college, Judd drove to Hollywood and studied acting under Robert Carnegie at Playhouse West. She supported herself working as a restaurant hostess. She eventually moved to Williamson County, Tennessee, on a family-owned farm to be near her mother and sister. Her acting career did not take off until the early 1990s.

In 1991, she made appearances on two television episodes of *Star Trek: The Next Generation*. She also had occasional appearances from 1991 to 1994 on the NBC drama *Sisters*. Her film debut came in 1992 with an appearance in *Kuffs*. She won her first starring role in the Sundance Film Festival Grand Jury Prize's dramatic winner *Ruby in Paradise*. She was selected by director Oliver Stone to play in the film *Natural Born Killers*. Judd would receive very positive recognition in her next few films: *Smoke*, *Heat*, and *The Passion of Darkly Noon*.

In 1996, she starred as Marilyn Monroe in the film *Norma Jean and Marilyn*. She found widespread acclaim for her roles in *Kiss the Girls* (1997) and *Double Jeopardy* (1999).

In the early 2000s, Judd achieved limited success in films such as *Someone Like You* (2001) and *High Crimes* (2002). She received a Golden Globe nomination for Best Actress in her 2004 performance in *De-Lovely*. That same year she starred in a widely criticized film, *Twisters*. Another box office disaster widely criticized was *Divergent* (2011). In 2012, Judd appeared in ABC's series *Missing*, for which she was nominated for a Primetime Emmy Award for Outstanding Lead Actress in a Miniseries or Movie.

In her personal life, Judd married Scottish racecar driver Dario Franchitti in December 2001 at Skibo Castle. Judd was opposed to having children making the comment, "it's unconscionable to breed with the number of children who are starving in impoverished countries." In April 2011, Judd wrote her memoir, *All That is Bitter and Sweet*. The marriage would end in divorce in 2013.

Judd became a regular attendee at the University of Kentucky basketball games. In 2009, she was awarded an Honorary Doctor of Humane Letters from Union College in Barbourville, Kentucky. In 2011, she earned a Mid-Career Master of Public Administration degree from the John F. Kennedy School of Government at Harvard University. In August

2016, she enrolled at UC Berkley to pursue a PhD in Public Policy at the Goldman School of Public Policy.

Judd has noted involvement in humanitarian and political causes. She is active in the international YouthAIDS programs. She is spokesperson for women's rights and equality. She has promoted animal rights causes. On November 10, 2009, she was the recipient of the fourth annual *USA Today* Hollywood Hero. She has actively supported national Democratic candidates. She gave serious consideration to running against Kentucky U.S. Senator Mitch McConnell in 2014 but declined after a series of vicious attacks ads by Conservative SuperPACs.

Her accomplishments in the entertainment industry are numerous. She appeared in over thirty-eight movies and in seven television series. She has received nominations and awards thirteen times. She has been recognized for her continued humanitarian and political causes. She is also an honorary Kentucky Colonel. She continues her support of the University of Kentucky athletic programs and carries the proud history of a Kentucky education.

Jennifer Lawrence
Louisville
Actress

She is acknowledged as the highest-paid actress in the world. She is recognized as the "most successful actor of her generation." Her films have grossed over $5.5 billion worldwide. This unique star was born and educated in Kentucky.

Jennifer Shrader Lawrence was born on August 15, 1990, in Louisville, Kentucky, to Karen and Gary Lawrence. Her mother is a manager of a children's summer camp. Her father is a construction worker. She has two older brothers. Her mother raised Jennifer to compete with her brothers as a tomboy. Jennifer attended the Kammerer Middle School in Louisville. She lacked self-confidence and saw herself as a "misfit" among her peers. She later stated, "I always felt dumber than everybody else. I hated it. I hated being inside. I hated being behind a desk. School just kind of killed me."

She overcame her feelings of inferiority and become a cheerleader and participated in several sports, including playing on the boys' basketball team, which her father coached. She was voted by her class as "Most Talkative." She also enjoyed visits to a local horse farm. Early on, she wanted to become a doctor. She performed for her father when he worked from home. She would dress up as a clown or ballerina. At the age of nine, she acted in her first role as a prostitute in a church play based on the Old Testament book of Jonah. She would continue to participate in church plays and school musicals.

When Lawrence was fourteen, she went with her family on a vacation to New York City. She was spotted on the street by a talent scout, who persuaded her and her parents to let her audition for agents. The agents were impressed, despite her parent's misgivings. She signed on with the CESD Talent Agency, which convinced her parents to let her audition for roles in Los Angeles. Her parents agreed only if she would finish high school. She was homeschooled in Los Angeles and finished high school in two years. Lawrence turned down several offers for modeling because she was committed to work in some early acting jobs. She appeared in several national television commercials and in guest roles in a few popular television shows, such as *Monk* (2006) and *Medium* (2007). Between jobs, she returned to Louisville and helped her mother, working as an assistant nurse in the summer camp.

In 2007, her parents, recognizing her potential success, moved with her to Los Angeles. Lawrence said of her family, "My parents saw me so truly happy that they sacrificed everything for my happiness. Without my family, I would be nothing." Lawrence found a key role in *The Bill Engvall Show*, in which she was a regular actor for three seasons from 2007 to 2010. In 2009, her performance earned her the Young Artist Award for Outstanding Young Performer in a TV Series. She was able to make several film appearances during that time. In 2008, she made her film debut in the drama *Garden Party*. That year she also appeared in *The Burning Plain*, which earned her the Venice Film Festival's Premio Marcello Mastoianni award for Best Emerging Actress. In 2009, she had a role in *The Poker House*, which earned her an Outstanding Performance award from the Los Angeles Film Festival.

She made a major breakthrough in her acting career with her role in *Winter's Bone* (2010). The film won the Grand Jury Prize at the Sundance Film Festival. For Lawrence, her performance earned her the National Board of Review for Breakthrough Performance and her first nomination for the Academy Award for Best Actress. She was the second youngest person to be nominated for that award. The next year Lawrence appeared in *Like Crazy* and the delayed production of *The Beaver*.

Lawrence again gained recognition for her acting role in *X-Men: First Class* (2011). The very successful box office film also gave Lawrence her largest audience viewing. Her success continued with her most-significant major role to date in the film *The Hunger Games* (2012). The film became the top-grossing film featuring a female lead and became "the highest-grossing action heroine of all time" for Lawrence. The film's success led to successful sequels, *The Hunger Games: Catching Fire* (2013) and *The Hunger Games: Mockingjay, Parts 1 and 2* (2014 and 2015).

She added to her successful film career in the 2012 production of *Silver Linings Playbook*. Her role earned her the Golden Globe and Academy Award Best Actress awards. At the age of twenty-two, she became the second youngest Best Actress to win an Oscar. She gave her Oscar to her parents to keep in the Louisville home. That year she also appeared in the *House at the End of the Street*. In 2013, Lawrence appeared in *The Devil You Know* and *American Hustle*.

In 2014, Lawrence starred in the less popular film *Serena*. She recovered her successful career with the sequels to the X-Men series: *X-Men: Days of Future Past* (2014) and *X-Men: The Apocalypse* (2016). She also appeared in *Joy* (2015) in which her acting role earned a third Golden Globe Award and a nomination for another Academy Award for Best Actress. She now was the youngest person to earn four Oscar nominations. The sole movie produced for her in 2017 was *Mother*!. In 2018, she starred in *Red Sparrow*. She starred in another sequel, *X-Men: Dark Phoenix*.

On a personal level, Lawrence had a romantic relationship with her co-star, Nicholas Hoult, from 2010–2014. She was then in a one-year relationship with Darren Aronfsky in 2017. She is avid supporter of many humanitarian causes, such as Planned Parenthood and world hunger programs. She established the Jennifer Lawrence Foundation, promoting numerous benevolent programs centered around Louisville, Kentucky. These programs include Uspiritus, St. Mary's Center, West End Boys Club, Boys and Girls Club, Make-A-Wish Foundation, Be the Match, Meghan's Mountain, Agape Flights, Fund for the Arts, Community Foundation of Louisville, Compassionate Schools Project, America Heart Association, Down Syndrome of Louisville, Dare to Care, and Kids Cancer Alliance.

Lawrence has received additional recognitions beyond those previously mentioned. *People* magazine named her in 2011 one of the "Most

Beautiful People in the World." Victoria's Secret named her in 2012 as having the "Sexiest Eyes." *Entertainment Weekly* named her in 2012 as "Entertainer of the Year." *Rolling Stone* magazine called her in 2012 "the most talented young actress in America." *Forbes* magazine named her as the highest paid actress in 2015 and 2016.

Perhaps recalling her upbringing in a house with two older brothers, Lawrence said, "I like when things are hard; I'm very competitive. If something seems difficult or impossible, it interests me." She has appeared in over twenty-five movies, nine television shows, and in one music video. Her various roles define her ability to be up for any challenge. She continues to show her love and interest in her Kentucky upbringing as a true innovator in the entertainment industry.

Patricia Neal

Packard

Actress

She began life in the coal mining country of Kentucky. She found success in Hollywood, winning awards and gaining acclaim for memorable roles she played. She also would earn national respect for overcoming the great challenges in her life—the death of a child, a series of debilitating strokes and grueling therapy to regain her place on the stage and screen. She worked with the Hollywood movie legends and equaled their acting performances.

Patsy Louise Neal was born on January 20, 1926, in Packard, White County, Kentucky. Her father was William Burdette Neal, a coal mine manager. Her mother, Eura Mildred Petrey Neal, was the daughter of a local doctor. Patsy had an older sister, Margaret Ann. Little is known of her early experiences in Kentucky, except her developing personal interest in dramatics.

When Neal was young, the family moved to Knoxville, Tennessee. There she attended Park Lowry Grammar School. At the age of ten, Neal attended an evening of monologues in the basement of the Methodist church. She would later write a note to Santa that read, "What I want for Christmas is to study dramatics." Neal attended Knoxville High School and participated in the dramatics programs. She was able to give monologues at various Knoxville social clubs. She received the Tennessee State Award for dramatic reading. She was chosen to apprentice at the prestigious Barter Theater in Virginia.

After high school graduation, Neal attended Northwestern University for two years as a drama major. She left school and went to New York City, where she served first as an understudy of a Broadway production of *The Voice of the Turtle*. She made her first true appearance in 1946 in *Another Part of the Forest*. Her performance won her the 1947 Tony Award for Best Featured Actress in a Play. She would also receive a famed New York Drama Critic's Circle Award for her notable debut performance. Both these awards were given to her before she was twenty-one years old.

Neal was signed by Warner Brothers and moved to Hollywood to begin a film career. A director changed her first name to "Patricia." She appeared in her film debut with Ronald Reagan in *John Loves Mary* (1949). She made a second film with Reagan in *The Hasty Heart* (1949). Her third film that year was *The Fountainhead*, starring Gary Cooper. During the filming of the movie, Neal, at age twenty-three, fell in love with Cooper, age forty-eight. They began a three-year relationship. During this period Neal continued filmmaking with *Bright Leaf* (1950) with Cooper, *The Breaking Point* (1950) with John Garfield, *The Day the Earth Stood Still* (1951) with Michael Rennie, and *Operation Pacific* (1951) with John Wayne. Her relationship with Cooper ended when she was persuaded by Cooper to have an abortion, and he would not agree to leave his wife and daughter. Neal would later say that the decision to have the abortion was one of her greatest regrets in her life. Soon after the breakup, Neal suffered from a nervous breakdown. Disappointed, she resigned from Warner Brothers.

Neal left Hollywood and returned to New York City and the Broadway theater. She was twenty-seven years old. She was persuaded to play a role in the revival of *The Children's Hour* (1952). At a social gathering she met noted British writer Roald Dahl. They would later marry in 1953 and have five children. Their marriage lasted thirty years but was a troubled marriage. Neal then starred in the stage production *A Roomful of Roses* (1955).

Neal became a member of the Actors Studio and returned to Hollywood. She made her successful return to films in *A Face in the Crowd* (1957). She was highly praised for her range of acting abilities. She also made numerous appearances on television in theatrical productions. She appeared in the stage production of *The Miracle Worker* (1959). Her other films were very memorable successes in *Breakfast at Tiffany's* (1961) and *Hud* (1963). Neal won the Academy Award for Best Actress for her performance in *Hud* with Paul Newman. She would receive her second award for her performance in the movie *In Harm's Way*, released in 1965.

Neal continued the balance between screen and stage into the 1960s in spite of personal crises. In December 1960, a four-month-old son, Theo, was crushed in his baby carriage between a taxicab and a bus on a New York street. The child was brain damaged, and Neal was devastated. Her husband, Roald, had to take charge of their depressing situation and moved the family to the English village of Great Misseden, Buckinghamshire. Two years later, their seven-year-old daughter Olivia died of measles-induced encephalitis. The lack of any modern medical facilities likely contributed to the death. In 1965, while Neal was pregnant, she suffered three burst brain aneurysms and was in a coma for three weeks. With her husband's supervision, sometimes deemed severe, Neal recovered and, on August 4, 1965, gave birth to a healthy daughter, Lucy.

It is amazing that it was through this time of emotional turmoil Neal continued to perform in her highly acclaimed films. In 1967, Neal was able to give a speech in New York at a charity dinner promoting care for brain-damaged children. In 1968, Neal had recovered to star in *The Subject Was Roses*, for which she was nominated for an Academy Award. She continued to perform in television presentations even though her film activity took a break. In 1978, the Fort Sanders Regional Medical Center dedicated the Patricia Neal Rehabilitation Center in her honor. The marriage ended in divorce in 1983, after Neal learned of Dahl's affair with a family friend. In 1988, Neal wrote her autobiography, *As I Am*. In 1999, she appeared in the film *Cookie's Fortune*.

Neal won several lifetime achievement awards and was active in fundraising and promotion of assistance for brain-injured children and adults. She died at her home in Edgartown, Martha's Vineyard, Massachusetts, on August 8, 2010, from lung cancer. She was eighty-four years old. She became a Catholic four months before she died. She was buried in the Abbey of Regina Laudis in Bethlehem, Connecticut.

Patricia Neal was a daughter of Kentucky and brought the tough grit of a coal mining family to all her challenges in life. She overcame great personal, emotional, and physical challenges. She left a legacy of memorable and innovative film roles that have given her continued acclaim.

Diane Sawyer

Glasgow

TV Journalist

She is an accomplished news journalist with many awards and national recognitions. She has worked in the White House for two administrations and has worked on two national television networks. She was the first female on primetime news programming. Her reporting has received high acclaim for her in-depth reporting and personal interviews with high profile national and international celebrities. She began her illustrious career in her home state of Kentucky and found the fertile soil of personal and professional growth that prepared her to compete in innovative journalism on a national level.

Lila Diane Sawyer was born on December 22, 1945, in Glasgow, Kentucky. Soon after Diane's birth, the family moved to Louisville, Kentucky. She is the second of two daughters born to Jean W. Dunagan and Ebron Powers Sawyer. Her mother was an elementary school teacher who instilled in her children the value of a well-rounded education. Her father was a Navy captain in World War II and a respected Republican politician and community leader, becoming the Jefferson County Judge/Executive. She would learn lessons from him about community service and public political education.

Diane began her life living in the shadow of her active and ambitious older sister, Linda. They attended Seneca High School in Louisville.

Diane was active singing in a local choir. She also served in the high school debate team and as editor of her high school yearbook. She was voted "most likely to succeed" by her classmates. Her sister became first runner-up in the 1962 Junior Miss Competition. Diane followed her sister the next year and became the 1963 Miss Junior Miss of America. She toured the country for several years as the pageant's representative. The travel for her was exciting and exposed her to the local news media. The two sisters would follow each other to the all-girl college, Wellesley. Diane graduated in 1967 with a Bachelor of Arts degree in English.

Anxious to begin a career, Sawyer returned to Louisville and applied for a job at WLKY TV, a local station in Louisville. Her looks and prominence as Junior Miss helped to earn her a position as the local "weather girl." That was the only position open for a female at that time. Sawyer used her education to expand the regular weather forecasting to include appropriate quotations and historical tidbits. She was promoted to a general assignment post but saw no future beyond that. She enrolled for one semester at the University of Louisville in Journalism. In 1969, her father was killed in a traffic accident.

With the loss of her father and realizing a dead-end situation at the television station, in 1970 Sawyer left Louisville and went to Washington, D.C. She interviewed for a position in the Nixon administration and was hired as an assistant to the White House deputy secretary, Jerry Warren. That role allowed her to write press releases. In just a few months, she was promoted to administrative assistant to White House Press Secretary Ron Ziegler and later to staff assistant to President Richard Nixon. Nixon at first called her "that tall girl" and later he changed it to "that smart girl." Sawyer learned to understand the great stress that came with the job. She stated, "I remember the terror, the terror of making a mistake. A mistake I made could alter history." Sawyer had brief affairs at that time with Nixon aide Frank Gannon and later with U.S. diplomat Richard Holbrooke.

The pressure of the job was greatly compounded by the Watergate scandal and the Nixon administration attempts to defend the president. After Assistant to the President John Dean's 1973 testimony before the U.S. Senate Watergate Committee, many of the White House workers, including Sawyer, began to doubt Nixon's innocence in the Watergate cover-up activities. In spite of her feeling, Sawyer remained loyal to the president and in 1974 worked with the Nixon-Ford transition team. She remained in her White House service temporarily for President Gerald

Ford. She eventually was asked to be among the small group of Nixon's staff to move to California to help Nixon with writing his memoirs and preparing for his 1977 television interviews with David Frost.

Frustrated with her experiences in politics, in 1978 Sawyer returned to Washington, D.C., as a general assignment reporter for CBS television network. Two years later, in February 1980, Sawyer was promoted to a political correspondent. She was a regular feature on *CBS Morning News*, eventually becoming co-anchor with Bill Kurtis. In 1984, Sawyer left the program to become the first female correspondent on the award-winning news magazine, *60 Minutes*. She credited Mike Wallace with being her mentor and best friend. She continued there for the next five years. In 1988, Sawyer married famed director Mike Nichols. The marriage lasted until his death in 2014.

In 1989, Sawyer moved to ABC News to co-anchor *Primetime Live* news magazine with Sam Donaldson. In 1998, Sawyer co-anchored *ABC's 20/20* with Sam Donaldson and Barbara Walters. That year she also co-anchored *Good Morning America* with Charles Gibson. She would have that position for eleven years. In September 2009, Sawyer was chosen as the successor to Charles Gibson as the anchor of *ABC World News*. For the years of 2010–2011, two of the three major network news anchors were women—Diane Sawyer and Barbara Walters. In September 2014, Sawyer resigned from anchor on ABC World News. Two months later, her husband of twenty-six years died of a heart attack at the age of eighty-three. Although the couple had no children, Nichols had two daughters and a son from a previous marriage.

Sawyer continued with ABC News doing special reporting. She has received numerous awards for her journalistic efforts. In 2000, she received a Daytime Emmy for excellence in morning programming. From 2005–2008, Sawyer was included in *Forbes* magazine's "List of The World's 100 Most Powerful Women." In 2007, she received a second Emmy for outstanding news and documentary program achievement. That year she also received a Peabody Award for her special reporting. In 2010, she received the Walter Cronkite Award for Excellence in Journalism. In 2012, she was awarded an honorary Doctorate of Letters from Brown University.

Diane Sawyer continues with her occasional special reports and personal interviews. She is a respected national and international journalist whose talent, education, and competitive drive originated from her Kentucky roots.

William Shatner
Woodford County
Actor

It may be a stretch to call this Canadian-born actor a Kentucky innovator. Most entertainers listed have early beginnings in Kentucky. But this actor made a choice to call Kentucky home after his prominent career. He continues to use his current Kentucky connections to provide innovative resources for personal pleasures and to benefit humanitarian causes.

William Shatner was born on March 22, 1931, in Montreal, Quebec, Canada. His parents were Anne Garmaise and Joseph Shatner, a clothing manufacturer. He has two sisters. The family lived in the Notre-Dame-de-Grace section of Montreal. His ancestors were Jewish immigrants from Eastern Europe and the family were Conservative Jews. He would later recall, "Montreal is a very cosmopolitan, sophisticated, erudite, glorious city today. But it wasn't quite that way when I was growing up. There was a lot of anti-Semitism. And I had to deal with that in an area of the city that had few Jews." Shatner attended Willingdon Elementary School and West Hill High School in Montreal. He performed as a child actor in radio programs for the Canadian Broadcasting Corporation. He was an active member of the Montreal Children's Theater. In summers, he was able to perform with the Royal Mount Theater Company.

He completed his higher education at McGill University in Montreal. Majoring in economics, he completed a Bachelor of Commerce degree in 1952.

Having had experiences early in his life with public performance opportunities, after graduation from college, Shatner became business manager for the Mountain Playhouse in Montreal. He later joined the Canadian National Repertory Theater in Ottawa, training in Shakespearean theater. In 1954, Shatner appeared in productions at the Stratford Shakespeare Festival in Ontario. That year he also played Ranger Bob on *The Canadian Howdy Doody Show*. In 1956, Shatner made several memorable appearances on nationally televised American productions of *Oedipus*, *Henry V*, and *Tamburlaine the Great*.

In 1951, Shatner made his movie debut in the Canadian film, *Butler's Night Off*. In the mid and late-1950s, he made appearances in other nationally televised American productions such as *Goodyear Television Playhouse*, *Studio One*, and *Playhouse 90*. In 1958, Shatner made his American film debut in *The Brothers Karamazov*. That year he began starring in a two-year Broadway production of *The Secret Life of Suzie Wong*. His role won him the 1959 Theater Award.

In the early 1960s, Shatner had roles in *Judgment at Nuremberg* (1951), *The Intruder* (1962), and *For the People* (1965). His real fame arrived with his performance in the 1966 premiere of *Star Trek*. The series lasted for three years with wide syndication after its cancellation.

In 1968, Shatner made a unique album recording, *The Transformed Man*, featuring dramatic readings of contemporary pop hits. He wrote a novel in 1989, *TekWar*. He later wrote his autobiography, *Up Til' Now* in 2008.

The 1970s were difficult years for Shatner. With his career established around the success of *Star Trek*, he received few major roles in film or television. To support his family, he accepted cameo appearances and made television commercials. His continued popularity in the role of Captain Kirk of the *Enterprise* led to a film, *Star Trek: The Motion Picture*, in 1979, with a sequel, *Star Trek II: The Wrath of Khan* (1982). These would be followed with several other sequels in the late 1980s and early 1990s.

Shatner appeared in several memorable films, such as *Airplane II: The Sequel* (1982) and the *Miss Congeniality* series (2000 and 2005). He found a new television role as a police officer in *T. J. Hooker*, which ran from

1982 until 1986. His appearance in 2003 on *The Practice* earned him his first Emmy Award for Outstanding Guest Actor in a Drama Series. The series led to a spin-off series, *Boston Legal*. The series earned Shatner his second Emmy Award in 2005, followed by two other nominations in 2006 and 2007.

Shatner has made many other appearances on television shows and minor roles in films. He continues to make commercials. He has been in twenty films and thirty television shows in his career. He has a great dislike of watching his performances on television and the movies. He has also made eight recordings and authored or co-authored nine books.

Shatner's personal life has been filled with a variety of successes and failures. He has been married four times. He has three children with his first wife Gloria Rand (1956–1969). His second marriage was to Marcy Lafferty (1973–1996). His third marriage was to Nerine Kidd in 1997. In 1999, Nerine drowned accidentally in their swimming pool. Her death was attributed to alcohol and drugs. His current wife is Elizabeth Anderson Martin. They married in 2001. Elizabeth is a horse breeder, and Shatner has had a lifelong love of horses. The couple moved to 360-acre farm near Versailles, Kentucky. They raise American Saddlebred horses. Since 1990, Shatner led in the creation of Hollywood Charity Horse Show, which raises money for local children's charities. They have been actively involved in raising money for charities in Kentucky and nationally.

William Shatner in his career has earned sixteen distinguished awards for his performances. He has balanced career with a desire to help others through mentoring and charities. He has maintained long-established friendships with fellow actors who hold him in high esteem. Shatner said, "You have to create your life. You have to carve it, like a sculpture." Although his connections with Kentucky came later in his life, his innovative career and personal interests serve the state very well.

Chuck Woolery
Ashland
Game Show Host

He hosted four of the long-running television game shows. In addition to this and hosting seven other television game shows, he also appeared in eleven films. Unknown to many, he had a number of musical recordings, one of which reached the Top 40 national ranking. He was born and raised in Kentucky and owes much of his talent and success to his family and professional experience beginning in Kentucky.

Charles Herbert "Chuck" Woolery was born on March 16, 1941, in Ashland, Kentucky. His father, Dan Woolery, was owner of a fountain supplies company. His mother, Katherine, worked early at a call center before becoming a homemaker. He has an older sister. Little is recorded of his early life and experiences in Ashland, other than being raised as a Presbyterian. Somewhere in his early years, he developed an interest in vocal music. He attended then Ashland High School and graduated in 1959.

After high school graduation, he served two years in the U.S. Navy. Returning to Kentucky, he attended Morehead State University, studying economics and sociology. For a while he worked as a sales representative for Pillsbury Company and later as a consultant for Wasserstrom

Wine in Columbus, Ohio. But his love and desire for a musical career surfaced.

Woolery left home for a future in Nashville. His first effort was joining with Elkin "Bubba" Fowler to form a 1960s-era psychedelic band The Avant-Garde. They were contracted by Columbia Records and produced three singles. In mid-1968, one of them, "Naturally Stoned," reached number 40 on the *Billboard* Hot 100 charts. Woolery also worked as a truck driver to supplement his income. His collaboration with Fowler ended, and in the 1970s, Woolery found limited recording opportunities with Warner Brothers Records and Epic Records. His efforts as a country singer failed, and with the helpful suggestion of comedian Jonathan Winters, he moved to Los Angeles.

In Los Angeles, Woolery made several television appearances and landed roles in several films. In 1974, Woolery received an opportunity to appear on the *Tonight Show with Johnny Carson.* On the show, he caught the attention of media mogul Merv Griffin. Although Woolery sang on Griffin's show, Griffin had a much different plan for Woolery. A newly made television game show, *Wheel of Fortune*, debuted on NBC network on January 6, 1975. It was hosted by Chuck Woolery and became a great hit. He gained a wide national audience and was thought to be very secure in the job. He decided to bargain for a much higher salary, competing with his rival Richard Dawson, who hosted *Family Feud.* Although NBC agreed to the salary parity, Griffin was very bothered by the chain of events and fired Woolery. His last show was on Christmas Day, 1981. He had been there for over six years. His replacement was Pat Sajak. Woolery would later reflect,

> At the time I thought my career was on the rise. I had no idea that it was *Wheel of Fortune* that was on the rise. The show escaped cancellation many times while I was hosting, so I wanted financial security in case NBC decided to dump it. Looking back at it, I let my ego get in the way of my decision making and it was a terrible mistake. I'm happy for the success Merv (Griffin) has had with the show. I have no idea if the show would have become a huge hit if I stayed on board.

Woolery continued his career path hosting other successful game shows. He hosted *Love Connection* from 1983 until 1994. He would also go on to host *Scrabble* (1984–1990), *The Dating Game* (1997–1999), and *Lingo* (2002–2007). Woolery later launched a nationally syndicated radio show and podcasts.

Woolery's personal life is one of sadness and yet hope. He has been married four times. In 1961, at the age of twenty, Woolery married Margaret Hayes. They had three children. The youngest was a son, Chad. Tragically, in January 1986, Chad was killed in a motorcycle accident. The death had a strong impact on Woolery. He said, "He loved me and I loved him. When Chad died, I was crushed. Something died with me that could be never replaced." The couple was divorced in 1971.

Woolery's second marriage was to actress Jo Ann Pflug in 1971. They remained together for eight years until divorce in 1980. His third wife was Teri Nelson. They married in 1985 and had two children. They divorced in 2004 after rumors surfaced of her infidelity. In July 2006, Woolery married hair stylist Kim Barnes.

Woolery has had to fight rumors of anti-Semitism and stories of his death. He is politically active for Republican causes and gun rights. He has endured his difficult life with a newfound Christian faith. He has brought a unique style and personality to television performance hosting popular game shows. He is a product of the Kentucky soil, which allows personalities to grow into innovative lives on a national scale.

Other Kentucky Innovators in Entertainment

Ned Beatty • *Louisville* • Actor
Foster Brooks • *Louisville* • Comedian
William Conrad • *Louisville* • Actor/Director
Lee Majors • *Middleboro* • Actor
Victor Mature • *Louisville* • Actor
Marie McDonald • *Burgin* • Actress/Singer
Grady Nutt • *Louisville* • Comedian
Warren Oates • *Depoy* • Actor
Annie Potts • *Franklin* • Actress
Helen Thomas • *Winchester* • News Reporter
Jack Warden • *Louisville* • Actor

Chapter Two

Fine Arts

(music, art, media)

Rosemary Clooney

Maysville

Actress/Singer

She began her life in a small Kentucky town amidst a dysfunctional family and poverty conditions. She learned to take care of herself and care for her four siblings. Fame and success were discovered away from Kentucky, but she often returned to share her accomplishments with that small town. She was a national figure widely respected for her unique talent and ability to overcome personal tragedies.

Rosemary Clooney was born on May 23, 1928, in Maysville, Kentucky. She was the daughter of Marie Francis Guilfoye and Andrew Joseph Clooney. She was one of five children in the family. Her father was an alcoholic unable to provide financially for the family. Her mother worked for a dress shop chain of stores that required much traveling away from the family. The siblings were often sent temporarily to live with relatives nearby.

Clooney found relief from the depressing family situation through music. The radio provided musical education and experiences through WLW station in Cincinnati. She had her stage appearance at the age of three in a downtown movie house, the Russell Theater. She and her sister, Betty, sang at campaign events for her grandfather's successful election as mayor. Raised as a Catholic, she attended Our Lady of Mercy High School in Cincinnati.

When Clooney was thirteen, her mother married a sailor and left for California with her son, Nick. The girls were all left with their undependable father. Several years later, her father, celebrating the end of World War II, left with the modest family savings and never returned. The children were on their own. They collected soda bottles and were able to buy meals at school. Just when the children were in danger of losing their home, Rosemary and Betty, "The Clooney Sisters," won an open audition at the Cincinnati radio station. They were hired for a regular late-night radio spot at $20 a week each.

The sisters' singing ability caught the attention of popular bandleader, Tony Pastor, who was passing through the region. Offered a contract to tour with Pastor's band, they signed only after the approval of their Uncle George, who agreed to accompany them as chaperone. The sisters then began several years of travel with the band. Betty and Uncle George had become tired of the grueling road life on a bus with little rest and many performances. Clooney would later write, "Three years is a long time to be on the road. Living out of a bus, ironing clothes on the hotel room floors, away from the people you love." When Clooney was offered a solo contract with Columbia Records, she left for New York City, and Betty and Uncle George returned home to Maysville, Kentucky.

At age twenty-one, Clooney was in high competition for success in the recording business. In the fall of 1949, she made an appearance on the *Ed Sullivan Show* and on the popular radio program *Camel Caravan*. In January 1951, she recorded her first big hit, "Beautiful Brown Eyes." Her career was advanced through the encouragement of associates and friends. Arranger Mitch Miller persuaded a resistant Clooney to record a song, "Come On-a My House." Despite Clooney's hesitancy, the song sold over 1,000,000 copies. Clooney was in demand for appearances on national radio and television programs. She also made her first film appearance in Paramount's 1952 movie *The Stars are Singing*. Clooney appeared at the film's premiere in January 1953 at her hometown of Maysville.

Her big break came when asked to co-star in the 1954 movie *White Christmas*, with Bing Crosby. Clooney had moved to Hollywood, California, and became part of the active social scene. On July 13, 1953, Clooney married actor Jose Ferrer. They would have five children. She continued to work throughout her pregnancies. In 1956, she had her own television program, *The Rosemary Clooney Show*. It had a successful one-year run. She recorded for several companies until 1960.

If the 1950s had been the highly successful years for Clooney, the 1960s would balance her life with painful personal tragedies. In 1961, she divorced Ferrer. She had a strained relationship with musician Nelson Riddle for several years. On November 22, 1964, she remarried Jose Ferrer. Confirmation of his affairs led to a final divorce in 1967. During this time, Clooney became addicted to sleeping pills. She was politically active in her support for John F. Kennedy in the 1960 election. Like most Americans, she was devastated by his assassination in 1963. She became good friends and an active supporter of Robert Kennedy in the 1968 Democratic primary election. On June 5, 1968, she was standing near him with two of her children at the Ambassador Hotel following the successful primary election rally when she heard the shots by Sirhan Sirhan that killed Robert Kennedy. The strain of her career, failed marriage, and drug dependence were too much for Clooney. She had a complete mental breakdown. She voluntarily admitted herself to the psychiatric ward at Mt. Sinai Hospital in Los Angeles for many years of therapy.

In the mid-1970s, Clooney's return to performing began at a slow pace. Her friends, such as Merv Griffin and Bing Crosby, provided the opportunities for her to appear on the national scene. Griffin invited her to appear on several television shows. Crosby invited her to join him on his 50th anniversary national tour. Clooney later wrote. "Bing's invitation to work with him was a breakthrough both personal and professional, like an apostolic blessing." She dealt well with another personal tragedy, the death of her sister Betty, due to a brain aneurysm, in 1976. Clooney established the Betty Clooney Center in Long Beach, California, a facility for brain-injured young adults. This was an innovative center in the United States.

In 1977, Clooney wrote her first autobiography, *This for Remembrance: The Autobiography of Rosemary Clooney, an Irish-American Singer*. Bing Crosby wrote the introduction to the book. In 1980, she bought a second home on Riverside Drive in Augusta, Kentucky, near Maysville. In 1997, Clooney married longtime friend and dancer Dante DiPaolo at the St. Patrick Church in Maysville, Kentucky. In 1999, Clooney wrote her second autobiography, *Girl Singer: An Autobiography*. A constant smoker, she was diagnosed with lung cancer in 2001. She underwent surgery, but six months later developed complications and died on June 29, 2002, at her Beverly Hills home. She was buried at Saint Patrick's Cemetery in Maysville.

Rosemary Clooney received numerous nominations for Grammy awards but never received any of the awards. In 2002, Clooney was presented a Lifetime Achievement Grammy Award but was unable to attend because of declining health. Clooney remained closely tied to her home state of Kentucky. In 2003, she was inducted into the Kentucky Women Remembered exhibit, and her portrait is on permanent display in the Kentucky State Capitol's rotunda. Many singers and performers would honor her in recordings her more memorable songs. She was a truly innovative person nurtured by strong Kentucky roots.

Don and Phil Everly
Central City
Rock 'n Roll Singers

Although only one of the Everly brothers was actually born in Kentucky, their father was a Kentucky coal miner. The brothers would remember their father's heritage through benefit performances and charitable gifts. Their talented songwriting and singing would be the innovative force behind future groups such as the Beatles, the Beach Boys, and Simon and Garfunkel. They would pioneer the sounds of country and rock and roll in recording history. They would gain fame in the United States, as well as the United Kingdom. Even with professional success, they would face challenges of personal demons largely unknown to their legions of followers.

Isaac Donald Everly was born on February 1, 1937, in Brownie, Kentucky, to parents Margaret Embry and Isaac Milford "Ike" Everly. Ike, age twenty-six, was a coal miner and talented guitarist. Margaret, age fifteen, was a talented singer. Not wanting to continue working in the coal mines or see his sons seek such work, the family moved to Chicago, Illinois. It was hoped that Ike could pursue a music career. On January 19, 1939, a second son, Philip Jason Everly was born. Soon after his birth, the family moved to Shenandoah, Iowa, where Ike and Margaret appeared on radio shows on KMA and KFNF. They would eventually have their own show.

Don and Phil attended schools in Shenandoah. While very young, the boys sang on the radio program. They were called "Little Donnie and Baby Boy Phil." The family later sang as The Everly Family. The boys grew in their singing talent and developed an interest in songwriting.

In 1953, the family moved to Knoxville, Tennessee. The brothers attended West High School in Knoxville. In 1955, after Don's high school graduation, the family parted, with the parents moving to Madison, Tennessee, and the boys moving to Nashville, Tennessee. The boys had drawn the attention of family friend Chet Atkins. He was the manager of RCA Victor's studio in Nashville. Phil began attending Peabody Demonstration School in Nashville, graduating in 1957. Their first attempt at a recording failed. But they persisted in the recording business with the help of various friends of Atkins. In February 1957, the brothers found their first major success with the song "Bye Bye Love." It had been turned down by thirty other acts, but the brothers' harmony and singing skill saw the recording climb the national charts to number two. The song became the brothers' first million-seller.

Their success reached beyond the United States to the United Kingdom. They produced additional big hits, such as "Wake Up Little Susie," "All I Have to Do Is Dream," "Bird Dog," "Problems," and "(Till) I Kissed You." The brothers toured the nation with Buddy Holly in 1957 and 1958. They eventually toured internationally on their own. In 1960, they signed with Warner Brothers Records. They continued to produce a number of successive hits, such as "Cathy's Clown," which sold eight million copies. Other hits followed in the early 1960s: "Walk Right Back," "Crying in the Rain," "That's Old Fashioned," When Will I Be Loved," "Like Strangers," "Lucille," "Temptation," and "The Price of Love." By 1962, the brothers had earned $35,000,000 from record sales.

A serious dispute over recording rights and royalties led the brothers to sever contractual ties with Acuff-Rose songwriters. For several years they began to write songs for other performers using pseudonyms. They established their own record label, Calliope Records. This short-lived attempt failed after a year. The brothers enlisted in the United States Marine Corps in October 1961. They were able to make one national television appearance on the popular *Ed Sullivan Show*.

Perhaps while on earlier tours and during their experiences in the military, the brothers both became addicted to amphetamines. Don's addiction became worse, with the addition of other drugs. The brothers also began to have sharp differences over performances and national political interests. By the end of the 1960s, the brothers were no longer successful in writing or recording. Their contract with Warner Brothers expired in 1970. They found several opportunities as replacement hosts for Johnny Cash's television show and a variety program, *Johnny Cash Presents the Everly Brothers*. The brothers renewed national touring, which ended on July 14, 1973, at Knott's Berry Farm in California when Phil smashed his guitar and walked off stage while Don finished the program. This ended their dual performance careers.

The brothers began separate careers as songwriters and backup performers for other artists with limited success. Don married three times, producing four children. Phil also married three times and produced two children. Ten years after their very public split, the brothers were persuaded to participate in a reunion concert.

On September 23, 1983, the brothers performed on stage at the Royal Albert Hall in London, England. They also tried studio recording of three new albums with limited success but paved the way for touring in the United States. In 1986, the Everly Brothers were inducted among the first ten into the Rock and Roll Hall of Fame. They kept in contact with their family connections in Kentucky and, starting on Labor Day weekend, 1988, performed annual Everly Brothers' Homecoming concerts in Central City, Kentucky. In 1997, the pair received a Lifetime Achievement Grammy Award. In 1999, Don and his son, Edan Everly, performed "The Everly Brothers for Kentucky Flood Relief."

In 2003 and 2004, the brothers joined Simon and Garfunkel in their "Old Friends" reunion tour. In 2004, a compilation album, *Country Classics*, was released, featuring their past recorded songs. That year the brothers were inducted into the Vocal Group Hall of Fame.

On January 3, 2014, Phil Everly died at Providence Saint Joseph Medical Center in Burbank, California. His years of smoking had taken its toll, leading to chronic obstructive pulmonary disease. His weak lungs were thought to have been inherited from his father, who died of black lung disease. His family established the Phil Everly Memorial COPD Foundation.

Don Everly lives in Nashville, Tennessee, with his family. Tributes continue to pour in for the Everly Brothers and their contribution to the music industry. Paul Simon said, "Phil and Don were the most beautiful sounding duo I ever heard. Both voices pristine and soulful. The Everlys were there at the crossroads of country and R&B. They witnessed and were a part of the birth of rock and roll."

Although their time in Kentucky was limited, their hearts and love for family kept them tied to the state. Their unique musical style and many recording hits illustrate their innovative performance style. Kentucky can proudly claim them as her own.

Red Foley
Blue Lick
Country Singer

He grew up in Kentucky and honed his musical talent in the backwoods. He rose from entertaining in his father's store to hosting and performing on nationally broadcast television shows. He is credited with popularizing country music for the middle-class national audience. His appealing public, God-fearing persona was countered by a hidden life of human failings.

Clyde Julian Foley was born on June 17, 1910, in Bluelick, Kentucky. His father ran a general store in nearby Berea. Foley developed an interest in music at a young age. This was encouraged by his family. He was called "Red" because of his red hair. At the age of nine, he was performing on a harmonica for the local residents in his father's store. His father received a guitar as partial payment on a store bill and gave the guitar to Foley. He seemed to master the instrument immediately, and before long, he was entertaining the customers with harmonica, guitar, French harp, piano, and trombone. The family moved to Berea, and Foley attended Berea High School. He was a good student athlete but kept his interest in music. When he was seventeen, he entered an Atwater-Kent amateur contest and won the Kentucky state finals. He was given a voice scholarship to Georgetown College. He worked as an usher and singer at a theater in Covington, Kentucky.

In 1930, during his freshman year at Georgetown, Foley was offered a chance to sing with the Cumberland Ridge Runners on the *National Barn Dance* radio program in Chicago. He joined with future entertainment stars Gene Autry, Smiley Burnette, and George Goebel. His seven-year run with the group proved to be very successful and professionally fulfilling. In June 1933, he produced his first single record, "Life Is Good Enough for Me and The Lone Cowboy." The show was now being broadcast nationally over the NBC network. His popularity was beginning to grow.

In 1933, Foley married Axie Pauline Cox. She died giving birth to their only child, a daughter named Betty. Soon after, Foley married Eva Alaine Overstake (Judy Martin), a WLS performer. The couple had three daughters. The oldest, Shirley Lee, would later marry popular recording star, Pat Boone. By now, Foley was writing and producing records under his own name. In 1935, Foley wrote and recorded "Old Shep," a touching song about a dog from his childhood memories.

In 1937, Foley moved to Cincinnati, Ohio, and formed the Renfro Valley Barn Dance. In 1939, the show moved to its permanent home in Renfro Valley, Kentucky. He was able to first work as a host on an NBC network program, *Avalon Time*, co-hosted by entertainer Red Skelton. In 1940, he signed a contract with Decca Records and returned to Chicago. He worked there for another seven years with the *National Barn Dance* company. In 1941, he was able to make appearances in two Western films. In 1944, he wrote and recorded "Smoke on the Water," a patriotic song that remained on top of the folk record charts for thirteen weeks. On January 17, 1945, Foley became the first country performer to record in Nashville, Tennessee. At the WSM-AM's Studio B, Foley recorded hits such as "Tennessee Saturday Night," "Blues in the Heart," and "Tennessee Border." In the summer of 1945, Foley traveled to New York City to record with Lawrence Welk and his orchestra.

In 1946, Foley moved to Nashville. He hosted and performed on the *Prince Albert Show*, part of the *Grand Ole Opry* that was carried on NBC radio. He would work in that position for eight years. His audience and reputation grew as his versatile musical styles broadened. He continued to develop his skills with songwriting and performance. Between 1947-49, Foley, joining with the backup group, the Cumberland Valley Boys, produced seven Top 5 hits. In the 1950s, Foley broadened his recordings to include popular gospel numbers "Just A Closer Walk with Thee," "Steal Away," and "There'll Be Peace in the Valley for Me." These were million-sellers for Foley.

In 1951, Foley's wife of eighteen years committed suicide. She had discovered that Foley had an ongoing affair with Sally Sweet. Foley cut back on his performances to devote more time to his daughters. He continued to write and record with other popular artists, such as the Andrews Sisters, Burl Ives, Ernest Tubb, Kitty Wells, and Anita Kerr Singers. He began hosting the *Red Foley Show* on Saturday afternoons on NBC radio from Nashville. It was eventually moved to ABC radio. On November 21, 1953, he was one of the first eight singers named to *Billboard* magazine's Honor Roll of Country and Western artists.

Unhappy with his near seclusion, depression, and growing struggle with alcoholism, Foley made a major change in his life and career. In July 1954, Foley, now married to Sally Sweet, and his family moved to Springfield, Missouri. He was persuaded to host the *Ozark Jubilee*. The popular show debuted on July 17, 1954, from the Jewell Theater. It was the launching pad for newly discovered musical talent, such as Brenda Lee and Porter Wagner. The show would continue until 1960.

During this time, Foley made a number of appearances on national television shows and state fairs. Foley faced federal income tax evasion charges for which he was later acquitted. He moved with his family to Los Angeles in the early 1960s, appearing in an ABC-TV sitcom, *Mr. Smith Goes to Washington*. He returned to Nashville in 1963 and performed and toured with the Grand Ole Opry. In 1967, Foley was elected to the Country Music Hall of Fame—the first Kentuckian selected. He was described as "one of the most versatile and moving performers of all time" and "a giant influence during the formative years of contemporary Country music and today as a timeless legend."

Foley's last appearance was on September 19, 1968, in Fort Wayne, Indiana. It was two Opry performances for the local Sheriff's Posse, which included Billy Walker and 19-year-old Hank Williams Jr. Foley had earlier sung "Peace in the Valley" at longtime friend Hank Williams Sr's funeral. Before the second show, Foley entered Walker's dressing room, where Walker shared his faith in Christ. Foley asked Walker, "Do you think God could forgive a sinner like me?" Walker said Foley shared with him all the terrible things he had done in his life. Walker responded to Foley, "Red, if God can forgive me, He can forgive you." Walker prayed with Foley.

Foley's last song on the program was "Peace in the Valley." Walker said after the song, Foley walked over to the stage and said to him, "Billy, I've never sung that song and feel the way I do tonight."

That night Red Foley experienced respiratory failure and died in his sleep. He was laid to rest in Woodland Memorial Park Cemetery in Nashville, Tennessee. Foley was an inspiration to future performers such as Jerry Lee Lewis and Elvis Presley. In 2002, he was inducted into the Kentucky Hall of Fame. On June 10, 2003, a Kentucky State marker (No. 2114) was placed at Foley's boyhood home in Berea. In 1970, Berea College established the Red Foley Memorial Musical Award to recognize students with musical contributions to the campus community.

Red Foley experienced a young life nurtured by Kentucky values and appreciation of musical talent. He found professional success away from Kentucky but was always mindful of where he began. He is a state treasure and derived his versatile musical style from those valued Kentucky roots.

Lionel Hampton
Louisville
Jazz Musician

He was called the "Gates of Swing." He was a jazz vibraphonist, pianist, percussionist, bandleader, singer, and actor. He performed with the greatest musicians of his day. He was recognized internationally and honored by two American presidents before his death. He left his Kentucky roots early and traveled extensively throughout his lifetime.

Lionel Leo Hampton (nicknamed "Hamp") was born on April 20, 1908, in Louisville, Kentucky. There is no information regarding his parents or his earliest experiences in Kentucky. Shortly after his birth, he and his mother moved to her hometown of Birmingham, Alabama. As a child, Hampton was exposed to the powerful music in his home church. He was raised as a Roman Catholic. He said later that the early church music experiences helped him to discover "the beat in me." The family moved to Kenosha, Wisconsin. It was there that Hampton took his first drum lessons from a nun at the Holy Rosary Academy.

His family moved again to Chicago, Illinois. His musical education received a boost by his joining the *Chicago Defender* Newsboys' Band. The new position required the teenager to sell newspapers. He found interest in the xylophone and took lessons from famed percussionist Jimmy Bertrand. At the age of fifteen, Hampton's experience with the band inspired a move to Los Angeles, California. He played drums for Reb Spikes "Sharps and Flats" and most notably with Paul Howard's "Quality Serenaders." Hampton developed a technique for doing stunts with multiple pairs of drumsticks while maintaining his steady rhythm. He made his recording debut in 1929.

He joined the Les Hite band in Culver City that accompanied Louis Armstrong at the Cotton Club. He also took the opportunity to study music at the University of California. Hampton developed an interest in the newly developed vibraphone. In 1930, he played the vibraphone on the first jazz recording featuring the instrument in improvised solos. The vibraphone was now most closely associated with Lionel Hampton. He left the Les Hite band and formed his own band in the Los Angeles Paradise Club. Performing there in 1936, he was discovered by famed bandleader Benny Goodman. He joined the trio of clarinetist Goodman, pianist Teddy Wilson, and drummer Gene Krupa. The quartet became the first racially integrated jazz group. He later stated, "As far as I'm concerned, what he [Goodman] did in those days—and they were hard days in 1937—made it possible for Negroes to have their chance in baseball and other fields."

The four years between 1936 and 1940 would be among the most productive of his career. During his time with Goodman in New York City, Hampton was able to make several recordings under his own name with memorable solo performances on songs such as "Dizzy Spells," "Avalon," and "Moonglow." In 1940, Hampton left the Goodman group to again lead his own group, the Lionel Hampton Orchestra. Two years later, he recorded his first major hit, "Flying Home." Other hits followed, such as "Hamp's Boogie Woogie," "Midnight Sun," "Million Dollar Smile," "Hey! Ba-Ba-Re-Bop," and "Central Avenue Breakdown." Hampton was including new and popular talent in his performances. Among those were Wes Montgomery, Clifford Brown, Art Farmer, Dexter Gordon, Quincy Jones, Jimmy Celeveland, Cat Anderson, Joe Williams, Charlie Mingus, Dinah Washington, Betty Carter, and Aretha Franklin.

On November 11, 1936, Hampton married Galdys Riddle. She became his business manager and created order in his life until her death in 1971. With her help, they founded two record labels, a music publishing company, and a company that built low-income housing in inner cities.

In the 1950s, Hampton and orchestra toured Europe, Japan, Australia, Africa, and the Middle East. They were goodwill ambassadors.

Hampton released what were considered his two most popular recordings: "September in the Rain" and "Stardust." There were numerous television appearances and reunions with former bands. In 1968, Hampton appeared at the Sanremo Music Festival in Italy. That year he received a Papal Medal from Pope Paul VI. The 1960s and 1970s saw a decline in Hampton's appeal, but he found steady opportunities for personal performances. In 1973, Hampton appeared at the Newport Jazz Festival, just a few months before the death of Gene Krupa. He was a featured performer at President Jimmy Carter's White House Jazz Party in June 1978.

In the 1980s, Hampton developed a strong affiliation with the University of Idaho and its annual jazz festival. The music department was named after him in 1987. He was still a popular international performer. In 1984, he was inducted into the Percussive Arts Society Hall of Fame. In 1986, he was inducted into the Big Band and Jazz Hall of Fame. On March 31, 1991, he suffered a stroke while on stage in Paris, France. In spite of his physical limitations with the addition of chronic arthritis, he was able to make occasional appearances and performances.

In 1992, President George H. W. Bush appointed Hampton to the Board of the Kennedy Center. In 1997, President Bill Clinton awarded Hampton the National Medal of the Arts. He died of heart failure on August 31, 2002, in New York City. He was buried in Woodlawn Cemetery in the Bronx, New York.

In his lifetime, Hampton received over twenty-eight awards, including fifteen honorary doctorate degrees. He had eleven acting credits. He expressed memorably, "Gratitude is when memory is stored in the heart and not in the mind." Lionel Hampton was an innovative international musician that Kentucky can proudly claim as one of its own.

Larnelle Harris
Danville
Gospel Singer

He is a man devoted first to God and then his family. His career takes second place to his family's activities. He remains a very private person. He set the gold standard in gospel music. He has recorded eighteen albums and won five Grammy Awards and eleven Dove Awards. He received his education and training in Kentucky.

Larnelle Steward Harris was born on July 6, 1947, in Danville, Kentucky. Little information is available about his parents and early childhood. He did start playing the drums at the age of nine. He attended Western Kentucky University, graduating in 1969, and trained in formal vocal performance. At the university, he met fellow student Cynthia Mitzi. They married and produced two children, settling in Louisville, Kentucky.

After graduation, Harris joined a popular gospel touring group, the Spurrlows. He began as a drummer and moved to vocal. His solo performances caught the attention of Bill and Gloria Gaither. In 1984, Harris joined the Gaither Vocal Band. He was propelled into the national spotlight, and his songs became popular beyond the gospel music audience. His solo performances were matched by his duets with Sandi Patty. The duo's big hits were "More than Wonderful" (1983) and the dramatic presentation of "I've Just Seen Jesus" (1985).

Harris was invited to perform at the White House in 1993 by President George H. W. Bush. During this time period, Harris had several songs as number one radio hits, such as "In It After All" (1989) and "All Along the Way" (1993). Harris made a number of memorable television appearances on national religious programs and on news talk shows. He was a consistent participant in the Gaither Homecoming shows.

Harris received a number of significant personal awards and honors. He received an honorary doctorate of music from Campbellsville University in central Kentucky. In 1993, he was inducted into the Western Kentucky University Hall of Distinguished Alumni. In 2007, Harris was inducted into the Gospel Music Association Foundation Hall of Fame. In 2009, he was inducted into the Christian Music Hall of Fame.

Harris and his wife have actively participated in the WHAS Crusade for Children local telethon in Louisville. Harris is a member and deacon in the family's home church. His many tours and performances have been scheduled around the family's priority schedule of activities.

In spite of the many awards and honors for Harris, none are more important than a single photo prominently displayed in his home. It is a photo of a well that he helped to build for a poor community in Africa that he had visited. Harris stated, "When you stack that up against Doves and Grammies, there really is no contest what is most important."

Harris continues to inspire audiences with his dramatic vocal performances. Certainly from his own experiences, he communicates the presence of God in the many human storms we all face. He said, "Storms are not pleasant, but they push us to find shelter with the only unmoving, unwavering thing we can find—and that is ultimately God." He shared about his life ministry to all people—from the East Room of the White House to the most poverty-stricken parts of the world. Kentucky can be proud to claim this man that the state helped to form.

Naomi and Wynonna Judd
Ashland
Country Singers

They were the most famous mother-daughter country music duet in history. From 1983 until 1990, they dominated all country music awards. They had their differences with each other but survived bouts of depression and physical dangers. Their association began in poverty in Kentucky and rose to national prominence performing for the president of the United States. In Wynonna's words, "We traveled from the outhouse to the White House."

Diana Ellen "Naomi" Judd was born on January 11, 1946, in Ashland, Kentucky. Her father, Charles Glen Judd, was owner of a gas station. Her mother, Pauline Oliver Judd, was a housewife who later became a riverboat cook. As a teenager, Naomi married Michael Ciminella. Their daughter, Wynonna, was born in 1964, when Naomi was eighteen years old. A second daughter, Ashley, was born in 1968. That year Naomi divorced Michael and raised the daughters as a single parent. Wynonna's name was changed to Judd after the divorce. To support her family, she worked a number of jobs as a nurse, for which she attended school at the College of Martin in California. She also worked as a clerk, secretary, and waitress. The family lived in poverty and moved often, eventually settling back in Kentucky.

Naomi shared a common interest in music with Wynonna. The two became a popular performing duo. Ashley developed an interest more in acting. Naomi and Wynonna formed The Judds. Wynonna played guitar and sang the lead while Naomi sang backup. The pair moved to Nashville, Tennessee, in pursuit of a music career. In 1983, they signed a recording contract with RCA Records. Over the next eight years, the pair sold over 20,000,000 albums with ten top singles on twenty different charts. They won five Grammys and dominated the country music awards until 1991. The pair performed well together but would often have strong differences off stage.

Naomi's life would see significant changes. In 1989, she married Larry Strickland of the Palmetto State Quartet. In 1991, her music career came to an abrupt halt with a life-threatening diagnosis of hepatitis C. The chronic liver disease caused her to focus only on recovery, which eventually came.

Wynonna's life also saw significant changes with her mother's illness. Wynonna began a solo career with continued success and recognition. In 1992, she debuted a widely acclaimed album and four Top Ten singles. She would produce three other successful albums in the 1990s. Her personal life was full of challenges. In 1994, she had an out-of-wedlock child, creating much criticism from the country music community. She eventually married the father, Arch Kelley, and they had a second daughter in 1996. The couple divorced in 1998.

Mother and daughter reunited for a reunion tour beginning on New Year's Eve, 1999. It was a major success and launched a revival of popular recordings, for the pair and Wynonna's additional solo albums. Naomi began a series of popular television show appearances, sharing experiences of her personal life, especially with kidney disease and chronic depression. She wrote her autobiography, *Love Can Build A Bridge.*

Wynonna experienced a number of personal battles. In 2003, she was arrested for driving while under the influence. Three weeks later she married longtime boyfriend, D. R. Roach. In 2006, she checked into rehab for food dependency. In 2007, she divorced her husband, who had multiple arrests for aggravated sexual battery on a child under the age of thirteen. In 2011, she published a romance novel, *Restless Heart.*

That same year, she married Cactus Moser and moved to Leiper's Fork, Tennessee.

Wynonna's life appears more settled with philanthropic activities with the USO, Habitat for Humanity, YouthAIDS, and various medical services for children and veterans. She has also made many television appearances sharing her life challenges, especially dealing with weight control. She has a new approach about life: "I used to wake up and say, 'Oh, God, it's morning.' Now I say, 'Good morning, God.'"

Naomi and Wynonna Judd have many successes on the professional level, as well as overcoming many personal challenges. While their relationship at times was very contentious, they never lost track of the fact that they were family. They also have strong awareness of their humble beginning in Kentucky.

Regrettably, Naomi Judd's battle with depression worsened the last few years. In early May of 2022, she took her own life just before induction into the Country Music Hall of Fame. Her sudden death has been an inspiration to many others to seek help in their own battles with depression.

Loretta Lynn
Butcher Hollow
Country Singer

She is probably one of the most famous coal miner's daughters in America. Her remote birthplace in Kentucky is also well known to many who have listened to her music and followed her life story in book and on film. She was a mother of four before she was twenty years old. She was a grandmother in her early thirties.

Loretta Webb was born on April 14, 1932, to Clara Marie Ramey and Melvin Theodore "Ted" Webb. Loretta, named after popular television and film star Loretta Young, was the eldest daughter and second of eventually eight children in the family. Her father was a coal miner in the Kentucky Appalachian hills. The family lived in poverty but enjoyed life together centered around music. With little other entertainment available (or affordable), nearly every family in the area was involved in music. The family performed often at church and local community events. Her father would die of black lung disease in 1959 before Loretta became a successful performer.

At the age of fifteen, she married Oliver "Doolittle" Lynn on January 10, 1948. "Doo" was a twenty-one-year-old war veteran known as a hell-raiser. Her relationship with him, would provide the background for much of her musical creations. When she was seven months' pregnant, they moved to Custer, Washington, a logging community. By the age of twenty, she had four children and was occupied with many household chores. She later said, "Before I was singing, I cleaned house; I took in laundry; I picked berries. I worked seven days a week. I was a housewife and mother fifteen years before I was an entertainer."

During her hectic life, she found some relief in music. After being impressed with her singing, Doo bought her a $17 Harmony guitar in 1953. She taught herself to play and began writing her own songs. They were songs of an autobiographical nature, dealing with everyday issues faced by many other women in that day. With Doo's continued encouragement she formed her own small band, the Trailblazers. They played in local nightclubs around the area in Washington and even across the Canadian border in Vancouver. While at a nightclub in Vancouver, a co-founder from Zero Records heard her performance and, in February 1960, persuaded her to make a recording on their label of "I'm a Honky Tonk Girl." With their first recording contract and records in hand, Loretta and Doo, in their old Mercury sedan, started out on a cross-country, self-promoting tour. They stopped at every radio station they could locate and pushed the DJs to play her record. Their strategy worked as the public expressed their approval and wanted to hear more from her.

By the time they reached Nashville, Tennessee, the record had reached the Top 20 of Billboard's Country and Western Chart. There she began cutting records for the Wilburn Brothers Publishing Company, eventually signing a contract with Decca Records. With skyrocketing success with her many new fans, by the end of 1960, she was named by Billboard magazine as No. 4 Most Promising Country Female Artist. She was able to make her first appearance on the famed Grand Ole Opry. She developed many professionally helpful relationships with the Opry performers, especially with Patsy Cline. She officially joined the Grand Ole Opry family on September 25, 1962.

During this time, Loretta faced challenges on several areas of her life. Doo was known to have cheated on her in their relationship. With six children (two sets of twins) to care for, their family life often erupted into heated arguments. Committed to stay together, Loretta used these personal experiences as subjects for her new songs. But she also had contractual issues with the Wilburn Brothers over publishing rights. It would be many years before the dispute was settled.

The songs produced through Decca records created a string of fifty-one Top 10 hits. Owen Bradley of Decca records was said to have been "smitten" with Loretta's innocence, individualism, infectious wit, independent spirit, humorous candor, refreshing frankness and immense talent." A list of just a few of her recordings reveals her personal experiences with married life:

"Before I'm Over You"
"Wine, Women and Song"
"Mr. and Mrs. Used to Be"
"If We Put Our Heads Together"
"The Home You're Tearing Down"
"You Ain't Woman Enough to Take My Man"
"Don't Come Home a Drinkin' With Lovin' on Your Mind"
"Your Squaw Is on the Warpath"
"We've Come A Long Way, Baby"
"Love Is the Foundation"
"One on the Way"
"Out of My Head and Back in My Bed"
"I've Got A Picture of Us on My Mind"
"Making Love from Memory"

Loretta did step into controversial waters with some of her more personal songs, such "The Pill" and "Rated-X," which were censored by some radio stations. Those songs only increased her fan base and relevance. She found a major boost to her career in teaming up with other performers, such as Conway Twitty. They became the most-awarded duet team in country music history. In 1971, Lynn was the first solo female country artist to perform at the White House, at the invitation of President Richard Nixon. She would perform for nearly every other administration after that.

In 1976, Lynn wrote her famous autobiography, *Coal Miner's Daughter*. The book and the associated recording propelled her into the public mind and exposed her to a new set of fans. In 1980, the movie *Coal*

Miner's Daughter was a major success with seven Academy Award nominations. Actress Sissy Spacek won the Best Actress Award for her portrayal of Lynn. Spacek even performed Lynn's songs in the movie.

In 1983, Lynn was inducted into the Nashville Songwriter's Hall of Fame. In 1972, she became the first woman to receive the Country Music Association's "Entertainer of the Year." In 1988, she entered the Country Music Hall of Fame. In the early 1990s, she cut back on her performances to tend to her husband's poor health. The couple had purchased a ranch in Hurricane Mills, Tennessee, where they raised their children and she could work at their recording studio. In 1993, she recorded a successful trio CD, *Honky Tonk Angels*, with Dolly Parton and Tammy Wynette. The trio was nominated for numerous Grammy and Country Music Association awards. In 1995, Lynn was presented with the Pioneer Award at the 30th Academy of Country Music Awards. Her world seemed to stop in 1996 with the death of Doo. She was lost in her world without him, which seemed to be in contrast with their contentious marriage experiences. She would later explain in her second autobiography in 2002, *Still Woman Enough*:

> I married Doo when I wasn't but a child, and he was my life from that day on. But as important as my youth and upbringing was, there's something else that made me stick to Doo. He thought I was something special. More special than anyone else in the world, and never let me forget it. That belief would be hard to shove out the door. Doo was my security, my safety net. And just remember, I'm explainin', not excusin'.... Doo was a good man and a hard worker. But he was an alcoholic, and it affected our marriage all the way through.

It would be another seven years before Lynn returned to the public spotlight. With successful recording produced in the early 2000s. Lynn was the first woman in country music to chart singles in five decades. In 2003, she published a cookbook, *You're Cookin' It Country*. That same year, Lynn was recognized with the Kennedy Center Honors. In 2010, she received a Grammy Lifetime Achievement Award. In 2013, Lynn was awarded the Presidential Medal of Freedom by President Barack Obama. Of Lynn, President Obama noted that "Loretta Lynn is a country music legend. Raised in rural Kentucky, she emerged as one of the first successful female country music vocalists in the early 1960s, courageously breaking barriers in an industry long dominated by men."

Lynn continued in recording successful songs and albums until 2017. She suffered a stroke on May 4, 2017, at her Hurricane Mills home and was hospitalized in Nashville. There are recording projects that she hopes to release in the near future.

Loretta Lynn has an innovative career with outstanding accomplishments. She has written over 160 songs and 60 albums. She has sold over 45,000,000 records worldwide. She is most awarded woman in country music with the following: three Grammy Awards, seven American Music Awards, eight Broadcast Music Incorporated Awards, thirteen Academy of Music Awards, eight Country Music Association Awards, and twenty-six fan-voted Music City News Awards.

Loretta Lynn brought the location of Butcher Hollow and the coal mining operation of the Kentucky Appalachian Mountains to the attention of mainstream America. She is proud of her deep Kentucky roots that gave rise to a talented musician and performer.

Bill Monroe

Rosine

Bluegrass Musician

The recognition of Kentucky as the "Bluegrass State" describes the unique music style created within its borders. The acknowledged "Father of Bluegrass Music" had strong roots and ties to his beloved home state. He brought the music style to the world and was instrumental in opening the door to future players of his musical standard.

William Smith Monroe was born on September 13, 1911, on the family farm in Jerusalem Ridge near Rosine, Kentucky. His father, James Buchanan "Buck" Monroe, was a farmer, sawmill, operator, and popular step dancer. His mother, Malissa Vandiver Monroe, was an accomplished musician who played the fiddle, accordion, and harmonica and who sang the traditional old-time ballads. She was also a homemaker for eight children, of which Bill was the youngest.

Like many of the other rural Kentucky families, the Monroes were a very musical family. The children learned from their parents and developed talents singing and playing musical instruments. Since there were a variety of common musical instruments already assigned to his siblings, Bill, as the youngest, had to settle for learning to play the least popular, the mandolin. It was said that his brothers removed four of the eight strings on his mandolin, so he wouldn't play it so loud. Bill was born with a condition that permanently fixed one eye crossed and limited his vision. He would suffer mental abuse from his siblings and other children.

The children were also influenced by their mother's brother, Pendleton Vandiver. He was physically handicapped and often stayed as a guest in their house. He was also a fiddler and was a popular singer of traditional ballads. When Bill was ten years old, his mother died. Several years later his father died, and Bill was sent to live with his "Uncle Pen." He continued his musical education and learned many of the old Kentucky ballads. They supported the family by playing at community dances and gatherings. They also played with a black blues musician, Arnold Shultz, who played the fiddle and guitar. That was a very unusual team, playing mostly in the segregated social gatherings in the 1920s. From Shultz, Monroe learned to appreciate the distinctive rhythm and style of black blues music.

In 1929, Monroe moved with two older brothers, Birch and Charlie, to Whiting, Indiana, to work at a Sinclair oil refinery. While there, they joined with several other family friends to form the "Monroe Brothers." The Great Depression proved economically challenging for the performers. They worked six days a week in Gary, Indiana, for WJKS for eleven dollars a week. The team broke up with Bill and Charlie, joining forces continuing the Monroe Brothers name. The pair found work with live performances on local radio stations. They traveled making radio station appearances in Indiana, Iowa, Nebraska, and the Carolinas. In 1935, Bill married Carolyn Brown. In 1936, the brothers worked for Crazy Water Crystals on WBT's *Crazy Barn Dance*. They were able to make a number of recordings with RCA Victor. From 1936 through 1938, they recorded over sixty tracks for the RCA Bluebird label.

In 1938, Charlie decided to leave the team. Bill moved to Little Rock, Arkansas, and formed the Kentuckians. They performed on KARK for a brief period. After disappointing experiences, Bill moved on to Atlanta and worked with the popular Crossroad Follies. While there, Bill formed his own band, called the "Blue Grass Boys." The name would be a tribute to his home state and lend a title to the unique style of music they would perform. The group included a banjo, fiddle, guitar, upright bass, and Monroe's mandolin. In October 1939, the band auditioned for the Grand Ole Opry on WSM in Nashville, Tennessee. They were hired and found a permanent home.

In 1940, Monroe made his first solo recording session for RCA Victor, performing "Mule Skinner Blues" with seven other songs. Monroe continued to work with the band's sound, with several players leaving and other new faces filling the open positions. In 1942, David "Stringbean" Akeman was added to play banjo with the band. The group began to develop a changing and appealing unique style, setting them apart from other bands. The big change occurred in 1945 with the addition of two new performers, Lester Flatt and Earl Scruggs. Flatt's steady rhythm guitar established the proper timing for the bluegrass style. Scruggs' unique three-finger banjo picking especially impressed the audiences and other professional musicians. The years of Monroe's experimentation paid off with his ideal bluegrass style now established. The model for this style was found in the band's recording of "Blue Moon of Kentucky." This original bluegrass band would continue their music style even though new players would replace those that left. In 1948, Flatt and Scruggs left to form their own group, the Foggy Mountain Boys.

In 1949, Monroe, having found the sound and style he had worked for, began what he called the "golden age" of his career. A number of what were considered bluegrass classics were written and recorded over the next few years. His personal experiences of sadness and joy became the basis for many of his later songs about family and fame. His high tenor voice added to the mournful sound accompanying the instruments. In 1951, Monroe bought land at Bean Blossom in Brown County, Indiana. The site became a park where many future, popular bluegrass shows would take place. He was sidelined for over four months on January 14, 1953, when his car was struck by a drunk driver. He suffered injuries to his back, left arm, and nose. His band continued but began to lose interest without the main attraction. A major challenge for the continued success of the band was the growing interest in the rock-and-roll sound. Monroe and bluegrass had become the inspiration for new musical interests, such as Buddy Holly, Carl Perkins, Elvis Presley, and even the Beatles. The interest in the pure bluegrass sound was found in a faithful remnant of followers.

The early and mid-1960s brought changes for Monroe and his band. First, the rise of folk music brought about a revival of interest in the bluegrass sound. Second, Monroe found an enterprising and effective manager for the band in the person of Ralph Rinzler. Rinzler began an orchestrated move of bluegrass music appreciation outside of the traditional Southern markets. He scheduled Monroe on Northern college campuses, incorporating the band with the growing folk music interest. During this time, Monroe was first acknowledged publicly as the "Father of Bluegrass." In 1965, the first Annual Blue Grass Music Festival was held at Fincastle, Virginia. In 1967, Monroe started his own festival at his Bean Blossom property in Indiana.

In 1969, Monroe was made an honorary Kentucky Colonel. In 1970, he was named to the Country Music Hall of Fame in Nashville. In 1971, he was elected into the Nashville Songwriter's Hall of Fame. He felt that his crowning achievement came in 1979, when he performed at Ford's Theater in Washington, D.C., for President Jimmy Carter. His heavy schedule was interrupted in 1981 with his diagnosis of cancer. He underwent successful treatment and continued a rigorous tour schedule.

On August 13, 1986, Monroe was honored when the United States Senate passed a resolution recognizing "his many contributions to American culture and his many ways of helping American people enjoy themselves. . . . As a musician, showman, composer and teacher, Mr. Monroe has been a cultural figure and force of single importance in our time." In 1986, he celebrated fifty years in the music business by starting on a rigorous fifty-state tour. In 1988, the Kentucky General Assembly named his song "Blue Moon of Kentucky" the official state song. In 1991, he was inducted into the International Bluegrass Music Hall of Fame. In 1993, he was honored with the Lifetime Achievement Award by the National Association of Recording Arts and Sciences. In 1995, he was presented the National Medal of Arts by President Bill Clinton.

He continued to perform on the Grand Ole Opry until March 1995. In April 1996, he suffered a stroke and was hospitalized. He died at the Northcrest Home & Hospice in Springfield, Tennessee, on September 9, 1996. He was four days shy of his eighty-fifth birthday. His funeral took place at the old Ryman Auditorium in Nashville. He was buried in his place of birth, Rosine, Kentucky.

Among the 150 musicians who appeared in his band, many have gone on to their own national careers. Monroe was the only American to have created an established new genre of music. He played for four sitting US presidents. He was a very private man, rarely interviewed, who kept his family life away from the public. His son, James, proudly continues to share his father's archives and official website. Monroe had a habit of giving out quarters to young people, especially those who sang in his presence.

Monroe was asked to describe what bluegrass music was. He response was "To me bluegrass is really *the* country music. It was meant for country people." When asked to describe its style, he answered, "It's got a hard rive to it. It's Scotch bagpipes and old-time fiddlin'. It's Methodist and Holiness and Baptist. It's blues and jazz and it has a high lonesome sound. It's plain music that tells a story. It's played from my heart to your heart, and it will touch you."

Bill Monroe is a true Kentucky innovator. He shared traditional Kentucky music and experiences through his talent and life experiences. He never forgot his roots and makes every Kentuckian proud of their common heritage.

Dottie Rambo
Madisonville
Gospel Music

She was the most prolific songwriter of her day. She was known as the queen of gospel music. She was proud of her deep roots and her discovered deep spiritual identity. Her Christian faith was her priority in life that threatened to cut her off from family and financial success. Maintaining her Christian commitments would lead her to numerous national music awards and honors by a multitude of famous recording artists.

Joyce Reba Luttrell was born on March 2, 1934, in Madisonville, Kentucky. Her parents were Jerald Vernon "Chick" and Elizabeth Luttrell. She was part of large family that enjoyed singing. She was raised in an Apostolic Pentecostal church with spirited music as an important part of their worship. Although the family, with many others in the Depression era, lived in poverty, she was able to receive a guitar that she learned to play by listening to the Grand Ole Opry on the radio. At the age of eight, she began to write country songs while sitting on the nearby riverbank. When she was ten years old, she was performing country songs on a local radio program. A year later she was performing with her family.

At the age of twelve, she had a life-changing experience in church and became a born-again Christian. Her personal commitment was so strong that she devoted herself to write and sing only Christian music. While her mother and other family members were supportive, her father was strongly opposed to her decision. Wanting to guide her into a more lucrative musical profession, he insisted that she stay with the country music genre. When she refused to accept his directions, he gave her an ultimatum to follow his advice or leave home. She was taken to the bus station by her mother, and with only a cardboard suitcase and a guitar, she left home and headed for Indianapolis, Indiana, to perform in a church.

In Indianapolis, she formed a musical trio, the Gospel Echoes, and toured the Midwest, often staying with pastors' families. In 1950, at a revival meeting she met another singer, Buck Rambo. Soon after their meeting, they married and began to tour together performing in small churches. She would write their songs and sing while playing the guitar. In 1951, their daughter, Reba, was born.

Word of their spiritual performances traveled to other performing groups. "The Rambos," as they were now called, were invited by Louisiana governor Jimmy Dickens to perform at the governor's mansion. Dickens was himself a popular country and gospel music recording artist. Dickens was impressed with the performance and signed her to a contract with his publishing company, Jimmy Dickens Music (BMI). He paid her a $3,000 signing bonus. Part of the agreement was that Dickens would be credited as a co-writer of her songs. For a while Rambo's daughter joined the group of performers.

The reputation of the Rambos increased with her performances and songs written for other performers. In 1967, she made a trip to Vietnam to perform for American troops—the first gospel group to sing there. In addition to the performances, the team also spent much time visiting with the troops and ministering in the field hospitals, aboard the USS *Kitty Hawk* and the USS *Ticonderoga*. Such love and concern impressed the soldiers and their families back home. Warner Brothers Records signed her for a two-record contract. The company wanted to sign only Dottie in strictly a rhythm-and-blues contract. She refused and continued on her own, eventually signing with Benson Records.

1968 was a very good year for Rambo. Other gospel groups were recording songs she had written. Her own album, *It's the Soul of Me,* earned her a Grammy Award for the Best Soul Gospel performance. It was a unique honor for a white woman singing with an all-black choir. *Billboard* magazine called her "Trendsetter of the year." She began appearing with national evangelical figures performing her songs. She would write her most famous song, "He Looked Beyond My Fault (And Saw My Need)." Her songs were recorded by popular artists such as Elvis Presley, Barbara Mandrell, Bill Monroe, Johnny Cash, Whitney Houston, Vince Gill, Dottie West, Pat Boone, Sandi Patty, the Oak Ridge Boys, and many others.

She made a number of television appearances on popular national television shows. She was the popular guest on many of the Christian talk shows. In 1980, she had her own program on Turner Broadcast Network, *The Dottie Rambo Magazine*. It was the No. 1 rated show on that network for six years. She has appeared on six of the *Gaither Homecoming* programs.

In 1989, Rambo suffered a debilitating ruptured disk that left her with severe back pain and paralysis in her left leg. She had a number of surgeries that, after several years, allowed her to walk again. To help with the financial burden, Rambo continued limited appearances on television shows. Another strain on Rambo's life occurred in 1992 when she and Buck separated. They were divorced in 1994.

During this time period, Rambo was recognized for her accomplishments. In 1991, she was inducted into the GMA Dove Gospel Music Hall of Fame. In 1992, she was honored by the Christian Country Music with the Songwriter of the Century Award. In 2000, ASCAP honored her with the prestigious Lifetime Achievement Award. In 2004, she was inducted into the North American Country Music Association International Hall of Fame. In 2006, she was inducted into the Kentucky Music Hall of Fame. Just before she received that award, she recalled, "I have a hard time receiving awards or rewards. But I can tell you this thing will be the one that drives me to tears because it's my home state." In 2007, she was inducted into the Nashville Songwriters Hall of Fame.

In 2002, Rambo made her 71st album, *Stand by the River*. It was her first solo album recorded in eighteen years. The album was very successful, helped by duets with Dolly Parton, and earned nominations for many music awards. She made her last album, *Sheltered*, in 2007. It was released posthumously in September 2009.

Although still somewhat physically handicapped, Rambo continued an active schedule touring across the country. On May 11, 2008, Rambo and her band were on a bus leaving Granite City, Illinois, heading for

Texas for a Mother's Day program. On Interstate 44, near Mt. Vernon, Missouri, in the night her bus was blown off the road in bad weather conditions. Rambo was killed, but her band recovered from serious injuries. Her funeral was held at Christ Church in Nashville, Tennessee, with over 4,000 people in attendance. She was buried at the Woodlawn Memorial Park Cemetery in Nashville. Her honors continued even after her death. She was inducted posthumously into the Christian Music Hall of Fame on June 14, 2008.

Dottie Rambo's life achievements are astounding. She wrote over 2,500 songs. Many she recorded, and many others were recorded by numerous recording stars of various musical genres. Many of her songs have what was "staying power." They continue to be popular and used in worship services today. Gloria Gaither said of her, "Dottie Rambo had the rare gift of a poet and the even rarer gift of being capable of creating both poetry and composing the perfect musical chariot to carry it to the soul. I stand in awe of that double gift."

Kentucky should be very proud to have had such an important role in her life—her upbringing, encouraging her musical gifts, and occupying that special place in her heart for all her life. She was a unique and innovative gift for the world from the state.

Mary Travers
Louisville
Folk Singer

She was a member of the most famous trio of the folk music era. She had very fortunate business associations with folk singers Pete Seeger and Bob Dylan that helped her team and personal career. Her music would serve as the rallying cry for anti-war and equal rights causes of the 1960s and 1970s. The songs still have relevance for the same issues today.

Mary Allin Travers was born on November 9, 1936, in Louisville, Kentucky. She was born into a very activist family. Her parents were Robert Travers and Virginia Coigney. They were both progressive journalists who tried to organize the local Newspaper Guild union. When Mary was two years old, the family moved to Greenwich Village in New York City. Her parents divorced soon after the move. Mary grew up in that unique community and attended the liberal, private Little Red Schoolhouse. She was surrounded by musical legends Paul Robeson and Pete Seeger. She began to idolize the new musical style of folk music by performers such as the Weavers, founded by Pete Seeger. She was drawn to nearby Washington Park Square on Sunday afternoons where the folk artists would perform. She had the opportunity to join in with the singers.

Travers dropped out of school in the eleventh grade to become a part of singing group known as the "Song Swappers." They had the fortune to serve as backup singers for several of Pete Seeger's albums. They were able to perform with him at Carnegie Hall in New York. In 1958, she joined a short-lived Broadway musical and then found her career at a standstill.

Travers had the continued good fortune of meeting just the right people. She met Paul Stookey and Peter Yarrow, who were managed by Albert Grossman. Grossman also managed an upcoming star, Bob Dylan. They were looking to form a beatnik-looking, new folk group envisioned by Grossman as "a tall blond woman, a good-looking man, and a jokester." The three fit his model and begin to practice performing as a trio, using some of the songs written by Dylan and Seeger. In 1961, they made their performance debut at New York's The Bitter End. In 1962, they released their first album, *Peter, Paul and Mary*, with popular songs such as "If I Had a Hammer" and "Where Have All the Flowers Gone?" They found instant success and by 1963 produced additional albums, *Moving* and *In the Wind*. One of their biggest hits on the new albums was "Puff, the Magic Dragon." They earned five Grammy awards for their songs and best-selling albums.

The trio became activists for the anti-war (Vietnam) and equal rights national movements. They made numerous appearances on national television and in various rallies around the country, including marching with Dr. Martin Luther King Jr. in Selma, Alabama. They participated in the 1963 March on Washington, D.C., led by Dr. King. They performed their songs before the huge crowd. They continued to record popular songs such as the No. 1 music chart-topper "Leaving on a Jet Plane," written by John Denver. They also mentored younger future recording artists, such as Gordon Lightfoot and Laura Nyro. In 1969, the trip earned their final Grammy for the best children's album, *Peter, Paul and Mommy*.

In 1970, after nearly a decade of performing, the trio disbanded. Each member tried to start solo careers, but none of them could achieve the success that they had as a trio. Mary recorded five solo albums with only moderate success. Finally, in 1978, they reunited for an anti-nuclear benefit and continued on with their national touring. They produced additional albums with many of the older hits. Their songs were timeless and became part of the new anti-war protestors and human rights activists.

The touring continued throughout the 1980s and into the 1990s. In 2005, Mary was diagnosed with leukemia. She received a needed bone-marrow transplant that provided enough relief for her to continue with the tours. But four years later, on September 16, 2009, she died of complications from the transplant and chemotherapy treatments. A memorial service was held for her on November 9, 2009, at Riverside Church in New York City. It was a four-hour service filled with music and tributes. She was seventy-two years old and was buried at Umpawaug Cemetery in Redding, Connecticut.

Mary's personal life was complicated with her own family's history and the strain of touring performances. In 1960, she had a brief marriage to John Filler that produced her first daughter. In 1963, she married Barry Feinsten and produced her second daughter in 1966. They divorced the next year. In 1970, she was briefly to married Gerald Taylor. In 1991, she married Ethan Robbins, living in Redding, Connecticut. They remained married until her death in 2009. She had two granddaughters.

In the fifty-year career of the trio, they earned five Grammy Awards, made thirteen Top 40 hits, and produced eight gold albums, with five becoming platinum. At her memorial service, co-founder of the Newport Folk Festival Theodore Bikel noted, "There were other people besides Mary who taught us that dissent was right and dissent was just, but only Mary taught us that dissent was also beautiful." Although Mary Travers became a national treasure, her roots were from Kentucky.

Merle Travis

Rosewood

Country Singer

He is another of the amazing musicians originating from the Kentucky coal mine area. He has a unique style of guitar picking named after him. He was a singer, actor, composer, instrumentalist, cartoonist, and even inventor.

Merle Robert Travis was born on November 29, 1917, in Rosewood, Muhllenburg County, Kentucky. His father was a coal miner. Like many of the families, they lived in dire poverty. Music was their life outside of the mines. As a young boy, he began with an interest in playing a five-string banjo. For his twelfth birthday, his older brother gave him a hand-made guitar. The community of musicians was quick to offer instructions on the guitar. Travis was very fortunate to have a most talented group of tutors. He learned his unique three-finger picking style from Mose Rager and black railroad worker Arnold Schultz. Another helpful neighbor was Ike Everly, the father of the later famed Everly Brothers. Travis improved on the three-finger picking style that would make him standout as a guitarist. The three-finger method was described as "a syncopated style of guitar fingering rooted in ragtime music in which alternating chords and bass notes are plucked by the thumb while melodies are simultaneously plucked by the index finger."

As an older teenager, Travis was already an accomplished performer playing in various bands for community events. He also found an income source working for the Civilian Conservation Corps. When he was eighteen, he visited his brother in Evansville, Indiana. There he played "Tiger Rag" on a local radio station and received offers to play with other local bands. In 1937, he was hired by Clayton McMichen to play with his Georgia Wildcats. The next year, he played with the Drifting Pioneers, a Chicago-based gospel group. The band moved to Cincinnati, Ohio, to perform on WLW radio station show *Boone County Jamboree*. The shows also featured other prominent musicians who were impressed with Travis's unique and complicated guitar style. He attracted the attention of Grandpa Jones and The Delmore Brothers. They formed a gospel quartet, The Browns Ferry Four, later becoming the Shepherd Brothers. They became one of the most popular white gospel groups of their time. They began recording for King Records in the 1940s.

With the onset of World War II, fearing being drafted, Travis joined the U.S. Marine Corps. After his time in the military, Travis eventually moved to Los Angeles, California. He was able to appear in several B-movie westerns and played with Ray Whitley's Western Swing Band. He then devoted more time to writing his own songs. In 1946, he was signed by Capitol Records and found successful status with several top ten hits. He produced a box set of records, *Folk Songs of the Hills*. It had only modest success.

Travis designed a solid body electric guitar that was built for him by Paul Bigsby. It was the forerunner and inspiration for Travis's friend, Leo Fender. In 1950, Fender would produce the popular Broadcaster guitar, favored by new musicians.

In 1953, Travis co-hosted, with his wife, Judy Hayden, a television show called *Merle Travis and Company*. Travis was a regular on the *Hometown Jamboree* and *Town Hall Party* television shows. Travis's fame as a songwriter grew with his song for Tex Williams, "Smoke, Smoke, Smoke That Cigarette." It was a million-seller that was followed in 1955 by the even more popular song for Tennessee Ernie Ford, "Sixteen Tons." Both these songs drew on his childhood experiences in Kentucky.

In the early 1960s, Travis's popularity declined with the arrival of the rock and roll invasion. It wasn't until the urban folk music revival of the late 1960s that he was rediscovered as many popular performers acknowledged their debt to Travis's picking style of music.

Travis's public success was countered by troubles in his personal life. He was a heavy drinker and was involved in a number of embarrassing public incidents. He also experienced several divorces and marriages during this time. He fell into some drug abuse. Some of his musician friends attempted to help him through the difficult period in his life. He was still able to perform on other record albums and make some television appearances with the other stars.

In the mid-1960s, Travis moved to Nashville, Tennessee. He found the continuing support of musical stars such as Johnny Cash and especially Chet Atkins. He had influenced both artists with his past songs and performances. In 1966, Travis's improving public image was boosted by his album *Songs of the Coal Mines*. He began to make many more television appearances, performing on popular shows and often joining with other musical performers. In the 1970s, he and wife number four moved to Tahlequah, Oklahoma. He signed a new contract with Los Angeles-based country music label CMH, and his re-released record sales again soared. In 1974, he joined with Chet Atkins, performing duets on their album *The Atkins-Travis Traveling Show*. It won the Grammy Award for Best Country Instrumental Performance. In 1977, Travis was inducted into the Country Music Hall of Fame.

Travis made occasional appearances on limited touring events. On October 20, 1983, he died of a heart attack at his Tahlequah home. His body was cremated, and his ashes were returned home and spread around a memorial erected in his honor near Drakesboro, Kentucky.

Merle Travis was a true innovator in country music. He used his experiences in Kentucky as the subject in many of his songs, but especially used the guitar style he learned from his Kentucky neighbors. His unique guitar style was described as a "trademark mature style [that] incorporated elements from ragtime, blues, boogie, jazz and Western swing, and was marked by rich chord progressions, harmonics, slides and bends, and rapid changes of key." His style became known in the country music industry as "Travis Picking."

Other Kentucky Innovators in the Fine Arts

David "Stringbean" Akeman • *Annville* • Country Singer
Stephen Curtis Chapman • *Paducah* • Christian Singer
Billy Ray Cyrus • *Flatwoods* • Country Singer
Skeeter Davis • *Dry Ridge* • Country Singer
Jackie DeShannon • *Hazel* • Singer/Songwriter
Crystal Gayle • *Paintsville* • Country Singer
Tom T. Hall • *Olive Hill* • Singer/Songwriter
Telma Hopkins • *Louisville* • Singer/Actress
Grandpa Jones • *Niagara* • Country Singer
Mose Rager • *Drakesboro* • Country Instrumentalist
Ricky Skaggs • *Cordell* • Country Singer

Chapter Three

Education and Literature

John James Audubon

Henderson

Wildlife Artist

He was born in a foreign country as the illegitimate son of a wealthy French adventurer. After later being adopted by his father, he lived a life of leisure that allowed him to become captivated by nature and wildlife, especially birds. He traveled to the United States and for a while settled in Kentucky, trying to establish a profitable business that would permit him time in the woods. His talent in art and access to unique bird models resulted in the most famous book regarding the birds of America.

Jean-Jacques Audubon was born on April 26, 1785, in Les Cayes, Saint Domingue, Hispaniola (now Haiti). His father was Captain Jean Audubon, a French adventurer working as a merchant, planter, and slave dealer. Jean-Jacques was the illegitimate son of Captain Audubon and his French servant Jeanne Rabin. She died soon after giving birth and Jean-Jacques and his sisters were sent to Nantes, France, to be raised by Captain Audubon's wife, Anne Moynet Audubon. The children were adopted by the Audubons in 1794, and their last names were changed to Audubon.

Being the son of a prominent Frenchman, Audubon was given a privileged education. He had very little interest in any of the academic areas. He found his greatest enjoyment in the woods and observing nature. He used his natural artistic talent to try and capture the objects of his observations, mostly birds. Trying to bring some degree of discipline to the now spoiled child, his father sent him to a French naval academy, where he spent four unproductive years. He failed to pass the naval entrance exam and returned home to Nantes. He resumed his preoccupation with drawing birds.

Earlier in 1789, Captain Audubon became concerned about the unrest in the Caribbean over slavery and sold his properties. He invested the proceeds in a 284-acre farm, Mill Grove, near Philadelphia, Pennsylvania. In 1803, a war with France and England started. Fearing his son being drafted, his father obtained a fake passport and sent his son to oversee the Mill Grove farm. His son's name was now changed to John James Audubon. Repeating his past habits, he gave little attention to the farm and devoted his time and energy in the new wooded surroundings. He made attempts to improve his recording and drawing of animal species discovered.

He enjoyed his time alone in the woods, drawing and hunting. He became a good athlete and developed skills in music, dancing, and horsemanship. He was a regular at nearby Fatland Ford and the farm of William Bakewell. He was attracted to their daughter, Lucy. They married in 1808, sold their Mill Grove properties, and moved to Louisville, Kentucky. Audubon set up a grocery store with a partner, Ferdinand Rozier. As usual, Audubon gave little attention to the business and spent his time in the woods. Attempts at other business ventures, including lead mining, proved equally unsuccessful. In 1810, the partners left Louisville, hoping to improve their experiences in Henderson, Kentucky. They set up a dry goods store. In spite of the poorly operated business, Audubon continued his interest in travel and observing nature. The partnership was dissolved.

Audubon had additional family responsibilities, with the birth of two sons and two daughters. Both daughters would die in infancy. In 1812, he received US citizenship. With many personal and business expenses and little additional income, Audubon went bankrupt. He even spent time in the Henderson jail for unpaid debts. He started a new partnership with his brother-in-law, Thomas Bakewell. For several years they were successful in starting a flour mill, investing in property, and buying and selling slaves. The businesses were of secondary interest as he continued spending time exploring nature. But in 1819, he again went bankrupt.

Concerned now about his family and simple subsistence, Audubon decided to leave Kentucky and go south to New Orleans. While sailing down the Mississippi River, Audubon earned money by drawing portraits and even teaching drawing. He continued his natural studies on the trip. Upon arrival in New Orleans, Audubon began tutoring students interested in drawing and selling portraits. Learning from her past experience, Lucy became the true breadwinner by becoming a governess. During this time, Audubon came upon a trick to make his drawings seem more lifelike. After he shot a bird, he would use wires to position it and prop it up so that it looked more lifelike. It was a great improvement of quality in his collections.

Audubon was prepared to search for a publisher of his unique collection of drawings. He could not find any interest in the United States. In 1826, on the recommendation of a friend, and with his wife's support, he set sail for England in search of a publisher. His arrival in England was at a great time for a naturalist. There was widespread interest in the American backwoods, especially ornithology. He found a publisher in London, Havell & Sons. In 1827, Audubon's book *Birds of America* was published, featuring 400 plates of his drawings in a four-volume set. It was an immediate success. Audubon went on tour around England and in Scotland, creating even more demand for his work. He even attracted the attention of British King George IV. He was described at that time as

> The tall and somewhat stooping form, the clothes not made by a West End but a Far West tailor, the steady, rapid, springing step, the long hair, the aquiline features and glowing, angry eyes—the expression of a handsome man conscious of ceasing to be young and an air and manner which told you that whoever you might be, he was John Audubon, will never be forgotten by anyone who knew or saw him.

In 1830, he was elected as a Fellow in London's Royal Society, only the second American after Benjamin Franklin. That same year he was elected to the American Academy of Arts and Sciences, for which he had been denied years earlier.

Audubon returned to the United States with fame and monetary success. He continued his exploration of the country, desiring to draw every bird species in America. He would eventually settle on an estate on the Hudson River in New York. He reunited with his family after an absence of three years. In 1843, he published *The Viviparous Quadrupeds of North America*, a work on mammals. His sight began to fail during the process of compiling research for the book. With the help of an assistant and collaborators, he was able to complete the work.

In 1848, Audubon suffered a stroke. It also affected his mind, leading to dementia. He said of himself, "I feel I am strange to all but the birds of America." On January 27, 1851, he died at his Hudson River home. He was buried in the graveyard at the Church of the Intercession in Trinity Church Cemetery and Mausoleum in Manhattan. Audubon received many honors around the world. In the United States, over twenty-eight museums and parks were created in his name, including each of his residences around the country. In 1886, the first bird-preservation society, the *National Audubon Society*, was named in his honor.

His published works have lasting quality that will be studied and enjoyed for years. His biographer, Francis Hobart Herrick, described the *Birds of America* as, "One of the most remarkable and interesting undertakings in the history of literature and science in the nineteenth century. Unique, as it was in every detail of its workmanship, it will remain for centuries a shining example of the triumph of human endeavor and the spirit and will of man."

In Kentucky, he is honored with the 692-acre John James Audubon Park in Henderson. Many of his famous drawings were made from the birds and animals of the state. He was a true innovator.

Ben M. Bogard
Elizabethtown
Clergyman

One of the important values for early Kentuckians was their religious faith. They had religious leaders who were quick to promote and defend their particular beliefs. One of those would become a national defender of faith and travel to several nearby states to organize a national denomination still active and strong today.

Benjamin Marcus Bogard was born on March 9, 1868, in Elizabethtown, Hardin County, Kentucky. He was the only son of six children born to M. L. and Nancy Bogard, tenant tobacco farmers. In 1873, the family moved to Caseyville, Union County, Kentucky. Bogard began his formal education there and attended the Woodland Baptist Church. He also participated in the evangelical camp meetings. As a teenager in February 1885, Bogard became a believer and was baptized in an icy pond to demonstrate his commitment to Jesus Christ.

In 1887, he was ordained as a Baptist minister and began attending Georgetown College near Lexington, Kentucky. In 1889, he continued his studies at the now defunct Bethel College in Russellville, Kentucky. In 1890, he married Lynn Oneida Meachum Owen, a widow with a daughter. They would later have a son. From 1892–1898, he pastored several churches in Kentucky and Missouri.

In 1895, while pastoring in Fulton in southwestern Kentucky, Bogard met John Newton Hall, who was leading a new movement called Landmarkism. Bogard became an active participant in the new movement. In 1899, Bogard and family moved to Arkansas as pastor of the First Baptist Church in Searcy, White County. He was also co-editor of the *Arkansas Baptist* denominational newspaper. In 1901, Bogard received an honorary doctorate degree from Southwest Baptist College in Bolivar, Missouri. In 1905, he left the Southern Baptist Convention and became an Independent Baptist. He pastored the First Baptist Church in Argenta (North Little Rock). In 1909, he became an itinerant minister and held revival meetings in several surrounding states. In 1914, he settled in Texarkana, Miller County, Arkansas. He founded what became *The Baptist and Commoner* newspaper and established the Arkansas Landmark churches and later led them to form the American Baptist Association, commonly called Missionary Baptists. In 1920, he became the pastor of the Antioch Missionary Baptist Church in Little Rock. He was the highest-paid Missionary Baptist pastor at that time. He stayed on as pastor for the next twenty-seven years.

In 1920, Bogard joined the Ku Klux Klan. It was a very popular national movement at the time and was viewed as anti-Catholic. During this time, religious people perceived serious threats from Darwin's theory of evolution, the growing spread of the Church of Christ, ecumenicalism, and Bolshevism. Bogard became an active defender of the faith against all these threats through writing but prominently through personal, public debates. He debated leaders of the Church of Christ. He became more popular when he challenged Clarence Darrow, defender of Darwinism, in debates in Little Rock. The state had placed an anti-evolution bill on the November 1928 election ballot. Darrow had been involved in the famous Scopes Monkey trial in Tennessee.

The November 1928 election was an interesting one for Arkansas. Beside the anti-evolution bill, the national presidential campaign was even more prominent. Running on the Democratic ticket was Alfred E. Smith, a Roman Catholic, for president and Arkansas U. S. Senator Joseph T. Robinson as vice president. Bogard strongly supported the anti-evolution bill and strongly opposed the Democratic ticket. The anti-evolution bill overwhelmingly passed by a two-to-one margin. It would be overturned in 1968 by the U.S. Supreme Court. In Arkansas, the strongly Democratic state favored the Democratic nominees, although they lost on the national ballot.

In 1931, Bogard helped establish the Missionary Baptist Seminary in Little Rock. In 1934, he debated with Aimee Semple McPherson, founder of the International Church of the Foursquare Gospel. They debated the role of miracles in the present age. In 1941, Bogard challenged J. Frank Norris, the fundamentalist leader from Fort Worth, Texas.

On May 29, 1951, Bogard died at his home in Little Rock. He was buried at Roselawn Cemetery in Little Rock. He left his estate to the Missionary Baptist Seminary and the Bogard Press in Texarkana, Arkansas. Conflicts continue in Arkansas between the Southern Baptists, Landmark Baptists, and Missionary Baptists.

Ben Bogard produced many scholarly written documents and is said to have participated in 237 debates between 1904 and 1948. He is honored in *Ripley's Believe It or Not!* for having preached for "sixty-one years without missing a single Sunday." He was a strong and capable defender of particular doctrinal issues but was a very divisive figure concerning denominational issues. He began his professional career in Kentucky and spread his innovative influences throughout the nation.

Edgar Cayce

Beverly

Mystic

He led a controversial life described by some as a mystic and a clairvoyant. Others saw him as a quack. He was described as "the sleeping prophet." From his self-induced trances, he claimed to glean knowledge of human healing and insights into future international events. Even after his death, he continues to draw devout followers and cynical critics. He began his unique career in Kentucky.

Edgar Cayce was born on March 18, 1877, near Hopkinsville, Kentucky. He was one of six children born to farmers Carrie and Leslie B. Cayce. As a child, Cayce played with imaginary friends and claimed to see and talk with his late grandfather. He was regular in church attendance as a member of the Disciples of Christ and regular in Bible reading. He was reportedly visited by an angel and told her (the angel) that he wanted to help others, especially sick children. He was not a good student but developed an ability to memorize pages of textbooks by "sleeping." He told his teacher that he saw "pictures of the pages of his books." With improving grades in 1892, he was considered by his teacher as one of the best students. He also developed an interest in photography.

Cayce could complete only a ninth-grade formal education. He began to experience the phenomenon of diagnosing his own physical ailments while in a self-imposed trance. With word of his abilities spreading, he was asked to perform what were called "readings" on other persons in need of physical cures. With only the person's name and location, he fell into his trance and responded best when asked questions by another person. On March 14, 1897, he became engaged to Gertrude Evans. She would assume the role of the questioner.

Cayce began an apprenticeship at the photography studio of W. R. Bowled in Hopkinsville after a severe and prolonged case of laryngitis. He supposedly discovered cures for his loss of voice through visiting hypnotists and eventually self- hypnotism. Cayce began a habit of offering free treatment through readings for the locals. In May 1902, he got a job in a bookshop in Bowling Green, Kentucky. There he roomed with two doctors, and he continued to give readings without charge. On June 17, 1903, he married Gertrude, and she moved to Bowling Green. With a relative, Cayce opened a photographic studio in Bowling Green. Cayce and Gertrude struggled with the morality and notoriety of the readings. Offers came from others to form a profitable business venture with his readings. These were quickly rejected. By 1907, fire had destroyed the photographic studio, and Cayce was forced to declare bankruptcy.

By 1909, he was debt-free. He found employment at the H. P. Tresslar photography firm. He was persuaded, after persistent pursuit by homeopath Wesley H. Ketchum, to establish a partnership with his readings. There was to be clear understanding that Cayce would receive no financial benefit from the readings. He would be furnished with a photographic studio and a separate office for his readings. During this time, the Cayces lost their second child, even with readings done to seek cures. Gertrude was diagnosed with tuberculosis and was supposedly miraculously healed through his readings. In 1912, learning of Ketchum's dishonesty with him and gambling practices, Cayce quit the partnership and left Kentucky to work in the Tresslar photographic studio in Selma, Alabama.

As word of his practices spread, his work increased. He hired a secretary, Gladys Davis, to record his readings. Readings moved from physical cures to philosophical questions. He even began to foresee the future, making many predictions of things to come. His previous denial of reincarnation was challenged along with his views on religion. It was reported that Cayce "was able to tap the mass of knowledge possessed by millions of other subconscious minds, including those who have passed over to the spiritual cosmic realms in death." Some tried to push Cayce into helping with their selfish interests by revealing winning horses in races. He decided to continue helping only those requesting help for the sick. He refused offers of performing on stage. He now readily accepted the idea of reincarnation and other metaphysical teachings.

In 1925, Cayce heard a voice during one of his trances telling him to move to Virginia Beach, Virginia. The voice said that "the sand's crystals would have curative properties to promote rapid healing." In Virginia Beach, the Cayces were helped financially by some well-meaning donors. Morton Blumenthal bought them a house. Others helped in financing a nearby hospital. On May 6, 1927, the Association of National Investigations was incorporated in Virginia. The organization would manage the hospital and maintain the associated scientific studies. On October 11, 1928, the hospital complex was dedicated, and the first patient admitted. Patients had to agree to join the association for legal protection. A long waiting list developed as several popular professionals joined the association.

The Depression years had a devastating financial effect on the total operations. On February 26, 1931, the Association was closed down. Cayce, upon requests from others seeking the same powers, established "study groups." He stated to the group that "the purpose of life is not to become psychic, but to become a more spiritually aware and loving person." On June 6, 1931, sixty-one people attended a meeting to continue his work, forming a new organization called the Association for Research and Enlightenment. In July 1931, the new organization was incorporated, and Cayce relinquished all the former properties back to Blumenthal.

Hugh Lynn helped the group to organize for education and training. The First Annual Congress of the Association was held in June 1932. Speakers and reading demonstrations were provided for the members. Although the scientific community remained unconvinced, the members took their enthusiasm back to their communities and established local interest groups. By 1941, there were over 500 members. They were able to raise funds for new facilities next to Cayce's home. In 1943, the only biography of Edgar Cayce was written by Thomas Sugrue. The publication brought new interest and additional members into the association.

With the renewed interest came more requests for readings. World War II also brought numerous requests from the families of soldiers for readings. Cayce's habit of conducting no more than four readings per day increased to six per day. It was physically straining and demanding. It was estimated that between June 1943 and June 1944, 1,385 readings were made. In August 1944, Cayce collapsed from the physical strain. He and Gertrude went to the Virginia mountains for rest. But in September 1944, Cayce suffered a stroke. He died on January 3, 1945. He was buried in Riverside Cemetery in Hopkinsville, Kentucky.

The Association in Virginia Beach contains files of over 14,000 readings done in Cayce's lifetime. His client list included many prominent people, such as Woodrow Wilson, Thomas Edison, Irving Berlin, and George Gershwin. Although there are questionable differences regarding the validity of the readings, the attention today seems to be centered more on his predictions. Like many psychics who claim to predict the future, there is a certain percentage that will come true—the vast majority are unfulfilled and are yet to come. Some of the more famous predictions noted were the end of World War II, the discovery of the Dead Sea Scrolls, the deaths of Franklin Delano Roosevelt and John F. Kennedy, and the rise of technological industries. Among the predictions that were not fulfilled was the return of Christ in 1998.

Edgar Cayce provided some valid curative assessments. He also failed to help with others. He had a love for people and refused to make a lucrative career with his "gift." He began his career in Kentucky and chose to have his remains returned to Kentucky. He was a unique individual with controversial practices and teachings.

Thomas D. Clark

Lexington

Historian

Although not born in Kentucky, he was responsible for preserving the documented history of Kentucky for future generations to research and appreciate. He enriched the history department of the University of Kentucky and educated over 25,000 students in history appreciation. He lived to be over one hundred years old.

Thomas Dionysius Clark was born on July 14, 1903, near Louisville, Mississippi. He was raised in a log cabin on a farm with a schoolteacher mother and a farmer father. He was raised at a particularly significant time in the history of the United States. It is likely that he would have encountered living history in the form of Confederate veterans, former slaves, and Choctaw Indians. He was educated early by his mother at home and attended classes through the seventh grade, mostly in his mother's classroom. Not unusual in that time, he dropped out of school and began working on the family farm and at a nearby sawmill. He soon lost interest in that kind of a future life.

When he was sixteen, Clark ignored his mother's urging to continue his education and took a job on a boat dredging the Pearl River. After a couple of years that work became unsatisfactory. When he was eighteen, he finally accepted his mother's advice. He registered to attend high school, the Choctaw Agricultural High School. He played football and received "reasonably basic preparation" after graduating in four years.

He had no money to continue his education. He received ten acres of good land from his father and committed his time and energy to produce a good cotton crop. He had a good crop of cotton that was sold, providing enough money to begin his first year of college at the University of Mississippi in September 1925. To support his remaining three years of college, he found maintenance work on a golf course. By coincidence, he worked with a gentleman named William Faulkner. Clark would not realize Faulkner's celebrity until much later in life. Clark fell in love with the study of history through a close association with his mentor, Charles S. Snyder, a history professor.

In December 1928, he began attending meetings of the American Historical Association in Indianapolis, Indiana. This was unusual for a student. He met other people who would encourage him toward his new direction of becoming a historian. Perhaps through contacts there, he received a scholarship to the University of Kentucky for a graduate degree. He completed his master's degree in just one year.

He was offered a fellowship at Duke University to work toward his doctorate degree. He centered his area of research on the American frontier, the development of Midwestern railroads, and slavery issues in the South. These aided him to produce his first two books. While a doctoral student, Clark married Martha Elizabeth Turner. They would have two children and remain together for sixty-two years. He received his doctorate in history in 1931.

He was asked to teach history courses at the University of Kentucky and to assemble library resources for the university. He was a very popular teacher with his unique storytelling style. He began by teaching five courses in British history. He had a very routine schedule, working hard teaching in the day and collecting and organizing historical materials well into the night. In 1937, he wrote *The History of Kentucky*, which would be used for his own classes. He eventually became head of the university's history department in 1942 and served until 1965.

Significant Kentucky historical records were being stored at the state capitol in Frankfort in deplorable conditions. When Albert "Happy" Chandler became governor, he ordered a cleanup of the state records. To the workers, that meant discarding the records. Four trucks were loaded to be delivered to Louisville and sold as scrap paper. Clark was informed about the situation late one night and raced to Frankfort. Standing by the trucks, he got the governor out of bed and apprised him of the situation. The papers contained military records of Kentuckians involved in the Battle of 1812, the Mexican War, and the Civil War. He was able to convince the governor to have these moved to the Lexington campus of the University of Kentucky under his care.

He was able to persuade a number of his students to assist in the organization of the papers for the university's research center. He was able to gather other significant resources from around the state to add to the special documents collection. He became recognized throughout the country for his historical contributions and interest in preserving documented history.

Clark wrote over thirty books on his portable typewriter. He had no interest in learning to use computers. He retired from the University of Kentucky faculty in 1968. From 1968 until 1973, he taught at numerous other universities in the country and even at the University of Vienna. He served as leader in many of the national historical organizations. He also served for forty-four years on the Kentucky State Archive Commission. In 1991, he witnessed the dedication of the Kentucky History Center in Frankfort, a project he had long promoted.

In 2004, he received the American Historical Association's Award for Scholarly Distinction. He continued to write and publish his books. He never ended his discovery of new resources for the Kentucky Historical Society. The center would bear his name in 2005.

After a brief illness, on June 29, 2005, Clark died in Lexington. He was survived by his second wife, Loretta Gilliam. His first wife had died in 1995. He would leave two children, three grandchildren, and five great-grandchildren. In 2006, the graduating class at the University of Kentucky presented Historical Marker #2232 in his honor.

The lasting legacy of Thomas Dionysius Clark will continue to enrich Kentuckians for many years. Students will benefit from his valiant efforts at organizing and preserving important state documents in their education aspirations. He chose to spend ¾ of his lifespan in the state he came to love.

Mordecai Ham
Allen County
Evangelist

He began his evangelistic ministry in his home state of Kentucky. His evangelistic meetings had thousands in attendance. Over a thirty-year period more than 300,000 new converts united with Baptist churches in Georgia, Alabama, Mississippi, Tennessee, the Carolinas, and Kentucky. He was controversial, having devout followers and dangerous social enemies. Among his converts were hardened criminals and future international evangelists.

Mordecai Flower Ham Jr. was born on April 2, 1877, in Scottsville, Allen County, Kentucky. His parents were Tobias and Ollie (McElroy) Ham. He came from a long line of eight generations of preachers, including his famous grandfather, Mordecai F. Ham Sr. It was assumed by all that Mordecai would follow in his ancestors' profession. Mordecai Jr. recalled, "From the time I was eight years old, I never thought of myself as anything but a Christian. At nine, I had definite convictions that the Lord wanted me to preach. . . ."

The family attended church at Greenwood in Warren County. Kentucky. Ham became an active church leader but was deeply bothered by the poverty conditions that preaching created for his father and grandfather. He felt like he needed good financial support before going into a preaching ministry. He attended Ogden College in Bowling Green, Kentucky. He was tutored in law study but was too young to take the bar exam. He found success as a traveling salesman for a grocery company. In 1897, he was crew manager for a picture-enlarging firm in Chicago, Illinois. He was called back to Kentucky in 1899 when his grandfather was near death. Ham recalled, "Seeing him die did more than anything else to convince me of the reality of Christian experience." He reconnected with his feeling about surrendering to a called ministry.

With a solid financial situation, he married Bessie Simmons in July 1900. After much consideration and prayer, Ham decided in December 1900 to quit his business and return his share to a partner. He borrowed $1,700 from a bank and devoted himself to eight months of intensive, personal training through reading books and Bible study.

In September 1901, Ham's first sermon was at the family church in Scottsville. His sermon, "The Absolute Lordship of Jesus Christ," greatly impressed the congregation. He received immediate invitations to preach at other churches in the town. His first revival followed soon after at Mt. Gilead Baptist Church. During the revival, Ham experienced a captivating encounter with the Holy Spirit that would provide the spiritual power for future revivals. He was ordained to the gospel ministry at Drake's Creek Baptist Church in Bowling Green.

In his first year of ministry, it was reported that he had made over 33,000 converts. His reputation was spreading both positively and negatively. He received numerous requests for revivals and, along with those, numerous threats on his life. As lives were being changed for the better, business was being lost at the more sinful local establishments. Personal tragedy struck on December 4, 1905, when his wife died of cerebral meningitis. He was greatly affected by her death. Losing much weight and in despair, he found some relief in January 1906 by sailing to the Near East and making a tour of the Holy Land.

He returned from the trip renewed in his spirit and evangelistic commitment. He had successful revival meetings in Texas, North Carolina, and Kentucky. Ham had trouble getting the full backing of local clergy with Ham's anti-Jewish and anti-Catholic pronouncements. This would follow him throughout his career. The particpants of immoral establishments joined with others in making personal threats.

Ham's life would change with revival services in August 1907 at Pleasureville, Kentucky. Dr. and Mrs. W. S. Smith, from Eminence, brought their fourteen-year-old daughter Annie Laurie to the services. Ham visited their home, and Annie Laurie developed a friendship with Ham. At the end of the revival services, Ham mentioned to Mrs. Smith that he wanted to take their daughter with him on his trip to Europe—as his wife. Ham had just turned thirty, and Annie Laurie had just turned fifteen. On June 30, 1908, the two were married. Three days later they sailed for Naples, Italy.

Upon their return to the United States, Ham continued his circuit of revival services with Annie Lurie playing piano. They would have three children and a happy marriage that lasted more than fifty years. They established their home in Anchorage, Kentucky. In 1912, Ham joined with musician W. J. Ramsey. The two would become known as "Ham and Ram." They would work together until 1945. In 1926, W. O. Saunders, a newspaper editor in Elizabeth City, North Carolina, was bothered by the anti-Jewish and anti-Catholic declarations of Ham. He produced what was called derogatorily *The Book of Ham*, which followed Ham wherever he had scheduled revival services.

1927 was a significant year of change for the Hams. He had prepared for a revival service at the First Baptist Church in Oklahoma City, Oklahoma. Getting off the train, he was met by forty leading members of the church. Their pastor had resigned, and they extended an invitation to Ham to be their pastor. Confident that there were members unhappy with his messages, Ham agreed if there was a unanimous vote by the church in calling him. Much to his surprise, the vote was unanimous, and Ham reluctantly accepted the call to serve as their pastor, beginning on June 19, 1927.

The vote in the church may have been unanimous, but the sentiment by some of the townspeople was not as welcoming. Ham had become a leading national proponent of the Prohibition Movement. He also had a fight with the American Association for the Advancement of Atheism. He became involved in the 1928 national election for president. Al Smith, Catholic governor of New York, was running against Herbert Hoover. Ham declared rather boldly, "If you vote for Al Smith, you're voting against Christ and you will be damned." On August 3, 1928, while crossing a street in Oklahoma City, Ham was hit by a car and dragged for half of a block. He was hospitalized for six weeks. Although church attendance and membership grew, he resigned from the pastorate on June 16, 1929.

The Hams returned to Louisville, Kentucky, and joined the Walnut Street Baptist Church. Over the next several years, Ham witnessed some very significant conversions in his revival services. In 1932, in Johnson City, Tennessee, Wyatt Lattimore, king of the local underworld, was converted. Many of his gang members were also converted. In 1933, in Little Rock, Arkansas, a heavyweight fighter and city roughneck was converted. He eventually pastored a church in New Orleans. In 1934, in Charlotte, North Carolina, young Billy Graham was converted, continuing the evangelistic traditions. Not until some years later would Ham appreciate the significance of what he felt was a comparatively unproductive revival service in Charlotte.

In 1935, Ham was honored with a D.D. degree from Bob Jones University. In 1936, he was elected president of the International Association of Christian Evangelists. He wrote *The Second Coming of Christ* and *Revelation*. He also wrote many Christian pamphlets. By 1940, Ham was beginning to slow down his pace, especially with traveling. He did start a radio ministry on the Mutual Broadcasting System, aligned with over fifty stations. He always included the words, "I'll meet you on the air, until I meet you in the air." In 1947, he began publication of a Christian paper, *The Old Kentucky Revivalist*.

In 1958, Billy Graham flew Ham to San Francisco, California. He joined Graham at a meeting in the Cow Palace. Graham proudly introduced the eighty-one-year-old evangelist to those in attendance. Three years later, on November 1, 1961, Ham died. He was honored by over 1,000,000 people who had heard his gospel presentations.

He was influenced by the evangelist Billy Sunday and influenced the evangelist Billy Graham. He was a controversial historical figure with devoted adherents and bitter enemies. He modeled the danger of evangelists getting involved in local and national politics. He was a master orator and plain-speaking communicator. Mordecai F. Ham Jr. was an innovator with strong ties to Kentucky.

Duncan Hines
Bowling Green
Food Critic

His rise to fame was accidental—not in the traditional professional and academic path. The American public was more familiar with the brand name than the person. His Kentucky roots provided the background for his unplanned and accidental professional success.

Duncan Hines was born on March 26, 1880, in Bowling Green, Kentucky. He was the youngest child of a former Confederate soldier. His mother died when he was four. His father sent him and one of his older brothers to live with his grandmother. His biographers indicate that Hines was a bit of a troublemaker and instigator. He attended Bowling Green Business University. Having asthma problems, he left for the American West.

He worked for Wells Fargo and the Green Copper Company. After several years, he worked as a traveling salesman based in Chicago. There he married his first wife, Florence. Having been spoiled by the home cooking of his grandmother, he became an observer of where to find good food during his sales travels. During the early 1930s, Hines began to document good places to eat and sleep around the country. This was before interstate highways and established food and motel chains.

Several years later, he and Florence divorced on the grounds of "cruelty." He moved back to Bowling Green. There was criticism of some of his personal business habits. He hired female secretaries based on their looks. He had a violent temper, exploding publicly over the most trivial events. He was also described as a snob and very vain. It was noted that he had a sign in his front yard announcing where he lived.

Although he was not personally a good cook, he was becoming one of the country's best food critics. Because of the many requests for information, Hines prepared a list of several hundred top restaurants discovered in the country. In 1935, he included printed copies of the list in his Christmas cards for family, friends, and business associates. The response to the list proved very popular and, in 1936, led Hines to expand the list into a book, *Adventures in Good Eating*. With good sales, the book was expanded further in 1937. In his 1939 edition, Hines noted:

> Corbin, KY. Sanders Court and Café
> 41- Jct with 25, 25E. ½ Mi. N. of Corbin. Open all year except Xmas.
> A very good place to stop en route to Cumberland Falls and the Great Smokies.Continuous 24-hour service.
> Sizzling steaks, fried Chicken, country ham, hot biscuits.
> L. 50 cents to $1; D., 60 cents to $1.
> Between 1936 and 1947, about two million books were sold.

Hines's business training and experience allowed him to expand this innovative venture. He expanded his writings to include the best hotels and motels. Descriptions and ratings were given to each. He was the national traveling authority by the mid-1940s. Following World War II, returning GIs and their families bought cars and were anxious to vacation and see the country. This only increased the demand for the limited traveling information.

His name recognition was high in the country. Capitalizing on that in 1949, he formed a partnership with businessman Roy H. Park. They formed Hines Park Foods, Inc., located in Ithaca, New York. They would allow the Hines name to endorse certain products, from ice cream to cake mixes. Hines would never allow anyone to buy a good review of their business from him. In the 1950s, he came up with the idea of posting metal signs that gave a particular business the Hines recommendation for travelers. The businesses were charged a fee for the signs. The stores recognized were also expected to promote and sell his books.

By 1955, Duncan Hines labeled products were bringing the company over $50 million in royalties. In 1956, the company merged with Procter & Gamble. The number of products endorsed expanded and his name came to symbolize quality for the consumer. On March 15, 1959, Hines died of lung cancer. He was buried in Fairview Cemetery in Bowling Green, Kentucky. A museum was founded in his honor at the Western Kentucky University.

Duncan Hines is still a very respected name in brand advertising. He is perceived as a beloved gourmet of quality food. He business background made him an innovative and successful entrepreneur. His Kentucky roots remained a strong force throughout his lifetime.

Harlan Hubbard

Bellevue

Artist/Author

He loved and lived in nature in the woods of Kentucky. He was an adventurer who wrote uniquely of his travels and painted scenes of his surroundings, mostly landscapes. He was a devoted husband and supporter of public education in the arts.

Harlan Hubbard was born on January 4, 1900, in Bellevue, Kentucky. Not much is known of his early childhood. When Hubbard was seven years old, his father died. His mother took him to New York City to be with his two older brothers. He attended Childs High School in the Bronx and continued his studies at New York's National Academy of Design. He received further education at the Art Academy of Cincinnati. In 1919, he returned to Kentucky, settling with his mother in Fort Thomas.

Hubbard became an observer of the natural life around northern Kentucky and the Ohio River. He had become dissatisfied with the growing industrialism and urbanization of the American society. He began keeping a daily journal of his observations and thoughts of his growing concerns. Comparatively late in life, Hubbard married Anna Eikenhout in 1943. She shared many of his concerns, and they would become true partners in life.

In 1944, they built a shantyboat at Brent, Kentucky. For the next eight years, they sailed down the Ohio and Mississippi Rivers. They recorded a detailed journal of their travels and experiences. In 1951, they arrived at the Louisiana bayous. In 1953, Hubbard published his first book, *Shantyboat.*

The Hubbards returned to Kentucky and settled in a place called Payne Hollow in Trimble County. In the woods close to the Ohio River, they enjoyed their living-off-the-land lifestyle. Harlan raised goats and fished in the river. He cut wood for the woodstove and discovered some useful items that had drifted down the river. Anna proved to be an industrious homemaker, preserving and preparing food for meals. Their water came from filtered roof water collected in a cistern. Every day the two read to each other, played music, and kept a journal. He spent many days painting landscapes of rural Kentucky and nearby Indiana.

They would travel to Indiana for shopping and especially to visit Hanover College. They became good friends with then-college president John Horner and his family. The Hubbards were given special privileges on campus and developed close relationships with many of the students. The students were often the guests at the Hubbards' home, and a mentoring relationship with some was established. In 1973, the home and their lifestyle were the subject for Hubbard's second book, *Simply Living at Payne Hollow.*

Through their good relationship with Hanover College and many friends and houseguests, word of Hubbard's writing and painting spread around the country. In 1988, Hubbard gave the college fourteen of his favorite paintings. He was very reluctant to sell his paintings. Hubbard was battling prostate cancer. A hospital bed was set up in their home, and Anna cared for him until her death in 1986. He died on January 16, 1988. His third book, *Shantyboat and the Bayous*, was published in 1990.

Hanover College established the Anna and Harlan Hubbard School of Living for the purpose to "help teach people how to make their lives a work of art." The Payne Hollow home has become a place for other artists to visit and enjoy. In 2016, the "Harlan Hubbard Studio and Preserve" in Fort Thomas was added to the National Park Service's Registry of Historic Places.

Robert Penn Warren

Guthrie

First U.S. Poet Laureate

He is the only American to have received a Nobel prize for both a novel and a book of poetry. He received these awards and wrote ten novels and thirteen collections of poetry, all while he was a full-time college professor. He was the first Poet Laureate of the United States.

Robert Penn Warren was born on April 24, 1905, in Guthrie, Kentucky. His father, Robert Franklin Warren, was a businessman. His mother, Anna Ruth Penn Warren, was a schoolteacher. He was their oldest child. Guthrie was located on the Kentucky-Tennessee border, and Warren attended Clarksville High School in Tennessee, graduating in 1921. He went on the Vanderbilt University in Nashville, Tennessee. He originally began to study science but was more interested in literature. Warren found encouragement and support from three English faculty members, and after joining them, he became the youngest member of a poetry interest group called the Fugitives. They published a newsletter that contained some of Warren's earliest poetry. In 1925, Warren graduated *summa cum laude*.

That same year, Warren entered the University of California at Berkeley in a English graduate program. He received his master's degree in

1927. He continued his graduate study at Yale University. In 1928, he left the United States for Oxford University as a Rhodes Scholar. He reconnected with fellow Vanderbilt alumni and Rhodes Scholar Cleanth Brooks. The two would work together, producing textbooks. Warren received his B.Litt. degree from Oxford in 1930.

That fall, Warren accepted a teaching position as assistant professor of English at Southwestern College in Memphis, Tennessee. It was the beginning of a continuous forty-three-year teaching career. That year he also married Emma Brescia of San Francisco. The next year he accepted a position at Vanderbilt University as assistant professor of English. He enjoyed the familiar surroundings and association with fellow faculty members. He began writing several novels that were ultimately rejected by publishers.

In 1934, Warren moved to Louisiana State University at Baton Rouge. He was again assistant professor of English. While there, he was a witness to the rise and fall of powerful state governor, Huey Long. As Warren learned of Long's political activities and influences, he later would use that background for one of his most popular future novels. At Louisiana State, Warren was joined on the faculty by his friend, Cleanth Brooks. The two collaborated on significant English textbooks: *An Approach to Literature* (1936) and *Understanding Poetry* (1938). He also found success in publishing. His collection of poetry, *Thirty-Six Poems*, was published in 1935. His first novel, *Night Rider*, was published in 1939. From 1939--1940, Warren received a Guggenheim Fellowship that allowed his study in Italy. He was there during the rise to power of Benito Mussolini. He continued his writing and also edited short stories by other Ssouthern writers.

In 1942, Warren became Professor of English at the University of Minnesota, with an increased salary and better title. He spent seven years in Minnesota. While there, he was also productive in getting many of his works published. Working again with Brooks, they had published other textbooks: *Understanding Fiction* (1943) and *Modern Rhetoric, with Readings* (1949). He was named Consultant in Poetry to the Library of Congress in 1944. His most famous work, a novel, *All the King's Men*, won the Pulitzer Prize for Fiction in 1947. The work was influenced by his knowledge of Huey Long's career while he was in Louisiana. In 1949, the film adaptation of his book won the Academy Award for Best Motion Picture.

In 1950, he moved to Yale University to become the Professor of Playwriting. After a failed first marriage, in 1952 Warren married Eleanor Clark. They would have two children. He wrote other novels and received honors for his collections of poetry. In 1958, he won the Pulitzer Prize for Poetry with his *Promises: Poems, 1954-1956*.

In 1954, Warren accepted an assignment from *Life* magazine to travel around the country to gather reactions to the Supreme Court's decision that year on public school integration. Being from the South and knowing the issues involved, Warren set out on trip that was potentially dangerous. He found the expected reactions of anger from concerned Southerners and fear from some African Americans. He wrote about his journey and the reactions in his 1956 book, *Segregation: The Inner Conflict in the South*. He wrote,

> We have to deal with the problem our historical moment proposes, the burden of our time. We all live with a thousand unsolved problems of justice all the time.... All we can do for posterity is to try to plug along in a way to make them think we—the old folks—did the best we could for justice, as we could understand it.

In 1961, Warren became the Professor of English at Yale. In 1970, he was awarded the National Medal for Literature. In 1973, he retired from Yale with the position of Professor Emeritus. In 1979, he won another Pulitzer Prize for Poetry with his *Now and Then: Poems 1976–1978*. In 1980, Warren was presented with the Medal of Freedom, the highest civilian award given in America. It was presented to him in the Rose Garden by President Jimmy Carter. In 1986, Warren was appointed the first Poet Laureate of the United States.

Warren and family lived the later part of his life in Fairfield, Connecticut, and Stratton, Vermont. On September 15, 1989, he died in Stratton from complications of bone cancer. He was buried at Stratton but requested that a memorial marker be placed in the Warren family gravesite in Guthrie, Kentucky. That same year, Vanderbilt University established the Robert Penn Warren Center for the Humanities, sponsored by the university's College of Arts and Sciences.

On February 26, 1986, Librarian of Congress, Daniel J. Boorstin, described Warren. He said:

> "Robert Penn Warren is a characteristically American man of letters in range and versatility of his writings and in his feelings for the promise and the frustrations of American life. He has high attainment in poetry, fiction, criticism, and social commentary.... If there is any person today whose work unites our America in its splendid variety, that person is Robert Penn Warren."

Warren brought much of his Kentucky background into his writings and his teachings. His awards and honors reflect the admiration that organizations and institutions held for him. His works are a lasting legacy of the man from Kentucky.

Other Kentucky Innovators in Education and Literature

Wendell Berry • *Henry County* • Writer/Activist

Chapter Four

Business, Science and Technology

James Gilbert Baker

Louisville

Astronomer

He was an award-winning scientist with innovative designs and applications for optical telescopes, and the first person to use a computer in his research on building lenses for telescope cameras. He helped the U.S. military in several war efforts through his satellite cameras. He began his education and professional training in his home state of Kentucky.

James Gilbert Baker was born on November 11, 1914, in Louisville, Kentucky. He was the fourth child of Jesse B. Baker and Hattie M. Stallard. He received his early education in Louisville. He graduated from DuPont Manual High School and attended the University of Louisville. He majored in mathematics and was greatly influenced by astronomy professor Dr. Moore. He used the university telescopes to explore the universe at night. He began the process of grinding his own telescope mirrors. In 1933, he helped establish the Louisville Astronomical Society. While at the university, he married Elizabeth Katherine Breitenstein of Jefferson County, Kentucky. In 1935, he received his B.S. degree and was awarded a Woodstock medal.

In the midst of the Great Depression, Baker began his graduate study in astronomy at the Harvard College Observatory. He earned his M. S. degree in 1936. In 1937, he was appointed a Junior Fellow in the honored

Harvard Society of Fellows and served until 1943. In 1942, he received his Ph.D. degree in astronomy and astrophysics from Harvard.

Baker began experimenting with designs for astronomical instruments with increased powers and wide-angle capabilities. His work caught the attention of Colonel George W. Goddard. With World War II underway, the U.S. Army was searching for improved aerial reconnaissance techniques requiring specific lens construction. Baker became the director in the Observatory Optical Project at Harvard from 1943 until 1945. After the war, Baker continued his associate professorship at Harvard but moved his lab to Boston University.

In 1945, he co-authored a book with George Z. Dimitroff, *Telescopes and Accessories*. In 1948, he received an honorary doctorate from the University of Louisville. That same year, he received the Presidential Medal for Merit for his military service in the Office of Scientific Research and Development.

In 1948, Baker moved to Orinda, California, and worked as a research associate at Lick Observatory. He studied there for two years before returning to Harvard in 1950. There, the high volume of design calculation was aided by the new Harvard Mark II computer. Baker became the first person to use numerical computers in helping with the complicated ray-trace application for cameras. He expanded his work to include delivery systems for the cameras. His family was also involved in the design creations.

He served as chairman of the U. S. Air Force Scientific Advisory Board. In that capacity, he became concerned with how his creations could be used for national security. In 1957, especially after the launch of Russia's Sputnik satellite, he was instrumental in designing the U-2 spy planes, making use of his camera systems. He and associate Edwin Land persuaded President Eisenhower to deploy these planes as reconnaissance around the world. His designs would also be a crucial part of President Kennedy's involvement in the Cuban missile crisis of 1962.

In 1958, Baker became a Fellow of the Optical Society of America. In 1960, he was elected as its president. He received numerous awards for his scientific contributions, including the folding optics for the Polaroid SX-70 Land Camera and the Paul-Baker telescope. He expanded his aerial reconnaissance work with the Air Force's SR-71 Blackbird plane. It was used until the 1990s.

In 1970, he was elected a member of the American Philosophical Society and the National Academy of Engineering in 1979. In 2000, he received the Pioneers of National Reconnaissance Medal noted "As a young Harvard astronomer, Dr. James G. Baker designed most of the lenses and many of the cameras used in aerial over-flights of 'denied territory' enabling the success of the U. S. peacetime strategic reconnaissance policy." In 2002, he was awarded the Space Pioneer Award by the U.S. Air Force.

Baker retired in 2003 but continued to work at his home. In his lifetime, he presented more than thirty professional papers and was owner of over fifty U. S. patents. He died on June 29, 2005, in Bedford, New Hampshire. He was survived by his wife, four children, and seven grandchildren.

Early in his career, Baker reflected on the inspiration for his work, "After all, it is the satisfaction obtained which benefits humanity, more than any other thing. It is in the satisfaction of greater human knowledge about the cosmos that the scientist is spurred on to greater efforts." This remarkably innovative man began with the rich groundwork of Kentucky education and inspiration.

Stephen Bishop
Edmonson County
State Explorer

He was a most unusual man with a most unusual background. He was the first person to effectively map out exploration of a cave. He had no formal education. He was a mixed-race slave. He became a popular cave guide and was the subject of several books written about his life. He died one year after he was freed.

Stephen Bishop was born in 1821 into slavery. While most slaves were located on plantations, Bishop was very different. He was described as part mulatto and part (American) Indian. In 1838, he was sold to Franklin Gorin, along with two other slaves and the land that included Mammoth Cave. The three were to serve as guides in the cave for tourists. They learned the tour routes from former white guides. Bishop began to stand out immediately as a unique guide. He was a showman with an interesting "singing voice." Gorin said of Bishop, "Stephen was a self-educated man. He had a fine genius, a great fund of wit and humor, some little knowledge of Latin and Greek, and much knowledge of geology, but his great talent was a knowledge of man."

Bishop soon became very bored with the routine cave tours and sought to explore new areas of the cave. He explored never-before-seen passages and made many discoveries. Much of the cave exploration ended at what was called the "bottomless pit." With help from an associate, Bishop formed a ladder across the pit and found new passages and rooms. He discovered the first body of water ever encountered in a cave. He also discovered strange blind fish, snakes, silent crickets, bear remains, and ancient Indian gypsum workings.

In 1839, Bishop, along with the other slaves and the Mammoth Cave lands, were purchased by Dr. John Croghan of Louisville, Kentucky. He met a house slave named Charlotte Brown on Croghan's estate. They married in 1843, and the next year, a son was born. After a few years assisting in a tuberculosis hospital necessitated by an epidemic, Bishop was sent back briefly to Mammoth Cave to draw a map of the cave system with his discoveries.

Bishop's map offered the first detailed drawing of a major cave system. It included ten miles of cave passages with dimensions and lengths, indications of water locations, and junction locations. His map showed the truly "mammoth" scale of the cave system. It was published in 1844 as a pull-out insert in Alexander Clark Bullit's *Rambles in Mammoth Cave in the Year 1844*. Bishop was given full credit for the map, which was very unusual for a slave. The map was in use for over forty years.

Bishop would continue his work as a cave guide. Cave visitor, Bayard Taylor, described him,

> He is a slight, graceful, and very handsome mulatto of about thirty-five years of age, with perfectly chiseled features, a keen dark eye and glossy hair, and mustache. He is the model of a guide—quick, daring, enthusiastic, persevering, with a lively appreciation of the wonders he shows, and a degree of intelligence unusual in one of his class. . . . I think no one can travel under his guidance without being interested in the man, and associating him in memory over which he is chief ruler.

Bishop's owner, Dr. John Croghan died in 1849, perhaps from the tuberculosis epidemic. That may have also affected Bishop's short life. In 1856, Bishop was freed, according to the wishes in Croghan's will. It was thought that Bishop wanted to buy the freedom of his wife and child and travel to Liberia. Unfortunately, in 1857, Bishop died before his wishes could be fulfilled. He was buried on a hill above the cave in what was later called The Old Guides' Cemetery. A later cave visitor was very impressed by the stories of Bishop and a chance meeting with Bishop's widow, Charlotte, so much so that he made provisions for a headstone to be placed at Bishop's grave. The marker reads "Stephen Bishop. First Guide & Explorer of the Mammoth Cave. Died June 15, 1859 in his 37 (sic) year."

Several books have been written about Bishop's life and accomplishments. In 1977, Mammoth Cave historian Harold Meloy wrote *Stephen Bishop: The Man and the Legend*. Roger Brucker wrote a novel, *Grand, Gloomy, and Peculiar: Stephen Bishop at Mammoth Cave*. Brucker noted, "Stephen was noted for being the first systematic cave explorer. He was the prototype for guiding, educating, and entertaining cave visitors. He was the economic engine that put Mammoth Cave on the map of American natural wonders."

Stephen Bishop was a true product of Kentucky. He spent his entire, all-too-short life, in the state. He marveled at the natural wonders of the state and sought to share that knowledge and experience with all who were fortunate to have encountered him as a cave guide.

George Devol
Louisville
Inventor, Unimate

Anyone who has ever walked through an automatic door entrance/exit, used a microwave, had an item scanned by a barcode reader, or purchased a car, you have been influenced by this inventive person. He began his life in Kentucky and would achieve international recognition for all of his unique creations.

George Charles Devol Jr. was born February 20, 1912, in Louisville, Kentucky. He was fortunate to have been born into a wealthy family that indulged his early interest in electricity and machines. His father was a traffic manager with Louisville & Nashville Railroad. He attended Riordan Prep School and was able to help run the school's electric light plant.

After graduation, he had no interest in higher education. He used his mechanical skills to try to develop a better sound quality for the new "talking pictures." He used his familiarity with vacuum tubes, photocells, and circuits. In 1932, he formed his own business, United Cinephone Corp. He found that the competition from major companies, like RCA and Western Electric, in that area was far beyond his level of experience and investment. He decided to give up that business.

He changed creative direction with his invention of the automatic door. Using the same vacuum tubes and photocells, he was able to create and license the discovery to Yale & Towne. They began a widespread production of the new automatic door system being used originally in grocery stores and expanding to other businesses. Using his original company, United Cinephone, and inspired by his success with the automatic door, Devol developed other now commonly used devices, such as an early barcode system. It was originally used for the Railway Express Agency and expanded to other businesses. He also developed optical registration controls, phonograph arms, and amplifiers. In 1939, he created an automated photoelectric counter system. It was first used at the New York World's Fair to count entering fairgoers.

In 1938, Devol married Evelyn Ruth Jahelka. They would have three children. She played an important role assisting him in his work.

As World War II began its impact on the country, Devol sold his United Cinephone business interest. He contacted Sperry Gyroscope trying to interest them in his ideas on radar technology. The company hired him as Special Projects Department Manager. He helped to create radar and microwave equipment. In 1943, Devol organized General Electric Industries in Greenwich, Connecticut. The company developed important radar countermeasures for the U.S. military that were used by allied planes on D-Day.

After the war, Devol continued his creative work in other areas. He developed a system for magnetic recording and digital playback devices. He also worked with others to develop the first microwave oven, called the "Speedy Weeny."

In 1954, Devol applied for a patent on a concept called Programmed Article Transfer. He wrote, "the present invention makes available for the first time a more or less general purpose machine that has universal application to a vast diversity of applications where cyclic digital control is desired." He found an interested investor and business partner in Joseph F. Engelberger, a family friend and chief engineer at Manning, Maxwell and Moore in Stratford, Connecticut. The company was later sold to Consolidated Diesel Electronic. The company agreed to finance the production of what was now called "Unimate"—the first robotic arm.

The first Unimate robot was sold to General Motors in 1961. The robotic arm machines were first used to handle hot and dangerous metals. Other automakers saw the practicality of the machines, and their use expanded to Chrysler, Ford, and Fiat manufacturers. Although the new machines proved very profitable and practical for General Motors, they received unfavorable support from auto labor unions worried about the loss of human jobs. In 1978, the improved Programmable Universal Machine for Assembly (PUMA) began increased production. The application also found international interest with Japanese automakers.

The new business venture was eventually sold to Westinghouse, with Devol hired as a consultant. In 1983, with advent of new affordable computers, Devol said the next step in automated manufacturing was for the robot to "be able to receive and use information from computers and give information to computers." In 1984, Devol sounded the alarm about the U.S. falling behind other countries in manufacturing capabilities. In 1985, Devol was elected to the Society of Manufacturing Engineers.

In 2005, Popular Mechanics magazine selected the Unimate as one of the "Top 50 Inventions of the Past 50 Years." In 2006, the Institute of Electrical and Electronics Engineers estimated that "there were more than 950,000 industrial robots in operation world wide." In 2011, he was inducted into the National Inventors Hall of Fame.

On August 11, 2011, Devol died at his home in Wilton, Connecticut. His wife had died in 2003. He was buried at Bald Hill Cemetery in Wilton.

George Devol Jr. received over forty patents in his life. The impact of his life and inventions continues to have an international scope. He began his life in Kentucky and found his innovative skills on Kentucky soil.

Larry Flynt
Lakeville
Publisher

He is a very controversial figure who leads an adult media conglomerate. He is a declared atheist who has challenged traditional church leaders. He is a champion of freedom of speech rights with a history of judicial battles. His sometimes public, eccentric actions have caused his temporary imprisonment.

Larry Claxton Flynt was born on November 1, 1942, in Lakeville, Magoffin County, Kentucky. It was the poorest county in the nation at that time. He was the oldest of three children born to Larry Claxton Flynt Sr. and Edith Arnett. They married when he was twenty-three years old, and she was just seventeen years old. His father was a sharecropper. His mother was a homemaker. With his father's absence and participation in World War II in Europe, Flynt was raised by his mother and maternal grandmother for his first three years.

In 1951, Flynt's four-year-old sister died from leukemia. Her death caused friction between his parents, and they separated in 1952 when Flynt was ten years old. He was then raised by his mother, who moved to Hamlet, Indiana. In 1954, Flynt had conflicts with his mother's new boyfriend and moved back to Magoffin County to live with his father. He attended Salyersville High School until the ninth grade. He ran away from home and, with counterfeit papers, joined the U. S. Army at the age of fifteen.

After an honorable discharge from the military, Flynt returned to Indiana to live with his mother. He stayed there only three months before moving back with his father in Kentucky. After a short time he was working as a wanted bootlegger. In July 1960, when his savings ran out, he joined the U. S. Navy. He became a radar operator and served on the *USS Enterprise*, which recovered John Glenn's space capsule. He was honorably discharged in July 1964.

In 1965, Flynt used his military savings to purchase a bar owned by his mother in Dayton, Ohio. He worked hard operating the bar and used the profits to purchase two other bars. He began use of amphetamines to compensate for his lack of sleep. He created a higher-class bar that he called the Hustler Club. New bars in Ohio were set up in Akron, Cleveland, Columbus, Cincinnati, and Toledo.

In January 1972, Flynt created the *Hustler Newsletter*. The popular two-page newsletter was expanded to sixteen pages in May 1972 and then doubled to thirty-two pages in August 1973. To cope with the financially crippling recession of 1973, Flynt turned his popular local newsletter into a sexually explicit magazine. He also began a national distribution of what became in July 1974 the first issue of *Hustler* magazine.

Flynt had continual battles with the public and some distributors, who refused to place the magazine on store shelves. In August 1975, his magazine gained national attention with the publication of nude photos of Jacqueline Kennedy Onassis, the former first lady. The photos were purchased from an enterprising paparazzo. The magazine issue sold over 1,000,000 copies in just the first few days of publication. In the 1970s, Flynt expanded to operate eight strip clubs in Ohio. In 1976, he created Larry Flynt Publications, a privately held company.

Flynt, as a millionaire, now aggressively waged legal battles to defend his right of free speech through his publications. He and his lawyer fought one of many legal battles in Lawrenceville, Gwinnnett County, Georgia. On March 6, 1978, Flynt and his lawyer approaching the courthouse, were shot by a gunman hiding in an alley across the street. Flynt survived the shooting but suffered permanent spinal cord injuries, leaving him partially paralyzed and requiring use of a wheelchair. He remained in much pain and became addicted to pain pills, leading to a stroke. This left him with some speech difficulties.

Sometime later, a white supremacist serial killer, Joseph Paul Franklin, confessed to the shooting. On November 30, 2013, having been tied to eight other murders, Franklin was executed in Missouri.

As the nation moved toward more conservative standards in the late 1970s and 1980s, Flynt and his empire faced more legal battles reaching to the U. S. Supreme Court. During the trials before the Supreme Court, he hurled obscenities at the nine justices. Chief Justice Warren E. Burger had him arrested for contempt of court. The charges were later dismissed. In a later trial, Flynt wore an American flag as a diaper and was imprisoned for desecration of the flag. In 1983, he was sent for two months to the Medical Center for Federal Prisoners in Springfield, Missouri. He was held there for psychiatric evaluations.

In 1988, a nationally prominent case, the Reverend Jerry Falwell sued Flynt. In an earlier issue, Falwell had been ridiculed in *Hustler*. Flynt won the issue in the Supreme Court and claimed that a friendship developed between him and Falwell. Flynt said, "I always appreciated his sincerity even though I knew what he was selling and he knew what I was selling."

Throughout the 1990s, Flynt continued to wage his own legal battles and assisted with defending other freedom of speech confrontations. In 1996, he published his autobiography, *An Unseemly Man: My Life as a Pornographer, Pundit and Social Outcast.* That same year, a movie based on his life, *The People vs. Larry Flynt*, won acclaim and an Academy Award nomination for Best Actor for Woody Harrelson.

In the 2000s, Flynt became politically active in opposing the war in Iraq and supporting LGBT rights and same-sex marriage. In June 2000, he opened the Hustler Casino in the Los Angeles suburb of Gardena.

Flynt's personal life is a revolving door of marriages and divorces that produced five children. He has been married five times. His current wife is Elizabeth Berrios. They married in 1998.

It is speculated that Flynt has a net worth of over $500,000,000. He is acknowledged to have bipolar disorder. He continues to be bound to a wheelchair. The turbulent experiences of his life in Kentucky probably had a great influence on his personality and life choices.

Benjamin Holladay

Nicholas County

Overland Stage

He was called the "Stagecoach King" of the Old West. He had an uncanny ability to invest and divest at just the right time for financial gain. He was a wealthy man with an obnoxious personality. He became friends with national military and religious leaders. He was an effective federal lobbyist, and his business evolved into steamships and railroads.

Benjamin Holladay was born on October 14, 1819, in Nicholas County, Kentucky. His father, William Holladay was from Virginia and migrated to Bourbon County, Kentucky, as a guide for wagon trains traveling through the Cumberland Gap. His mother was Margaret "Peggy" Hughes. Little is known of his early early years in Kentucky, where he was raised until his late teenage years. He developed an interest in the freight business and traveled toward, at that time, the Mexican city of Santa Fe. Along the route, he decided to settle in Weston, Missouri. He found employment as a store clerk. He later became a courier for General Alexander Doniphan of the Missouri militia. During the Mormon Wars of 1838, he witnessed Doniphan's refusal to follow orders to kill the Mormons. A relationship was established between Holladay and the

Mormon community, including Brigham Young. That friendship would prove valuable for Holladay in future years.

Holladay returned to work at the store until he started his own tavern and hotel in 1840. He started the McCormick Distilling Company. In 1846, with the Mexican-American War underway, Holladay experienced financial success, providing war supplies for Missouri's General Stephen Watts Kearny. With his accumulated wealth, Holladay moved to California in 1852.

Holladay used his past stage line experience to supervise newly developed routes that avoided conflict with the native Indian tribes. In 1861, he won a contract for mail service to Salt Lake City, Utah, and established the Overland Stage Route (the Overland Trail), with help from his friend Brigham Young. In 1862, he purchased the year-old, failing Pony Express. He developed a southern route for travel and mail service between New York, St. Louis, Memphis, El Paso, Tucson, and San Francisco. Important rest stops that provided traveling comforts for passengers and additional income for Holladay were set up every ten to fifteen miles along the route.

Samuel Clemens (Mark Twain) gave a detailed description of these station stops in his 1872 book, *Roughing It*. The station buildings were long, low huts, made of sundried, mud-colored bricks, laid up without mortar (adobes, the Spaniards call these bricks 'adobes', and Americans shorten it to 'dobies.'). The roofs, which had no slant to speak of, were thatched and then sodded or covered with a thick layer of earth, and from this sprung a pretty rank growth of weeds or grass. It was the first time we had ever seen a man's front yard on top of his house.

He supervised a large work force of "station attendants, drivers, conductors, smithies, cartwrights, mules, horses and equipment." Over the next few years, Holladay developed six other routes and won lucrative government delivery contracts totaling over $6,000,000. In 1866, Holladay sold his stage routes to Wells Fargo Express for $1,500,000.

Holladay purchased mansions in Oregon, Washington, D.C., and in New York on the Hudson River. Holladay speculated that railroads would be the future of travel in the West. He began early investments into the increasing steamboat transportation. In August 1868, he moved to Oregon and began construction of a railway line from Oregon to California. Using some unscrupulous and illegal methods, he purchased lands and construction rights. With the help of investments by German bankers, work progressed. He also created river port docks and warehouses. With the national financial Panic of 1873, work stopped, and Holladay faced financial ruin. The stock market crash in September 1873 left him essentially bankrupt. In 1874, German investors were not paid and sent Henry Villard as their representative to visit Holladay. In 1876, Villard took over control of the railroad project.

Villard gave interesting descriptions of Holladay. He described him as "illiterate, coarse, boastful, false and cunning." Villard was also known as being born to command, clever, shrewd, and completely unscrupulous. Business associate Joseph Gaston gave further insights into Holladay's personality as "wholly destitute of fixed principles of honesty, morality, or common decency." Gaston noted that when Holladay bought a large home from Doctor Rodney Glisan, "he remodeled it and immediately installed a harem of high-class prostitutes."

Little is recorded of Holladay's family life. He did have a wife from the European upper class, Mrs. De Pourtales. They had two daughters. When his wife died after the second daughter's birth, the children were sent to live with grandparents.

Holladay died at his Portland, Oregon, home on July 8, 1887. He was buried in Portland at Mount Calvary Cemetery. He had been a major force in opening up the West to dependable routes of travel and commerce. He gained significant wealth and lost it in over-speculation. He learned the lessons of human nature and business from his Kentucky roots.

G. Scott Hubbard

Elizabethtown

NASA Scientist

He is currently a professor in the Department of Aeronautics and Astronautics at Stanford University. He worked as a National Aeronautics Space Administration (NASA) scientist for twenty years. He was instrumental in the development of the Mars Pathfinder and the Lunar Prospector Mission.

G. Scott Hubbard was born on December 27, 1948, in Elizabethtown, Kentucky. Very little information is available on his family and early life in Kentucky. He became interested in music and still plays a guitar in a jazz group. He developed an interest in space exploration. When he was nine years old, his interest in the possibility of life elsewhere in the universe was spurred by reading science writings of George Gamov, Fred Hoyle, and Isaac Asimov. He received his undergraduate degree in physics and astronomy at Vanderbilt University in Nashville, Tennessee. He completed his graduate education in solid state and semiconductor physics at the University of California at Berkeley.

Beginning his forty-year career in research and development, Hubbard created a small startup "high technology" company in the San Francisco Bay area. He was also a staff scientist at the Lawrence Berkeley National Laboratory. He eventually found his way to the NASA research center.

He brought his innovative concepts of space exploration with new concepts and ideas to NASA. In 1998, he founded NASA's Astrobiology Institute. He was the creator of the adventurous Mars Pathfinder mission with the Mars Rover. He was known as the "Mars Czar." He also served as manager for the very successful Lunar Prospector Mission. From 2002 to 2006, he was the director of NASA's Ames Research Center in the Silicon Valley in California. There he worked as supervisor for over 2,600 people, with an operating budget of $700,000,000. He was able to develop the NASA Research Park working with Google and Intel.

In 2003, Hubbard was the only NASA representative on the national Columbia Accident Investigation Board. He worked to demonstrate the physical cause of the Columbia Space Shuttle disaster.

During his twenty-year period with NASA, Hubbard received seven, highly honored medals for his research and development work. Among the medals were the Distinguished Service Medal and the Presidential Meritorious Achievement Medal. In 2012, he wrote an award-winning book about his work on the Mars project, *Exploring Mars: Chronicles from a Decade of Discovery*. He has also authored over fifty scholarly papers for professional presentations.

Hubbard has received recognitions and honors from associated professional organizations. He is a member of the International Academy of Aeronautics and received their Engineering Science Award. He is also a member of the American Institute of Aeronautics and Astronautics and received their Von Karman medal in Astronautics, and in 2006, he received the Carl Sagan Memorial Award. He was awarded an Honorary Doctorate degree from the Polytechnic University of Madrid, Spain. He received the Challenger Learning Center Distinguished Achievement Award.

Hubbard continues to be involved critical space observations in the B612 Foundation. That is created to protect the earth from asteroid strikes. He continues writing and speaking to reach into the universe, visualizing Mars as "our second home." He continues in futurist observations by noting that "My prediction is that human beings will change in ways that both enable and react to space exploration." He looks back on the many new technologies that past space exploration have benefited mankind. He sees even greater and more beneficial technology in future space explorations.

G. Scott Hubbard, who leads a very private personal life, is a true international and even terrestrial innovator. He has not finished his potential list of accomplishments. All of this began as a child of Kentucky.

Casey Jones

Cacey

Railroad Engineer

His entire life was centered around first becoming then being—a railroad engineer. He was recognized for his unique ability as a railroad engineer in keeping trains on time. His bravery was equaled by his professional skills. He was the source of legends after his death. Even his death has a mixture of truth and legend.

John Luther Jones was born on March 14, 1864, in rural southeast Missouri. His parents were Frank Jones, a schoolteacher, and Ann Nolan Jones, a homemaker. When Jones was a young boy, his parents became aware that rural southeast Missouri held no future for them. They moved the family to Cacey, Kentucky. From that town, Jones received his nickname "Casey."

The American railroad operations expansions were a source of fascination for young Jones. Little is known of his early education. When he was fifteen years old, Jones moved to Columbus, Kentucky, where he worked as a telegrapher, brakeman, and fireman for the Mobile and Ohio Railroad. His personality and work habits impressed the other workers. In 1884, he moved to Jackson, Tennessee, where he was promoted to the job of flagman. He lived in a boarding house in Jackson and began a relationship with the proprietor's daughter, Joanne "Janie" Brady. They married on November 26, 1886. They would have two sons and a daughter.

On March 1, 1888, Jones moved to a new company, the Illinois Central Railroad (IC). He worked as fireman on a train line running from Jackson, Tennessee, to Water Valley, Mississippi. In 1891, after a yellow fever epidemic hit the freight train crews, Jones was finally promoted to his lifelong goal of engineer. He quickly established a professional reputation for punctuality. Legend says that people set their watches by his freight train scheduled runs. He also set a personal calling card with his unique train whistle blow. It was called the "whippoorwill" with its "long-drawn-out note that began softly, rose and then died away to a whisper."

In 1893, the World's Columbian Exposition (World's Fair) was held in Chicago, Illinois. IC was responsible for providing transportation services for visitors to the fair grounds. When the company asked for volunteer engineers, Jones was accepted. He and his family moved to Chicago for the summer. It was the first experience Jones had as an engineer for a passenger train. He and his family enjoyed the experiences. In Chicago, Jones was introduced to the newest and most modern, updated freight train called Engine 638. At the fair's conclusion, Jones received permission to drive the train back to Water Valley, Mississippi. He would also operate the train on the usual runs to Jackson, Tennessee.

In February 1900, Jones was transferred to Memphis, Tennessee. He was given responsibility for a passenger train, Engine 382, also called "Cannonball." His new run was from Memphis to Canton, Mississippi. He worked and maintain close friendships with his crew, especially fireman Simeon T. "Sim" Webb.

On April 30, 1900, Jones and Webb returned from a run back to the Memphis station. They were notified that a fellow engineer had reported too ill to drive his assigned schedule. Jones and Sims offered to do a double shift and take the delayed run. They were to take an empty six-car Engine No. 1 to Canton. They left the station at 12:50 a.m., seventy-five minutes behind schedule. With a lighter-than-usual load, they became determined to make up for the lost time. The weather was foggy, reducing visibility. By the time they reached Goodman, Mississippi, the train was nearly back on schedule. They were informed that at Vaughn, there were three other trains off on a sidetrack. One of the trains was very long and overlapped onto the main line. All the elements (speed, weather, obstruction, miscommunication) were in place for a major disaster. As Jones rounded a curve at seventy-five miles-an-hour, Sims first saw the red lights of the caboose and the blocked main line. He yelled to Jones. Jones yelled for Webb to jump from the train. Webb recalled hearing the whistle blow as a warning. Webb landed and was unconscious but was unhurt. Jones was able to continue to simultaneously back throttle the train and blow the warning whistle. He was able to slow the train down to thirty-five miles an hour before the collision. At 3:52 am, he smashed into the last few freight cars of the stalled train but was able to spare the passengers from any serious injury. Jones was the only casualty. Legend said that when his body was recovered, his hands were still on the throttle and whistle handles. Crewmen from the other trains placed his body on a stretcher and carried him to the depot half-a-mile away.

Jones' body was carried by train the next day to his hometown in Jackson, Tennessee. Funeral services were held in St. Mary's Church. He was buried in Mount Calvary Cemetery. His wife, Janie, later described Jones as "a lovable lad—six-foot four and a half inches in height, dark-haired and gray-eyed. Always he was in good humor and his Irish heart was a[s] big as his body."

Legends and conflicting accounts of his heroics began to appear in print. An official accident report was released on July 13, 1900, by the officials of IC. It stated that "Engineer Jones was solely responsible having disregarded the signals given by Flagman Newberry." The reported findings were challenged by many, including fireman Webb. He swore that they never saw the flagman or any signs and claimed Jones was a true hero.

Mixed stories began to surface of Jones's experiences as an engineer. In 1895, he was supposed to have saved a young girl from his train by racing to the front of the train and standing on the cowcatcher, grabbing the girl before the train would have hit her. There were other accounts of Jones's risk-taking operation infractions that resulted in nine career citations. It is likely that there was a mixture of good and bad deeds performed by Casey Jones.

His life became the source of many country songs, books, and movies. There are markers that recognize his home and the train collision. His is a unique life story that had its major life influences from his time in Kentucky.

William Lipscomb
Lexington
Chemistry

He was a Nobel Prize-winning chemist whose research and discoveries brought advances in the scientific understanding of the human body. He was recognized nationally and internationally, winning many other prestigious awards. He had his early educational foundation and innovative dreams in Kentucky.

William Nunn Lipscomb Jr. was born on December 9, 1919, in Cleveland, Ohio. During his first year his parents moved the family to Lexington, Kentucky. His father was a physician and encouraged his son's interest in all matters of science. His mother was a music teacher and encouraged his interest in the fine arts. Lipscomb recalled later, "My early home environment...stressed personal responsibility and self-reliance. Independence was encouraged especially in the early years when my mother taught music and when my father's medical practice occupied most of his time."

As a child, Lipscomb made regular visits to the Observatory of the University of Kentucky, adding to his scientific interests. When he was eleven years old, his parents gave him a popular Gilbert chemistry set. This launched his attention to the world of chemicals and chemical creations. He conducted numerous experiments and added components from the small chemistry set by ordering equipment and additional chemicals from suppliers, helped by his father's medical discounts. He was also aided by his father's personal library. He made his own fireworks and experimented with colors, odors, and explosions.

In high school, Lipscomb was encouraged by the chemistry teacher Frederick Jones. Lipscomb poured through advanced college books in various aspects of chemistry. Although his knowledge of chemistry was greatly expanded, his class grade in chemistry was only a C. He had not prepared for taking the tests that were the basis of his grades. He took other science courses and became interested in physics. He entered a state contest on the subject and won first place. His independent chemistry experiments led him to receive the Bausch and Lomb science award in 1937.

That year, he entered the University of Kentucky on a music scholarship. He continued his mostly independent chemistry experiments, reading graduate-level books from leading chemistry educators around the nation. He graduated with a Bachelor of Science degree in 1941 and won the American Chemical Society's Award for Distinguished Service in the Advancement of Inorganic Chemistry. He also won the Peter Debye Award in Physical Chemistry. The university presented him with the Sullivan Medallion.

Having received several acceptances and a few rejections from graduate schools, Lipscomb enrolled at the California Institute of Technology (Caltech) where he earned a teaching assistantship in physics for twenty dollars a month. After one semester, he changed directions and began studies in chemistry with renowned Professor Linus Pauling. He worked with Pauling in research and development of materials that had an impact during World War II. His students referred to him as "the Colonel," out of respect for his Kentucky roots. He was awarded his Doctor of Philosophy degree in Chemistry in 1946.

Following graduation, Lipscomb joined the faculty of the University of Minnesota. He served there for thirteen years. He was named a Guggenheim Fellow in 1954. In 1959, he joined the faculty of Harvard University as a professor of chemistry. In 1960, he was named a Fellow of the American Academy of Arts and Sciences. His book, *Boron Hydrudes*, was published in 1963. That year, he received an honorary doctorate degree from the University of Kentucky and received in 1965 their Distinguished Alumni Centennial Award.

During his long tenure at Harvard, Lipscomb and colleagues focused their research on developing X-ray diffraction techniques. They were able to "map the molecular structures of numerous boranes and their derivatives." They later focused on the atomic structure of proteins, with interest in the working of enzymes. These complicated but innovative discoveries are explained in detail in the papers and books of Lipscomb.

In 1973, Lipscomb was made a member of the Honorable Order of Kentucky Colonels. For his academic work and research, Lipscomb was awarded the Nobel Prize in Chemistry in 1976. That same year, he was awarded an honorary doctoral degree from the University of Munich. He was also made a member of the Royal Netherlands Academy of Arts and Sciences. He retired from the Harvard faculty in 1990 after completing thirty-one years of tenure. He would continue his independent research and share his discoveries with other interested scientists and professional organizations.

Lipscomb's personal life was reflective of his mother's influence. He was a clarinetist performing classical music with chamber groups. He was also an active tennis player. In 1944, he married Mary Adele Sargent. They had three children. She died in 1983. His second marriage was to Jean Evans in 1983. Lipscomb died on April 14, 2011, at the age of ninety-one, in Cambridge, Massachusetts.

Lipscomb had described an interesting work philosophy, saying, "For me, the creative process, first of all, requires a good nine hours of sleep at night. Second, it must not be pushed by the need to produce practical applications." This highly innovative scientist owed his academic basics and interests to his Kentucky home.

Garrett Morgan

Paris

Inventor, Gas Masks

He was an inventor with only a sixth-grade formal education. He developed a number of important inventions that would save many lives. His inventions are very much a part of the life today. He was honored by local citizens as a true hero. He was friends with John D. Rockefeller and J. Pierpont Morgan. He was an African American.

Garrett Augustus Morgan was born on March 4, 1877, near Paris, Kentucky. He was the seventh of eleven children born to Sydney Morgan and Elizabeth Reed. His mother was a former slave with African and American Indian backgrounds. She was the daughter of a Baptist minister. His father was a former slave of Confederate Colonel John Hunt Morgan, of Morgan's Raiders fame.

Morgan attended the Branch Elementary School in Claysville, near Paris, in Kentucky. He completed the sixth grade. Like many others of his day, Morgan quit school, and at age sixteen, he left Kentucky and traveled to Ohio in search of more substantial employment. He originally started in Cincinnati as a handyman for a wealthy landowner. While working and receiving better wages, Morgan was able to employ a tutor to continue his education. He had an interest and natural curiosity about all things mechanical.

In 1895, Morgan moved to Cleveland. He married Madge Nelson, but the marriage soon ended in divorce. He developed interest in sewing machine operations and repairs. He developed a belt fastener for the sewing machines and improved their efficiency. He was growing a wide reputation for his ability at repairs. He began experimenting with chemicals to decrease the heat from the friction of the sewing needle. The results were his creation of what became a very successful hair straightener for wiry hair. He was able to set up the G. A. Morgan Hair Refining Company.

In 1907, Morgan opened his own sewing machine and shoe repair shop. In 1908, he married a Bavarian seamstress, Mary Anne Hassek. They would have three children. That same year, Morgan helped to establish the Cleveland Association of Colored Men. In 1909, he and his wife expanded their business to include the Morgan's Cut Rate Ladies Clothing Store. He was now employing thirty-two workers.

Morgan continued his inventive ideas. In 1912, he developed what became the first "smoke hood" (breathing device). It was to provide a "safer breathing experience in the presence of smoke, gases, and other pollutants." He received a patent for the device and began public demonstrations and sales campaigns through his National Safety Device Company. Although the device was receiving high praise from safety officials, the real-life, dramatic use came to public attention on July 24, 1916. An explosion occurred in a tunnel being dug under Lake Erie by the Cleveland Water Works. Thirty-two workers were trapped in the tunnel, which was filled with smoke, dust, and poisonous gas. Morgan was contacted at his home for help. Along with his brother, Frank, the two men raced to the scene. With the smoke hoods in place, they entered the tunnel and began to retrieve the workers during many trips. The crowds cheered the heroics, and although several died, many were rescued. News of the event and the Morgans' heroic act spread around the country. Morgan received a gold medal from the citizens of Cleveland and from the International Association of Fire Engineers. Orders for the smoke hoods rapidly increased from fire stations around the country, especially in the North. It is sad to note that when some of those placing orders discovered that Morgan was African American, they canceled the orders. Morgan's smoke hood would be adapted and effectively used by forces in World War I with the use of gas warfare. Thousands of lives were saved from their use.

Morgan was the first black man in Cleveland to own a car. He was very aware of the dangers of city driving with carriages still on the road. The early stop light system simply had only two lights, a stop and go. Morgan witnessed many traffic accidents due to the lack of delay between the two lights. He created a stop light with three lights, stop, go and caution (a warning light). He sought a patent for his new creation that was granted in November 1923. The system was quickly used throughout the United States, Britain, and Canada. He eventually sold the rights of his invention to General Electric for $40,000, a high price in the mid-1920s. He continued his inventive activities designing a woman's hat fastener, a round belt fastener, and a friction drive clutch.

Morgan continued his interest in promoting African-American causes, local and national. He made donations to black colleges, opened an all-black country club (Wakeman Country Club), and launched the *Cleveland Call*, an African-American newspaper. He was an active member of the National Association for the Advancement of Colored People. In 1931, he became politically active, running unsuccessfully as an independent candidate for the Cleveland City Council.

In 1943, Morgan developed a serious case of glaucoma, resulting in the loss of 90 percent of his vision. Although limited in physical ability, he maintained an active life, organizing a fraternity for black students at Cleveland's Western Reserve University. He continued to struggle with physical ailments during his remaining years.

One of his last goals was to attend the Emancipation Centennial in Chicago in August 1963. Unfortunately, he died a month earlier on July 27, 1963. He would receive many honors and recognitions for his life's work. An elementary school in Lexington, Kentucky was named after him. He was included in the 2002 book *100 Greatest African Americans*, by Molefi Kete Asante.

It is difficult to estimate the number of lives saved by Morgan's inventions. However, it is no secret how many people today are protected and benefitted by his inventions. Kentuckians should be privileged to claim him as a native son.

Thomas Hunt Morgan

Lexington

Physiology

He was a pioneer in the study of genetics, a dedicated researcher and academician. He was a devoted family man, respected nationally and internationally for his scientific discoveries. He was a product of Kentucky.

Thomas Hunt Morgan was born on September 25, 1866, in Lexington, Kentucky. He was the son of Charles Hunt Morgan and Ellen Key Howard Morgan, born into a family that came from very prominent ancestry. His father's brother was the infamous leader of the Confederate Morgan's Raiders. His mother's grandfather was Francis Scott Key, who composed the "Star Spangled Banner." Following the Civil War, the family, who had supported the Confederate cause, lost much of its property and wealth. Before the war, his father had been American consul at Messina, Sicily, but had difficulty finding any post-war political assignment.

Growing up in the hills of rural Kentucky, Morgan found enjoyment in the study of natural history. By the age of ten, he had collections of birds, bird's eggs, and fossils. He was able to continue his interests by working for several summers with the U. S. Geological Survey in Kentucky. At the age of sixteen, Morgan entered the preparatory department of the State College of Kentucky (now the University of Kentucky). He took a heavy academic load, strong in the sciences. It was reported that he nearly flunked his French class because the instructor had been held captive during the war by Morgan's Raiders. Morgan graduated as valedictorian in 1886 with a bachelor's degree in science.

Following graduation, Morgan spent the summer working at the Marine Biology School in Annisquam, Massachusetts. He would spend as many future summers as he could in such work. A new school was founded that was focused on research. Johns Hopkins University had appeal for Morgan, and he began his graduate work in zoology. He worked with knowledgeable instructors who encouraged his independent research style. He received a generous research fellowship to allow him to continue his graduate studies. In 1890, he received his Ph.D. from Johns Hopkins. He was awarded the Adam Bruce Fellowship and that summer was able to visit Europe, studying at the Marine Zoological Laboratory in Naples, Italy. He was greatly influenced by several prominent zoologists, which led to his interest in experimental embryology.

Returning the United States, Morgan accepted an offer as associate professor of biology at Bryn Mawr College for Women. He had the opportunity for continued research and taught classes in biology. In 1894, he was granted a year's absence to return to Naples and study at the laboratories of Stazione Zoologica. He was again influenced by the experiments of fellow scientists. He was particularly interested in the sea urchin reproduction system.

In 1895, Morgan returned to Bryn Mawr as a full professor. He continued his research and classes. He was recalled as a pleasant fellow, even-tempered with a good sense of humor. He wrote his first of many books, *The Development of Frog's Eggs*, in 1897. He became a member of a number of national scientific organizations, including the Genetics Society of America and the American Morphological Society, becoming their president in 1900.

In 1904, Morgan received an offer from Columbia University as professor in experimental zoology. The position allowed him more time to pursue experimental research. He accepted the position. Between semesters, on June 4, 1904, Morgan married Lillian Vaughn Sampson. She had been a graduate student in biology at Bryn Mawr. They would have four children. Lillian put her continued graduate studies on hold until after the birth of their children. She would be a wonderful assistant for Morgan in laboratory experimentations. They always, in spite of the tedious research, made family time an important part of their daily schedule.

At Columbia University, Morgan began experimentation with the common fruit fly, also known in the scientific world as *Drosophila melanogaster*. Thus started what would be referred to as Morgan's *Drosophila* period of experimental discoveries in genetics in what would be called his "fly room." Darwin's theory of the "survival of the fittest" called into question through discovery of genes and chromosomes. Determination of sex and personal characteristics was more on the crossover of genes within chromosomes. Morgan encouraged his students' experimentation with this theory of study. In 1913, one of his students developed the first genetic map. Morgan and his students wrote *The Mechanics of Mendelian Heredity* in 1915. This opened the door for a new field of research.

In the early 1920s, Morgan left the bulk of the "fly room" research to his students. He began to consider genetic research for other organisms, including humans. He was a strong opponent to other research in the area that would later lead to support of racism and human engineering. Morgan was near retirement and had spent twenty-five years at Columbia.

In 1927, Morgan received an offer to establish a school of biology at the California Institute of Technology. He accepted the offer and moved with his family in 1928. He wanted to develop new areas for biological study different from his previous research studies. He expanded his research focused on genetics and evolution through "experimental embryology, physiology, biophysics and biochemistry." He helped to establish the Marine Laboratory at Corona del Mar. He was able to attract other similarly minded researchers to his new school. He continued to record his findings in other books, including *Heredity and Sex* (1913), *The Physical Basis of Heredity* (1919), *Embryology and Genetics* (1924), *Evolution and Genetics* (1925), *The Theory of Genes* (1926), *Experimental Embryology* (1927) and *The Scientific Basis of Evolution* (1935).

Morgan received many honors and awards for his discoveries. He was awarded an honorary doctorate from the University of Kentucky. In 1924, he received the Darwin Medal. In 1933, he received the Nobel Prize for "his discoveries concerning the role played by chromosomes in heredity." In 1939, he received the Copley Medal of the Royal Society of London. A number of his students would receive Nobel Prizes for their continued advances originating from Morgan's research. His membership in many other national and internal scientific organizations led to other awards and recognitions, too numerous to mention.

Throughout his life, Morgan suffered from a chronic duodenal ulcer. He continued working in his private lab until he died of heart failure in Pasadena at his home on December 4, 1945, at the age of seventy-nine. Colleagues remembered him "as a generous man with an infectious enthusiasm for his work. As a mentor Morgan had a knack for spotting and fostering talent, and many of his students went on to make important contributions to the field."

Thomas Hunt Morgan was an innovator in the field of genetic research and discovery. He would pave the path for future studies in the prevention and cure of diseases. He was prepared for his academic career through his early observations and education in Kentucky.

Harlan Sanders

Corbin

Founder KFC

He was a failure in many things. He couldn't keep a job because of insubordination and fighting. Any good job he found was lost to modernization. He lost his wife and children because of his inability to provide financially for them. At retirement age, he was still a failure. Late in his life, he found his true calling and became a billionaire. His name is associated with one of the most widely recognized brands today.

Harlan David Sanders was born on September 9, 1890, in Henryville, Indiana, close to the Kentucky border. He was the oldest of three children born to Wilbur David and Margaret Ann Dunlevy Sanders. His father was a farmer, until a broken leg forced him to work as a butcher. His mother was a strict homemaker who warned her children of "the evils of alcohol, tobacco, gambling, and whistling on Sundays." They were devout attenders of church.

In 1895, Sanders' father came home with a fever and died that night. To support the family, Sanders' mother found work in a tomato cannery, which required her to be gone for days at a time. This required Harlan, age five, to care for his two younger brothers, which required preparing meals. By the age of seven, he was recognized by the family for his skills at cooking. At the age of ten, Sanders found work as a farmhand.

His mother remarried to William Broadus in 1902, and the family moved to Greenwood, Indiana. In 1903, experiencing physical abuse from his stepfather, Sanders dropped out of the seventh grade and went to work on a nearby farm. He soon left for Indianapolis, getting a job painting carriages. He later moved to southern Indiana to work again as a farmhand.

In 1906, Sanders left the area to live with his uncle in New Albany, Indiana. His uncle arranged to get Sanders a job as a streetcar conductor. Later that year, Sanders obtained a fake birth certificate and enlisted in the U.S. Army at the age of fifteen. He saw service in Cuba and was honorably discharged in February 1907. He moved to Sheffield, Alabama, where his uncle lived. His uncle arranged for Sanders to get a job with the Southern Railway. Later, moving to Jasper, Alabama, he found work with the Northern Alabama Railroad, becoming a fireman, stoking the steam engine. In 1909, he then worked in Jasper for the Norfolk and Western Railway. He married Josephine King, and they had three children. The family moved to Jackson, Tennessee, where he worked as a fireman with the Illinois Central Railroad. At night, Sanders begin studying law through a correspondence course through the La Salle Extension University. He lost his job after a fight with a coworker. He went to work for the Rock Island Railroad, and his wife and children left to live with her parents.

Sanders began his practice of law in Little Rock, Arkansas, for three years. He sent for his wife and children to live with him in Little Rock. His law career ended when Sanders got into a fistfight with his own client in the courtroom. He returned to live with his mother in Henryville, Indiana. For the next few years, Sanders moved around (Jeffersonville, Louisville, and Columbus), trying to find permanent employment with unsuccessful results. He worked for another railroad, sold life insurance, and established a ferryboat company that was successful. He used the earned company shares to purchase an acetylene lamp manufacturing company. The company failed due to the advent of modern electric lamps.

Sanders moved to Winchester, Kentucky, to work as a tire salesman. In 1924, he lost that job when the tire manufacturer closed. He then went to work operating a Standard Oil service station in Nicholasville. In 1930, the station closed because of the Great Depression. That same year, the Shell Oil Company asked Sanders to operate a service station in North Corbin, Kentucky. He could have the service station rent free, paying a percentage of his sales. He began to serve meals to his customers—including his famous fried chicken. The service station was located on a major, well-traveled, north-south route through Kentucky. His business began to prosper. He began an effective activity of advertising, including painting signs on barns along the highway. A competitor, Matt Stewart, began to paint over his signs. When Sanders confronted Stewart, accompanied by Shell officials, Stewart shot and killed one of Shell's men, and Sanders shot and wounded Stewart. Stewart was later convicted of murder, but Sanders was never charged. The service station's food service required Sanders to build a restaurant nearby. In 1935, Kentucky Governor Ruby Laffoon commissioned Sanders as a "Kentucky Colonel." The popularity of the food grew by word-of-mouth. In 1939, it was also boosted by a notice in Duncan Hines' popular *Adventures in Good Eating*.

In July 1939, Sanders bought a motel in Asheville, North Carolina. Four months later, the North Corbin restaurant and new motel were destroyed by fire. They were both rebuilt and enlarged. In 1940, Sanders had refined his chicken frying process. With his secret recipe of eleven herbs and spices, Sanders initiated the practice of frying the chicken in a pressure cooker instead of a frying pan. That reduced the cooking time from thirty minutes to only nine minutes.

World War II saw a drop in the tourism business and Sanders sold his Asheville motel. Needing additional income, Sanders sought employment in Seattle, Washington. He turned to operating a cafeteria for government workers in Tennessee. During this time, Sanders' mistress, Claudia Ledington-Price, managed the North Corbin businesses. In 1947, he and his first wife officially divorced. He married Claudia in 1949. After the war, increasing tourism and new automobiles led to a dramatic rise in tourism and business for Sanders. In 1950, Sanders was re-commissioned as a Kentucky Colonel by Governor Lawrence Wetherby. It was at this time that he began to wear the famous white suit and string tie.

In 1952, Sanders sold a franchise of his chicken recipe and frying technique to Pete Harman, operator of the largest restaurant in Salt Lake City, Utah. Harman experienced a 300% sales increase in the first year, largely through sales of fried chicken. It was there that the concept of Kentucky Fried Chicken was originated. Other restaurant owners sought franchises and paid Sanders $0.04 per chicken sold. In 1955, Sanders was dealt another cruel blow as the newly constructed Interstate 75 left the road in North Corbin largely unused by tourists. Business declined, and Sanders sold the North Corbin businesses. At the age of sixty-five, Sanders received a $105 a month Social Security check and drew on his limited savings.

Reflecting on his earlier franchise successes, Sanders set out across the country, offering franchises to restaurants along major traffic routes. He proposed to cook his chicken for the owners, and they were interested enough to agree to a franchise paying $0.05 per chicken sold. Sanders also expanded the market into Canada, Mexico, and Jamaica. Claudia would mix and ship the required spices to the restaurants. The increased financial income allowed Sanders and his wife to open a new restaurant and establish a company headquarters in Shelbyville in 1959. In 1962, Sanders obtained a patent on his chicken frying process. In 1963, he trademarked the phrase "It's Finger Lickin' Good." Their company expanded quickly to over six hundred locations.

In 1964, Sanders, now seventy-three years old, sold the Kentucky Fried Chicken Corporation for $2,000,000 to business partners. Sanders arranged to keep the Canadian businesses and was employed by the partners as a spokesman for the company, being paid a salary of $250,000 per year. He traveled 200,000 miles a year for the company and made TV commercials and publicity appearances. In 1956, Sanders moved to Mississauga, Ontario, to supervise his Canadian franchises.

In 1968, the couple openedThe Colonel's Lady's Dinner House restaurant in Shelbyville. In 1971, Heublein purchased the American company. As was his custom, Sanders visited many of the American franchises in travels. Heublein began to alter some of the recipes, trying to save preparation expenses. Sanders was furious, especially over the gravy they were now serving. He began to publicly decry the gravy as "slop" and "wallpaper paste to which sludge has been added." In 1973, Sanders sued Heublein for using his image to promote the inferior food. Heublein tried to stop the couple having the competing restaurant in Shelbyville. A settlement was reached where Sanders was paid $1,000,000 to agree not to criticize the company, and the couple was allowed to operate the restaurant.

Now with assets nearing $1,000,000,000, Sanders began to consider charitable works. He said, "There's no reason to be the richest man in the cemetery. You can't do any business from there." The couple created the Colonel Harland Sanders Trust and the Colonel Harland Sanders Charitable Organization. It provided scholarships and funds for medical facilities.

In June 1980, Sanders was diagnosed with acute leukemia He died at Jewish Hospital in Louisville, Kentucky, on December 16, 1980, at the age of ninety. His body laid in state in the rotunda of the Kentucky Sate Capitol in Frankfort after a funeral service at the Southern Baptist Theological Seminary Chapel. He was buried in his usual white suit and string tie in Cave Hill Cemetery in Louisville. By the time of his death, there were an estimated 6,000 KFC outlets in 48 countries worldwide, with $2,000,000,000 in annual sales.

He had a close friendship with Dave Thomas, founder of the Wendy's hamburger chain. He was also known for his strong use of swear words, especially when his recipes were not followed. Toward the end of his life, he became a converted Christian. In 1970, he and his wife were baptized in the Jordan River. He developed close friendships with Billy Graham and Jerry Falwell.

Although not born in Kentucky, he proudly referred to himself as a Kentucky Colonel. His appearance and his chicken gave rise to the idea of Southern hospitality and good food. His ongoing brand name will forever bring credit to the state where he was interred.

Philip A. Sharp

Falmouth

Physiology

He is an American geneticist and molecular biologist who co-discovered RNA splicing. He is a Nobel Prize winner and has received numerous national and international scientific association awards. He was from East Kentucky and received his early education and undergraduate work in the state.

Philip Allen Sharp was born on June 6, 1944, in Falmouth, Kentucky. His parents were Katherine Colvin Sharp and Joseph Walter Sharp. His father operated the family farm. Both parents came from large families that provided young Sharp with many grandparents, aunts, uncles, and cousins. Sharp attended the public schools in Pendleton County, which included McKinneysburg Elementary School, Butler Elementary School and High School, and Pendleton County High School. He had a well-rounded educational experience, including participation in sports and a growing interest in math and science. With strong encouragement from his parents, Sharp prepared to enter college. He saved the money he earned from raising cattle and growing tobacco for college expenses.

Desiring a smaller college, Sharp enrolled in a small, liberal arts college in the foothills of Eastern Kentucky, Union College. The school, located in Barbourville, was able to prepare students for further educational opportunities. He majored in chemistry and mathematics. In 1964, while at Union College, Sharp married a fellow student from New Jersey, Ann Holcombe. They had three children, and as Sharp would recall, "they came at opportune times in his academic career."

On the recommendation of a Union College professor, Sharp applied for admission to the Department of Chemistry at the University of Illinois. He was offered a fellowship and pursued his doctoral studies in chemistry. He completed his PhD in chemistry in 1969 with his dissertation on "the description of DNA as a polymer using statistics and physical theories." He was able to continue his postdoctoral studies at the California Institute of Technology. He became acquainted with the works of another famous Kentuckian, genetic scientist Thomas Hunt Morgan. He continued his studies there and moved to the Cold Spring Laboratory.

In 1974, he was offered an opportunity to go the Massachusetts Institute of Technology. In 1978, he cofounded a pharmaceutical company called Biogen Ltd. He later served as director of the Center for Cancer Research (now known as the Koch Institute for Integrative Cancer Research) from 1985 until 1991. His family found a home in Newton, Massachusetts, where Ann taught a preschool class. Sharp and colleagues explored the structure of genes DNA and RNA splicing in human cells seeking a possible cure for cancer. In 1991, Sharp became the head of the biology department until 1999. That year he was named as Institute Professor, the highest honor given. From 2000 until 2004, he was founding director of the McGovern Institute for Brain Research. In 2006, he confounded a small biotechnology company called Magen BioSciences, Inc.

Sharp's research discoveries and practical applications for humans have led to numerous awards and recognitions. The most prestigious was the Nobel Prize in Physiology of Medicine in 1993. In 1980, he received the Eli Lilly Award in molecular biology and the U.S. Steel Award from the National Academy of Sciences. He also received the General Motors Cancer Research Foundation's Alfred P. Sloan Jr. Prize. On May 4, 1991, he was awarded the honorary degree of Doctor of Humane Letters from Kentucky Union College. Sharp has served on the President's Advisory Committee on Science and Technology. He is an elected member of the National Academy of Sciences, the Institute of Medicine, the American Academy of Arts and Sciences, the American Philosophical Society, and the Royal Society, UK. In 1999, he won the Benjamin Franklin Medal for Distinguished Achievement in the Sciences of American Philosophical Society. In 2006, he was presented the National Medal of Science award by President George W. Bush. In 2015, he received the Othmer Gold Medal.

In addition to other awards and recognitions, Sharp has had published over 255 articles in peer-reviewed and other journals. Recently, a middle school in his hometown in Pendleton, Kentucky, was named after him. His discoveries have opened the possibilities for the challenging goal of curing cancer in the future. Kentucky can be proud to have produced this innovative scientist.

Nathan Stubblefield

Murray

Inventor, Wireless Radio

While notable inventors in major research laboratories around the nation and the world were experimenting in the similar fields, he found success in his home in the hills of Kentucky. There is still debate over what he actually invented. There is no question that he did invent something of great importance to the field of communication.

Nathan Beverly Stubblefield was born on November 22, 1860, in Murray, Kentucky. He was the next oldest of seven sons born to William "Captain Billy" Jefferson Stubblefield and Victoria Bowman. His father became a Confederate army veteran and a lawyer. Nathan's education began with tutoring by a governess. He later attended the Female and Male Institute, a boarding school near Farmington. In 1869, his mother died of scarlet fever. In 1874, his father died, ending his formal education. He lived with his stepmother. Stubblefield became obsessed with reading current scientific publications, especially editions of *Scientific American* and *Electrical World*. He also developed an interest in science fiction writings. He was greatly impressed by the earlier inventions of Samuel Morse, Alexander Graham Bell, and Thomas Edison.

In 1881, Stubblefield married Ada Mae Buchannan. They had nine children. For a number of years, he supported his family by farming part of his family's land. He was able to develop his scientific interests into successful inventions. On November 3, 1885, he was issued a patent for a device that lit coal oil lamps inside of the lamp chimney. In 1886, he began selling and installing acoustic telephones. Competition from local Bell Telephone companies caused him to lose interest in the acoustical devices. In 1892, Stubblefield developed a true wireless telephone. He demonstrated his invention to a local friend, Rainey Wells. He had experimented with battery power sources from the earth. Neighbors described strange lights at night coming from the hills around his cabin. The new telephone used natural conduction through the earth.

On January 1, 1902, Stubblefield demonstrated his device before a large crowd at the Calloway County Courthouse in Murray. He and his son set two boxes about 200 feet apart on the lawn. They were able to talk clearly and distinctly to each other through the boxes. The crowd seemed to be unimpressed, and Stubblefield returned home upset. However, the *St. Louis Post Dispatch* newspaper heard of the event, and Stubblefield approved their request for a personal demonstration at his home. This time the boxes were set about a mile apart, the voices were clearly heard, and his son played the harmonica. After the newspaper article appeared, Stubblefield was invited to Washington, D.C., for a demonstration. This time a box was placed on the steamship *Bartholdi* on the Potomac River, and other boxes were placed along the shore. His success led to other demonstrations in Philadelphia and New York. He received patents for his telephone in Canada and the United States.

In 1902, Stubblefield agreed to a commercial use of his invention and founded the Wireless Telephone Company of America. He was named director of the company and "received stock in exchange for the patent rights of his device." A recognized scientific publisher, A. Frederick Collins, became a part of the company. There is much speculation about the true role of Collins in the company. Stubblefield felt he was being swindled by a group within the company and opted to drop out of the agreement. It seemed to him that the men's only interest was in selling stock for their financial gain. Years later, Collins and a group of men were convicted in 1913 of mail fraud in another failed business venture.

Worried about his invention being stolen, Stubblefield moved into a crude shack near Almo, Kentucky. In 1907, he ran a home school called

The Nathan Stubblefield Industrial School. He created an upgraded system to his wireless phone that was patented in his name in 1908. He devoted his time and energy totally to his inventions. He became reclusive, avoiding all social contact. The family's farm was sold off, and his family left him soon after his return. Neighbors continued to report seeing strange lights and hearing weird noises coming from his home. It was reported that his wireless messages were now able to be transmitted over ten miles.

The real creations that he made during this reclusive time may never be discovered. Before his death, he did tell a kind neighbor, Mrs. L. E. Owens,

> I've lived fifty years before my time. The past is nothing. I have perfected now the greatest invention the world has ever known. I've taken light from the air and the earth as I did with sound.... I want you to know about making a whole hillside blossom with light....

Two weeks later, on March 28, 1928, concerned neighbors tried to contact him. It was a cold and rainy day. The neighbors and town officials found the outside door locked. They broke through the door and discovered his body in his bed. He had been dead for several days. It was initially thought that he had died of malnutrition and fatigue. It was later decided that he suffered from heart disease. Inside his cabin, the temperature was very warm. There was no fire. They discovered "two highly polished metal mirrors which faced each other, radiating a very great heat in rippling waves." The mystery was never solved.

He was buried in Bowman Cemetery near Murray. On the campus of Murray State University, a simple historical marker (#87) and monument was placed to remember his life and contributions. A collection of Stubblefield's papers and photos are located at the University of Kentucky at Lexington and the Chamber of Commerce in Murray. In 1948, the first radio station in Murray, Kentucky, chose the station's call letters, WNBS, to honor Nathan Beverly Stubblefield. Kentucky declared 1992 as Nathan Beverly Stubblefield Year.

Some called him a psychic who exploited psychic phenomena. Some called him 'The Real Father of Radio." Both claims are misplaced and incorrect. His inventions were truly innovative. It was said that "the implementation of his earth energy technology would have changed the nature of American Society were it permitted free market expression in its day." While other more famous inventors around the world received more publicity and recognition, Kentucky can claim a native son as an addition to the list of great inventors of that age.

John T. Thompson

Newport

Inventor, "Tommy Gun"

His inventions were used by the military, local law enforcement agencies, and organized crime gangs. He was an innovative designer and efficient administrator for the military in the Spanish-American War and the First World War. He received his early education, developed his professional interests, and experienced his initial professional service in Kentucky.

John T. Thompson was born on December 31, 1860, in Newport, Kentucky. His father was Lt. Col. James Thompson, distinguished Civil War soldier, who had graduated from the United States Military Academy at West Point. His father later taught military science as a professor at Indiana University. His mother was Maria Taliaferro. Thompson grew up on various army posts in Kentucky, Tennessee, Ohio, and California. Proud of his father's military career, Thompson decided at age sixteen to pursue a similar career. In 1877, he attended Indiana University for one year before transferring to the United States Military Academy at West Point. His father died in 1880 and did not see him graduate. In 1882, he graduated eleventh in his class of twenty-one.

He was commissioned as a second lieutenant and stationed with the U.S. Second Artillery unit at his hometown in Newport, Kentucky. Over the next eight years, he was trained at several engineering and artillery schools. In 1890, he was transferred to the Army Ordnance Department, in which he served for much of his military career. He began to specialize in small arms for the military.

With the start of the Spanish-American War, he was promoted to Lieutenant Colonel and appointed Chief Ordnance Officer under General Shafter. In Cuba, Thompson was able to effectively organize a previously confused supply system and provide munitions in a timely manner. He was responsible for the uninterrupted delivery of 18,000 tons of munitions during the war. He was promoted to the rank of colonel.

Thompson's credibility allowed him to create a special unit for the use of rapid-fire weapons. Working with Second Lieutenant John H. Parker, they moved fifteen Gatling guns to Cuba for use by the new unit. Army leadership had not been supportive of using rapid-fire weapons in battle, fearing a waste of ammunition and ineffective aiming. The new unit proved to be very effective, having a positive influence in the battle of San Juan Hill. After the war, now appointed chief of the Small Arms Division for the Ordnance Department, Thompson set out to prove to the Army leadership the value of updated pistols and rifles in combat.

Having already served the military for thirty-two years, in 1914, Thompson retired from military service. The delayed entry of the United States into World War I allowed Thompson to take the position of Chief Engineer at the Remington Arms Company. He supervised the construction of the Eddystone Plant in Chester, Pennsylvania. It was the largest small arms plant in the world. They manufactured guns for the British and Russians for use in World War I. Thompson spent much of his time experimenting with a weapon that was called a "trench broom." It was needed to help clear the enemy trenches used in the European war theater.

With the U.S. entry into World War I, in 1917, Thompson re-enlisted in the military. He was promoted to the rank of brigadier general. He served as Director of Arsenals, supervising the production of small arms. He was later decorated with the Distinguished Service Medal for his efforts. After the war, in December 1918, he retired again and continued work on his automatic rifle. He completed his work on what became known as the Thompson submachine gun. He received a patent in 1920 and became president of the Auto Ordnance Corporation. With the war at an end, need for the weapon was limited to local law enforcement agencies. In 1921, 15,000 guns were manufactured by Colt's Patent Fire Army Manufacturing Company. By 1928, the sales had dwindled, and Thompson left as head of the Fire Army Manufacturing Company.

Throughout the 1920s and 1930s, Thompson would witness the use of his machine gun by local organized gang members and law enforcement agencies. Films would introduce the Thompson submachine gun to a public audience. Thompson died on June 21, 1940, at the age of seventy-nine at his home in Great Neck, Long Island, New York. He was buried on the grounds of the United Sates Military Academy in West Point, New York.

His innovative weapon would find use throughout World War II and future wars. His purpose was to save American lives through more effective armaments. His early training and career in Kentucky led to his lasting creation.

W. T. Young
Lexington
Food Processor

He was a successful businessman, an effective business manager, a political advisor, and an innovative racing horse breeder. He loved his home state and invested his wealth heavily in her future. He was a kind man with many friends around the state.

William T. Young was born on February 15, 1918, in Lexington, Kentucky. His parents were Willis S. Young and Margaret Thompson. Little is known of his early life in Lexington. In 1939, he graduated from the University of Kentucky with a Bachelor of Science degree as a mechanical engineer. He was an active member of the Sigma Alpha Epsilon fraternity. He had brief employment with the Bailey Meter Company in Cleveland, Ohio. When World War II began, he served as a captain in the US Army. He lived in Philadelphia and following his discharge from the Army as a major in December 1945, he returned home to Lexington.

In 1946, Young married Lucy Hilton Maddox. They would remain together for over fifty-six years. They had two children, a son and a daughter. His father-in-law was in the peanut business in Georgia. Most likely encouraged by his father-in-law, Young started W.T. Young Foods, Inc., with his wife's assistance in 1946. The company made Big Top peanut butter. His business grew into the leading producer of peanut butter in the United States. In 1955, he sold the company to Procter &

Gamble. The brand name was changed to the now more familiar Jif. Young remained as manager of operations for the next several years.

Young's success and reputation allowed him to become involved in many other business activities. In 1957, he founded W. T. Young Storage, Inc., and Lexington Cartage. He began service on several key business boards. He was chairman of Royal Crown Cola from 1966 until 1984. He was a board member of Kentucky Fried Chicken and the First Security National Bank and Trust Company of Lexington. He became the largest single shareholder of Humana health insurance company.

1972 was the year when Young's interest turned to his involvement in Kentucky's most popular activity, horse racing at the Churchill Downs track. Young went with a friend, Alex G. Campbell Jr. to watch his friend's filly win the race. He was persuaded to go into partnership with him to invest in future racehorses. Young bought land from Lucas Combs near Lexington that would develop into Overbrook Farm. The farm eventually grew into 2,400 acres. He created a knowledgeable team to help with the breeding business. A veterinarian, Robert Copelan, was part of the team. He noted, "We called him 'The Chief.' He had a hand in everything. Because of his engineering skills, he was able to put everything into a practical sense. He had that special disposition that made everything run smoothly."

One of the most notable team members was horse trainer Dr. Wayne Lukas. Throughout the 1990s and 2000s, the team was able to raise in house a number of successful horses that won key races, including the Kentucky Derby and the Breeders' Cup. In 1994, Young received the Eclipse Award for Outstanding Breeder. In 1996, when their horse Grindstone won the 122nd Kentucky Derby, Young said, "This is a very special moment for me. I'm no import. I'm from Kentucky. I was born here. I came back here after the war."

Young found time to become involved in other state activities. In 1979, when Kentucky Fried Chicken CEO John Y. Brown Jr. was elected governor of Kentucky, he chose Young to serve as chairman of the executive cabinet. He also served the state as chairman of the Kentucky Economic Development Corporation. He was also involved in community activities, such as the YMCA, Junior Achievement, Spindletop Research, the Red Cross, and the Cancer Drive.

Young was committed to helping the local educational institutions. The University of Kentucky was a beneficiary of Young's financial assistance. In the university's campaign for a new library, Young led in the fundraising effort as a trustee with a personal donation of $5,000,000. The $58,000,000-building bears his name. Young worked for an endowment to purchase books for the library. The $65,000,000 endowment was the largest endowment for any public university at the time. He helped to raise $7,500,000 for a new house for the Sigma Alpha Epsilon fraternity.

Another university in Lexington is Transylvania. In 1982, Young set up the Thomas Jefferson Scholarship Program, offering ten four-year scholarships per year. It was later expanded to twenty-five scholarships per year. Serving as chairman of the school's board for twenty-three years, he helped to raise $75,000,000 in capital campaigns. During that period, the school saw great enrollment increases.

On January 12, 2004, Young was near his winter home in Gulf Stream, Florida. He was at a banquet and had just introduced the after-dinner speaker, Jim McKay, when Young collapsed. He never regained consciousness and died of a heart attack at the age of eighty-five. His wife had died on January 13, 2002. Former Kentucky Governor and friend said upon his death, "He'll be missed by all who knew him, but what a legacy and imprint his life has left, especially on Lexington and the state of Kentucky."

His legacy lives on through his children, his continued winning horses from Overbrook Farm, and the countless number of students benefitting from his generous financial gifts to the University of Kentucky and Transylvania. He was a true Southern gentleman who personified the most positive image of the state.

Other Kentucky Innovators in Business, Science and Technology

Robert Grubbs • *Paducah* • Chemistry
"Papa" John Schnatter • *Anchorage* • Papa John's Pizza
George Whitesides • *Louisville* • Chemistry
Terrence W. Wilcutt • *Russellville* • Astronaut

Chapter Five

Politics

(Executives)

Alben Barkley

Graves County

U. S. Vice President

He was an effective U.S. senator, supporting the beneficial programs of several US presidents. He would lead the Senate in its business. He was a key leader and speaker at the Democratic National Conventions. He became a vice-president of the United States in the first major role as an active part of the president's cabinet. He was called "Veep."

Willie Alben Barkley was born on November 25, 1877, in a log cabin near Lowes in Graves County, Kentucky. His parents were John Wilson Barkley and Electra Smith Barkley. They were tenant tobacco farmers and very religious, his father being an elder in the Presbyterian Church. He and his seven siblings were often left in the care of his grandparents. Barkley worked on the family farm and attended school in Lowes. In 1891, his father sold their farm and moved to Clinton, where he worked as a tenant wheat farmer. In 1892, Barkley attended Marvin College, a Methodist school in Clinton. He received a scholarship in exchange for work as a janitor at the school. He was an active member of the school's debate society. His experiences at Marvin persuaded him to convert to Methodism. In 1897, he graduated with Bachelor of Arts degree.

That fall, he attended Emory College in Oxford, Georgia, where he was again part of the debate society. He was also a member of the Delta

Tau Delta fraternity. Lack of financial support caused him to quit after the first year. He returned to Clinton and had a temporary teaching job at Marvin. In December 1898, he moved with his parents to Paducah, Kentucky, where his father found work in a cordage mill. Some sources indicate that he briefly attended the University of Virginia Law School in Charlottesville. Dissatisfied with his name, he was able to legally change his name to "Alben William" Barkley.

In Clinton, Barkley worked as a law clerk for several local lawyers. Making use of their libraries, he continued his studies of the law. In 1901, he was admitted to the bar and began his practice in Paducah. He joined the local Broadway Methodist Church and served as a lay preacher. On June 23, 1903, he married Dorothy Brower. They would have three children.

Barkley began his long career in politics in December 1904, when he declared his candidacy for the local McCracken County prosecuting attorney. His campaigning and likability among the rural residents helped him to win the election. He would serve until 1909 when he was elected county judge and continued service until 1913. His popularity increased with his sound financial dealings and progressive advances for rural constituents.

When an opening appeared in his congressional district, Barkley declared his interest in running for the position. He faced three opponents, including a former employer, John K. Hendrick, who had sought to run unsuccessfully in other past elections. Hendrick attacked Barkley heavily, decrying his youth and inexperience and labeling him a socialist for supporting federal funding of highway construction. Barkley used his plain-speaking talk and humor to answer Hendrick. He said, "When the pope died some years ago, nobody would tell Hendrick, for fear he would declare for the job." In the 1912 election year, Wilson and the Democrats found popular national support. That helped Barkley win in the primary and general election.

He was an effective orator and organizer for domestic concerns and international policy. He largely supported Wilson's neutrality in World War I. When war was finally declared by the U.S., Barkley, age forty, considered resigning from politics and enlisting for military service. Wilson talked him out of it. After the war, he failed to get enough support for Wilson's desire for the U.S. to enter the League of Nations. With the election of Warren G. Harding as president, Barkley found himself at odds with many of Harding's economic proposals. Barkley seriously considered a run for Kentucky governor in 1926 but chose instead to run for a U.S. Senate seat. He served six successive congressional terms until 1927.

Barkley was a well-liked congressman and built up a good organization in the state, which allowed him to run for the U.S. Senate in 1926. He faced no opposition in the primary race. He won the Senate race by a vote of 287,997 to 266,657. In 1928, he was under serious consideration to be nominated as the vice-presidential candidate with New York Governor Al Smith. Smith's advisors waited until after Barkley had seconded Smith's nomination before letting him know that they were going with Arkansas Senator Joseph T. Robinson. Barkley removed his name from nomination for vice president and made the Robinson nomination unanimous.

In the 1932 Kentucky U.S. Senate race, Barkley won with greater numbers. The Democrats gained control of the U.S. Senate and the new majority leader, Joseph Robinson, named Barkley his assistant. They helped President Franklin Roosevelt secure passage of the New Deal legislation. For the midterm elections in 1934, Barkley was an effective speaker. He supported the New Deal programs and Democratic candidates, traveling on a twenty-state tour. He was asked to be the keynote speaker at the 1936 Democratic National Convention. When Robinson died in 1937, there was a fight for the new majority leader. Under Roosevelt's subtle influence while maintaining neutrality, Barkley was elected by one vote.

In 1938, Barkley would face his most difficult battle for another term as U.S. Senator. He faced a strong primary challenge from the current, popular Kentucky governor, A. B. "Happy" Chandler. The primary was in reality a challenge to Roosevelt's New Deal policies, which Chandler opposed. His strong state organization was a formidable challenge for Barkley. The forty-year-old Chandler accused Barkley, sixty, of being too old and out-of-touch with people in the state. In addition to Roosevelt's in-state tour supporting Barkley, Barkley himself demonstrated his physical abilities by conducting his own state tours involving eight to fifteen speeches per day and traveling about 4,500 miles a week. Chandler printed campaign materials with state funds and sought campaign funds from state employees. Such practices were not illegal but unethical.

Barkley won the primary election, winning seventy-four of the state's one hundred and twenty counties. It was the first political defeat for Chandler. Barkley would go on to win the general election vote by 62 percent.

Back in the U.S. Senate, Barkley continued his strong and effective leadership. In 1940, recalling Chandler's unethical campaigning as governor, he helped to pass the Hatch Act, prohibiting campaigning by federally funded state employees. He was a possible candidate for president in 1940 until Roosevelt decided to run for a third term. Barkley was chosen as the permanent chairman and key speaker of the 1940 Democratic Convention. Many supported him for the vice president position on the ticket, but Roosevelt chose Henry A. Wallace. The Democratic slate easily won re-election with the development of involvement in World War II.

Barkley's senate leadership position enabled him to secure significant legislation approval in the Lend-Lease Act, War Powers Act, and emergency Price Controls. He expressed concern for the Nazi mistreatment of the Jews. He failed to get a bill approved to outlaw poll taxes. During the war, a split between Barkley and Roosevelt occurred over a revenue bill that Roosevelt vetoed. Roosevelt also refused to nominate Barkley for a Supreme Court vacancy. Angered, Barkley resigned as the Senate floor leader. Roosevelt sent him word urging him not to resign, and the Senate caucus unanimously re-elected him as floor leader.

The 1944 election found the Democrats very dissatisfied with Roosevelt's vice president, Henry Wallace. Roosevelt refused to dismiss him. Barkley was highly recommended as a replacement, but Roosevelt felt Barkley was too old. In a compromise with the party leadership, Missouri Senator Harry S. Truman was chosen as Wallace's replacement. The ticket easily won the wartime election. Barkley also easily won his Senate election in Kentucky.

With Roosevelt's death in April 1945, Truman became president. Barkley was very supportive of Truman and helped to get Senate approval for key legislation, including support for the United Nations. The 1946 mid-term elections found the Republicans controlling both the House and the Senate. In spite of that, *Look* magazine named Barkley the second-most fascinating person in the country, behind General Dwight D. Eisenhower.

Barkley's wife suffered from heart disease and became an invalid. Not being a wealthy man, Barkley made sacrifices for the care of his wife. He increased his speaking schedule for supplemental income.

He sold their home to move into a less expensive apartment. His wife died on March 10, 1947. Barkley won the Collier Award in May 1948 and donated his $10,000 prize to the University of Louisville School of Medicine in his wife's honor.

In the 1948 national election, it was assumed by many that Truman would not be re-elected. Truman initially asked Supreme Court Justice William O. Douglas to be his running mate. Douglas refused and Truman asked Barkley. At first offended by being a second choice, Barkley accepted, and the Democratic National Convention enthusiastically approved the ticket. His acceptance speech was a powerful and motivating experience for the convention delegates. He introduced the term "do-nothing Congress," referring to the Republican-controlled Congress's failure to pass any meaningful legislation. Truman followed up with the idea by calling Congress back into session and still failing to accomplish anything. Much attention has been given to Truman's "whistlestop" campaign. But the seventy-year-old Barkley was up to the challenge. That fall he made over 250 speeches in thirty-six states. Democrats won a surprising victory and the now seventy-one-year-old Barkley became the oldest man elected as vice president. His grandson had a difficult time calling him vice president and just called him "Veep," a title used by the press. In 1949, he remarried to Jane Hedley.

President Truman knew what is was like to be vice president and outside of the presidential activities. He made sure Barkley was very active in his administration from the outset. Truman made certain that Barkley attended all cabinet meetings. Barkley was also a member of the created National Security Council. Truman ordered the U.S. Army Institute of Heraldry to create a seal and flag for the vice president. He increased the salary and expense budget. With Truman's preoccupation with the Korean War, Barkley became the administration's key spokesman. He aggressively campaigned for Democratic candidates during the 1950 mid-term elections. His pace proved to be too much, and he returned home to recuperate from what his doctor called a "tired heart." On March 1, 1951, his fellow congressmen presented him with the Congressional Gold Medal for his thirty-eight years of legislative service. President Truman personally appeared on the Senate floor to present him with the medallion.

In spite of his age, in the 1952 election campaign, Barkley was considered a serious candidate for the Democratic nomination for president.

Party leadership fell in behind the reluctant Illinois Governor Adlai Stevenson II. Barkley withdrew his nomination in support of Stevenson. On July 22, he gave his farewell address to the convention. He received a thirty-five-minute ovation before his speech and a forty-five-minute ovation afterward.

But Barkley's political service was not over. He continued making speeches around the country. In 1954, he challenged Kentucky Republican Senator John Sherman Cooper. In spite of supportive Republican visits by President Eisenhower, Vice President Nixon and Illinois Congressman Everett Dirksen, Barkley returned to his aggressive campaign practices. He worked sixteen hours a day in the state. He won the election and the win gave the Democrats a one-vote margin in the Senate. In the Senate, several prominent senators offered to exchange their front row seats of honor for Barkley's back row seat for freshmen. Barkley refused.

On April 30, 1956, Barkley was speaking at Washington and Lee University. He explained why he chose to remain on the back row of the Senate. Quoting from Psalm 84:10, he said, "I would rather be a servant in the House of the Lord than to sit in the seats of the mighty." Those were his last words as he fell into the microphone, having suffered a heart attack. He was buried in Mount Kenton Cemetery near Paducah, Kentucky.

Not many politicians have such long careers in politics, free from scandals and admired by the state residents. He represented Kentucky well and served the nation with effective legislative leadership. He was respected by his colleagues and U.S. presidents.

John Breckinridge

Lexington

U. S. Vice President

He was the youngest man elected as U.S. Vice President. He lost a presidential election to Abraham Lincoln. He was a brilliant military commander for the Confederate Army. He was labeled a traitor and a hero. Some thought he should have been hanged.

John Caleb Breckinridge was born on January 21, 1821, in Lexington, Kentucky. He was born into a very prominent family, tracing their political, military, and educational activities from the time of the Revolutionary War. His parents were Joseph Cabell Breckinridge and Mary Clay Smith. He was the fourth of their six children and their only son. Breckinridge's father was the Kentucky Secretary of State at the time of his birth. One month after his son's birth, the family moved into the Governor's Mansion in Frankfort to be near his work. Two years later, his father died of a fever striking Frankfort. The family was forced to move back to Lexington to live with his father's mother. Breckinridge's grandmother spent much time with him, sharing stories of the famous relatives' activities and traditions. She instilled in him much of the Southern attitudes towards culture, race, Northerners, politics, and religion. He attended the Pisgah Academy in Woodford County.

After a serious disagreement between Breckinridge's mother and mother-in-law, the family moved to Danville, Kentucky, to live with his married sister. Her husband was the president of Centre College, where Breckinridge enrolled in November 1834. He received his Bachelor of Arts degree in September 1838 and developed an interest in studying law. After a semester studying at the College of New Jersey (now Princeton University), he returned to Lexington, assisting Judge William Owsley. On November 1840, he continued his study of law at Transylvania University in Lexington. He received his Bachelor of Law degree on November 25, 1841. The next day he was licensed to practice law.

He and a former classmate, Thomas W. Bullock, moved to the Iowa Territory in Burlington to establish their law practice in a less competitive environment. Greatly disappointing his Whig relatives, Breckinridge became active as a Democrat. He returned to Kentucky to try to patch things up between his mother and the in-laws. While there, he was sidelined by the flu. While in recovery, he met Bullock's cousin, Mary Cyreme Burch. With love blossoming, the Iowa law business was closed, and the partners returned to Kentucky. Breckinridge married Mary on December 12, 1843. They settled in Georgetown, Kentucky, and had six children. In 1845, the family returned to Lexington, where Breckinridge formed a partnership with James B. Beck.

Breckinridge tried to volunteer for military service in the Mexican-American. After political connections were cleared, he was appointed as major of the Third Kentucky Infantry Regiment. Arriving in Mexico City at the conclusion of the fighting, his regiment saw no military combat action. On July 16, 1845, he returned to Kentucky, where his regiment was disbanded. He declined offers to enter political races for local Democratic positions. He actively campaigned for national Democratic tickets.

The issue of slavery was beginning to become divisive in the state. Breckinridge was also caught in the middle as he owned five slaves and yet was a member of the Freemasons and the First Presbyterian Church in Lexington, which both opposed slavery. Able to see both points of view allowed him latitude in his successful run for the state House of Representatives in 1849. In 1851, he ran successfully for the U.S. Congress in Kentucky's Eighth District. During this period, Breckinridge had developed a close friendship with Henry Clay. Upon Clay's death, Breckinridge's eulogy impressed many people.

In 1853, Breckinridge ran for re-election to Congress. He won in another close race. He was able to gain assignment on the important Ways and Means Committee. He was torn between the constant debates on secession, which he opposed, and state's rights, which he supported. A reapportionment bill changed Breckinridge's district, making it unlikely for his re-election. He returned to Lexington to practice law. He was instrumental in promoting "the advancement of horse racing in his native state and was chosen president of the Kentucky Association of the Breeding of Horses."

He was a delegate to the 1856 Democratic National Convention in Cincinnati. He had supported Stephen Douglas as the presidential nominee. James Buchanan was selected, and Breckinridge was nominated for vice president, a move that would bring support from Douglas' followers. Breckinridge campaigned vigorously for the ticket nationwide. The Whig Party was split with the formation of the Republican Party. The Democratic ticket won the election. At the age of thirty-six, Breckinridge was the youngest vice president to be elected. He was inaugurated on March 4, 1857.

Aware of Breckinridge's early support for Douglas, Buchanan kept Breckinridge at a distance from administrative activities. Breckinridge presided over the U.S. Senate "gracefully and impartially." On December 12, 1859, the Kentucky Assembly chose Breckinridge to fill the vacant Senate seat.

The 1860 Democratic National Convention was in chaos. Stephen Douglas was seen as the favorite. Their meeting in Charleston, South Carolina, ended without a presidential nominee. Pro-Southern delegates walked out of the meeting dissatisfied. On June 18, the convention reconvened in Baltimore. Breckinridge was seen as the least offensive candidate after other compromise plans were refused. He accepted the nomination from the split party. The division allowed the Republican candidate, Abraham Lincoln, to win the election. On March 4, 1861, it was Breckinridge's duty as vice president to announce Lincoln's victory to the Senate.

Breckinridge, with others, sought to keep Kentucky neutral as seven Southern states seceded from the Union. On April 12, with the firing on Fort Sumter, there was a strong push for Kentucky to take a side. Breckinridge continued his service in the Senate, much in a minority position. He was the only senator to vote against Lincoln's plans for the war effort. He was deemed a traitor by many for his Southern sympathies. With the attacks in Kentucky by both Confederate and Union forces, Breckinridge left to return to Lexington. Kentucky had now declared allegiance to the Confederate cause. He left for the Confederate-held territory in Bowling Green, Kentucky. He stated, "I exchange with proud satisfaction a term of six years in the Senate of the United States for the musket of a soldier." He enlisted in the Confederate Army and was indicted for treason on November 6. 1861. In the U.S. Senate, he was declared traitor.

On November 6, 1861, he was given command as brigadier general of the 1st Kentucky Brigade. Over the course of Civil War, Breckinridge distinguished himself in battle. He fought in twelve significant battles: Shiloh, Baton Rouge, Stones River, Jackson, Chickamauga, Chattanooga, New Market, Piedmont, Lynchburg, Monocacy, Bull's Gap, and Marion. He was promoted to major general on April 14, 1862. On February 6, 1865, Confederate President Jefferson Davis appointed Breckinridge as Secretary of War. He was now convinced of the South's defeat. With the news of Lee's surrender, Breckinridge and other Confederate leaders fled Richmond to Greensboro, North Carolina. Breckinridge ordered the surrender of all Confederate troops. On April 18, when he received news of Lincoln's assassination, he said, "Gentlemen, the South has lost its best friend." His words would prove very true.

Breckinridge, fearing capture and arrest, fled to the Bahamas and then to Cuba. He made a trip to Britain and then to Canada, where on September 13, 1865, he was reunited with his wife and family in Toronto. In May 1866, the family moved to Niagara, Canada. His wife's failing health prompted the family to move to Europe. For two years, the family toured much of Europe. In June 1868, the family returned to Niagara.

On December 25, 1868, President Andrew Johnson proclaimed amnesty for all former Confederates. After receiving assurances of safety, the family moved back to Lexington in February 1869. He continued his practice of law and worked for an insurance company and as legal counsel for a railroad company. He refused all requests to return back to politics. In 1873, he began to experience health problems, most likely from his war injuries. After repeated surgeries, he died on May 17, 1873. He was buried in the Lexington Cemetery. A memorial statue was placed on the Fayette County Courthouse lawn in Lexington in 1887. It was removed in 2015 with the groundswell of Confederate memorial removals.

Breckinridge struggled with his feelings about racial relationships. In March 1870, he publicly denounced the activities of the Ku Klux Klan. In 1872, he supported legislation legalizing black testimony against whites in court. He was innovative in his legal, political, and military decisions. He remained forever faithful to his beloved state of Kentucky.

A. B. "Happy" Chandler
Coryton
Governor

He was a paradox in political and racial practices. He was a pragmatist, willing to do whatever it took to win. He was a jovial person who could also be mean and vindictive. He established his own rules in whatever professional career he entered. Even, so he accomplished much good for the people he served.

Albert Benjamin "Happy" Chandler was born on July 14, 1898, in Corydon, Kentucky. He was the first son of Joseph Sephus Chandler and Callie Saunders. His mother was only fifteen years old and gave birth to another son in 1899. She left the family and the state in 1891. His father, a farmer, and family relatives raised the two sons. When Chandler was eight years old, he was often left on his own. He supported himself by his newspaper route and doing odd jobs in the neighborhood.

He attended Corydon High School, where he excelled in sports activities. He was captain of the baseball and football teams. He graduated in 1917. Encouraged by his father to enter the ministry, Chandler chose to enroll in Transylvania College in Lexington. To meet the financial needs, Chandler worked for local residents. He continued his active leadership role in the school's sports programs. He was captain of the basketball and baseball teams and quarterback for the football team. He was a member of Kappa Alpha fraternity and Omicron Delta Kappa honor society. With his broad smile and jovial nature, he was given the nickname "Happy." He began officer training, but the war ended before he could see active duty. He graduated in 1921 with a Bachelor of Arts degree.

After several failed attempts to enter professional baseball, he decided to study law. He attended Harvard Law School but had difficulty raising the needed funds. After a year, he returned to Kentucky and continued his study at the University of Kentucky Law School. He found financial support through assistant coaching sports programs at Versailles, Centre, and the University of Kentucky. He continued his academic honors as a member of the Order of the Coif and received his Bachelor of Law degree in 1924. He was admitted to the bar in 1925 and began his law practice in Versailles. On November 12, 1925, he married Mildred Watkins, a teacher at Margaret Hall School for Girls. They would have four children. Chandler continued his local assistant coaching while practicing a successful law firm. He found time to become involved in many local civic organizations.

In 1928, he became chairman of the Woodford County Democratic Committee. In 1929, he was elected as a representative for the 22nd district in the Kentucky State Senate. In 1931, he was among the favorites to run for Kentucky lieutenant governor. He was a favorite of the political bosses and his nomination created political enemies within the state. He did not get along well with Governor Laffoon. There was a strong disagreement over the governor's new sales tax. Chandler began to plot for the party nomination for governor in the 1934 election. When the governor was away from the state, Chandler, as acting governor, called for a nominating convention instead of the usual primary election system. He knew his chances were better in the party structure than in a state primary. The bill was passed, and Chandler signed it as acting governor before Laffoon's return to the state. This enabled Chandler to win the party nomination and his first term as governor in the general election. In 1935, he began his term.

Governor Chandler adopted major changes within the state. He guided a repeal of the sales tax through the legislature. He found new revenue sources through implementing new excise taxes and the state's first income tax. He reorganized the state government, eliminating many of the boards and committees. The savings from these actions allowed him pay off the state's debts and improve the state's education and infrastructure systems. He discouraged the integration of the University of Kentucky, losing black support.

Ambitious for higher political office, Chandler ran for the 1938 U.S. Senate primary against Alben Barkley in a bitterly fought campaign. President Roosevelt came to Kentucky and leaned his support toward Barkley. Barkley in polling was a two-to-one favorite. Chandler said, "We Americans are a peculiar people. We are for the underdog, no matter how much of a dog he is." Barkley would eventually win the nomination in an overwhelming victory. Chandler took advantage of a vacant U.S. Senate seat and resigned as governor, assured that the new governor would chose him to fill the senate vacancy. He became the Kentucky U.S. senator in 1939.

Chandler was an inconsistent supporter of President Roosevelt's New Deal programs. He was offended when the president did not support Chandler's recommendation for a Supreme Court vacancy but instead approved Kentucky senator Alben Barkley's recommendation. He became an opponent of Barkley, even when Barkley was the Senate majority leader. In 1942, Chandler won re-election for a second term as senator. He faced opposition from the black community in Kentucky.

Ambitious for even higher national political office, Chandler gathered support for a nomination as vice president at the 1944 Democratic National Convention. His enemies in Kentucky prevented the delegation from giving their support to him. His support dwindled, and the convention chose Missouri Senator Harry Truman as Roosevelt's running mate. A year later, after the announcement of Roosevelt's death, Chandler had even more bitter feelings toward his political enemies in Kentucky.

In April 1945, the owners of the baseball commission voted to elect Chandler as the new commissioner after the death of Kenesaw Mountain Landis. Chandler had promoted some pro-baseball legislation during the war. Chandler accepted, perhaps because of the much-higher salary offered. He immediately made enemies of the some of the owners by not actually beginning his service as commissioner until November 1945. He had interest in some pending Senate legislation and resigned from the Senate while the war was still in progress.

Chandler, besides upsetting some the owners, also had difficulty with the press, mostly from the East Coast. They perceived him as a "Kentucky windbag" and primarily a politician. He also created enemies when he moved the commissioner's office from Chicago to Cincinnati in 1946.

He did win support for his stand against the Mexican league trying to steal major ball player with higher salaries and benefits. Chandler aggressively dealt with the players with strong threats and penalties. He prevailed in most cases. He also dealt effectively with inter-club rivalries and managerial conflicts.

The most significant action from Commissioner Chandler was his support of Brooklyn Dodger General Manager Branch Rickey's signing of Jackie Robinson. As commissioner, Chandler had the right to void the contract of the first black signed to a major league team. He stood firm in his support of Rickey and Robinson and the integration of Major League Baseball. He also made serious threats against those team members demonstrating against Robinson. This paved the way for other black players to have their chance in major league baseball. Don Newcombe, later Dodger player said, "Some of the things he did for Jackie Robinson, Roy Campanella, and Don Newcombe when he was commissioner of baseball—those are the kinds of things we never forget." He said that "Mr. Chandler had cared about blacks in baseball when it wasn't fashionable."

Chandler proved to be an effective business for baseball. In 1947, he sold the radio rights to that year's World Series for $475,000 and, with the funds, established the first pension fund for Major League Baseball players. In 1949, he set up a seven-year contract with Gillette and the Mutual Broadcasting System for $370,000 to broadcast the series. The funds were added to the pension fund. With the same two companies, in 1950, he negotiated a six-year $6,000,000 contract to telecast the series. All those funds went into the pension fund. He helped establish a $5,000 base contract for all players. He became known as "the players' commissioner." That was high praise for Chandler but did not set well with the owners who hired him. In 1948, he was an active supporter of the Dixiecrat division of the Democratic Party, opposing President Truman's integration policies. A two-thirds majority of baseball team owners was required for the renewal of his contract as commissioner. He received a majority vote but not the two-thirds requirement. He negotiated to leave as commissioner on July 13, 1951.

Chandler returned to Kentucky to continue his law practice. He also worked for several companies and corporations. He began building a political base and announced a run for the Democratic primary for governor. He faced enormous pressure from his opponents and political enemies in the state. He won the primary and went on to handily win the governorship, taking office in 1955.

It was a challenging time for Chandler. State budget issues dominated the legislative activities. In spite of budget shortfalls, he allocated $5,000,000 to establish a medical center at the University of Louisville that would later be named after him. The 1954 Brown v. Board of Education ruling requiring desegregation of public schools hit Kentucky hard. Attempts in 1956, by the public, to disrupt integration of the local schools prompted Chandler to authorize the use of the Kentucky National Guard and tanks to quell near riots in several locations. He still had ambitions for the national office of president in the 1956 Democratic National Convention. He left disappointed with the nomination of Adlai Stevenson. He refused to meet President Truman, who was visiting Kentucky to promote the Democratic candidates. He failed again in his efforts to gain the presidential nomination at the 1960 Democratic Convention.

On January 3, 1962, Chandler announced his plans to run for a third term as governor. He faced strong opposition in the primary from his enemies and supporters for a younger candidate. He failed to gain the nomination. He tried unsuccessfully again in 1967. In 1968, he was seriously considered as a running mate for Alabama Governor George Wallace's presidential Independent Party ticket. He tried a run for governor again in 1971 but narrowly failed to get the nomination. The new governor appointed Chandler to the University of Kentucky's board of trustees without voting rights. His voting rights were given to him in 1987. At a board meeting discussing divesting of investments in South Africa, Chandler remarked, "You know Zimbabwe's all nigger now. There aren't any whites." The statement drew immediate criticism from student groups, demanding his resignation from the board. The university president and the governor refused to force Chandler's resignation. The controversial statement would follow him the rest of his life.

In 1989, Chandler published his autobiography, *Heroes, Plain Folks, and Skunks*. He died of a heart attack in Versailles on June 15, 1991, at the age of ninety-two. He was buried in the churchyard of Pisgah Presbyterian Church near Versailles.

Chandler received numerous awards and honors in his lifetime. In 1957, he was one of the ten inaugural members of the Kentucky Sports Hall of Fame. In 1959, he was awarded the Bishop's Medal of the Episcopal Church and received the Cross of Military Service from the United

Daughters of the Confederacy. In 1965, he was named to the University of Kentucky Hall of Distinguished Alumni. In 1982, he was chosen by the Major League Baseball Veterans Committee for induction into the Baseball Hall of Fame.

He was a product of Kentucky and perhaps the paradoxes in his life were reflective of the paradoxes within the state of Kentucky. He accomplished much for racial equality while continuing to exhibit racial insensitivity. His continued grudges against his political enemies divided his party loyalties. But he never wavered in his loyalty to the state he loved.

Abraham Lincoln

Hardin County

U. S. President

No U. S. president has ever been the subject of more books, plays, movies, and historical debates. No U. S. president has ever been more worshipped and adored while also having been more hated and despised. He led a divided nation while enduring his own personal grief. With all that has been written, it is a challenge to separate the facts from the legends that have evolved about this man.

Abraham Lincoln was born on February 12, 1809, near Hodgenville, Hardin County, Kentucky. He was raised in a small log cabin. He was the middle child of Thomas and Nancy Hanks Lincoln. When he was two years old, the family moved to a farm in nearby Knob Creek. He received a limited formal education, distracted by required farm chores. In 1816, his father sold his lands and moved the family to Indiana, just across the Ohio River. Two years were spent preparing a home and the land for farming. Tragedy struck the family in the summer of 1818. Abraham's mother died of a widespread disease called milk poison. The children became mostly self-supporting, while the father worked the farm.

In the winter of 1818, his father remarried to Sarah Bush Johnson, a Kentucky native. She was a widow with three children. She was a good mother to Lincoln and encouraged him in basic education. Lincoln became an avid reader and was mostly self-educated. His father hired him out to work for neighbors. In 1830, the family moved to Illinois on the Sangamon River. His world opened to him when he took a flatboat of goods to New Orleans and reportedly walked back home. In 1832, when disease began to spread near their home, the family moved again to Cole County. Lincoln, being a grown man by then, chose not to go with the family and settled on his own in the growing town of New Salem, Illinois.

Life in New Salem was more appealing to Lincoln than farm life. He found employment co-owning and operating a store and mill. At the store customers and visitors would share stories and experiences of travels. Lincoln also developed a talent and reputation as a good storyteller. He became an active participant in the New Salem Debating Society. He would develop skills in persuasive speaking and logical thinking by debating issues of the day.

A new experience came to Lincoln with the involvement in the Black Hawk War of 1832. A volunteer regiment was formed in New Salem, and Lincoln, tall and lanky, was elected as their captain. He saw no combat but was deeply moved by viewing corpses on the battlefields they passed through. He developed a friendship with a fellow soldier, John Todd Stuart.

After the war, Lincoln began a serious study of the law. He entered the race for the Illinois legislature but lost to his friend, Stuart. They maintained a close friendship, and both men would win election to the Illinois General Assembly in 1834. Stuart became a leader of the state's Whig Party and influenced Lincoln's participation. He was also a successful lawyer in Springfield, Illinois. Lincoln joined him and studied law under him. In September 1836, Lincoln was admitted to the bar and began his practice of law with Stuart. He won re-election to the Illinois legislature in 1836, 1838, and 1840. Lincoln also provided legal representation for the Illinois Central Railroad. In Springfield Lincoln became engaged to a well-educated Kentucky resident, Mary Todd. Their on-and-off-again relationship culminated in marriage on November 4, 1842. Her family did not approve of the marriage, noting Lincoln's moods of depression. The couple had four children.

In 1857, Lincoln made a run for a vacant Illinois U. S. Senate position but was defeated for re-election because of his unpopular political views. He was against involvement in the Mexican-American War and wanted to abolish slavery in the District of Columbia. Lincoln switched party allegiance to the new Republican Party. Lincoln returned to Springfield to continue his practice of law.

Lincoln continued to express his views regarding slavery. He strongly opposed slavery in the new recognized states and territories but was willing to allow its continuation in the original states. He saw slavery as a "moral, social and political wrong." His views were challenging for the current and popular Illinois U. S. Senator Stephen A. Douglas. The two agreed to a series of debates across Illinois. Douglas's position was to allow self-determination of the new states and territories regarding the slavery issue. Lincoln used his good speaking skills with memorable stories that were often repeated. One of the more important was in his "house divided" speech. He clearly stated the issue on a national level: "A house divided against itself cannot stand. I believe the government cannot endure permanently half slave and half free." Such sentiments created supporters in the North and enemies in the South.

In 1860, the Republican National Convention nominated Lincoln for president. The Democrats were divided over John Breckinridge and Stephen Douglas. A third party emerged, the Constitution Union Party. All of these provided the victory for Lincoln with a 40% of the popular vote, but with 180 of the 303 electoral votes. He lost all Southern states. Before he was inaugurated in March 1861, South Carolina seceded from the Union, followed by six other states.

When President Lincoln called for 75,000 troops to stop South Carolina's rebellion and capture of Fort Sumter, three other states seceded. With his limited experience in military leadership, Lincoln turned to books and read volumes on military tactics and procedures. Those would prove to be invaluable with his troubles with military leaders.

Just as the Confederacy faced its own set of problems, Lincoln faced his. He had a contentious cabinet with often opposing views. He had generals with greater egos than abilities in combat. He had open rebellion in the Northern states by those opposed to the war and enlistments. There were political opponents to Lincoln's usurping of basic constitutional rights in a time of war. All these issues, in addition to the growing number of battlefield deaths and major battlefield losses, caused Lincoln and others to assume defeat in the 1864 election. Several things helped to change the course of the war and the result of the election. With the use of the newly created telegraph system, Lincoln was able to communicate quicker with his generals regarding battlefield tactics and necessary command changes. The use of the Union railroad system provided faster arrival of troops. The big events helping Lincoln were the Emancipation Proclamation of January 1, 1863, and the July 4, 1864 news of Sherman's victory over Atlanta.

In spite of the war, Lincoln and Congress were able to pass significant legislation. In 1862, the Revenue Act was passed, creating the first income tax in support of the war cost. That same year, the Morrill Act established the state university system throughout the country. Also in that year, the Homestead Act was approved, giving settlers in the West 160 acres of free land after five years of homesteading. With scrupulous behind-the scenes-activities, Lincoln was able to get the Thirteenth Amendment approved, eliminating slavery throughout the nation.

In Lincoln's inauguration address on March 4, 1865, he stated his desire for the unity of the states. He appealed to audience to have "malice towards none and charity for all." On April 9, 1865, Confederate General Robert E. Lee surrendered the bulk of Southern forces to General Grant at the Appomattox Courthouse. When the news reached the president in the nation's capital, celebration erupted at the impending conclusion to war.

Not all in Washington, D. C., were celebrating. President Lincoln, his wife, and his guests left for the April 14 evening of entertainment at Ford's Theater, Confederate sympathizer John Wilkes Booth and cohorts attempted to dismantle the Union leadership. Booth shot Lincoln, and attacks were made on other cabinet members. The following morning, April 15, 1865, Lincoln died. Along with his death was the death of the hope for a kinder Reconstruction for the Southern states.

Lincoln was buried in Springfield, Illinois. In 1876, a small gang attempted to steal his body. His body was removed to more secure resting place covered by 4,000 pounds of concrete. In 1922, the Lincoln Memorial was dedicated in his honor. His name is to be found on many cities and schools, as well as a university and a national highway.

The news of his death caused widespread mourning in the North and even in some Southern states as they realized the future consequences. Legends, both positive and negative, began to spread about the man and his life. Many of his sayings were recorded for future generations. Some of these have great relevance for our generation:

> 'Nearly all men can stand adversity, but if you want to test a man's character, give him power.'

'Be sure to put your feet in the right place, then stand firm.'
'No man has a good enough memory to be a successful liar.'
'You can fool all of the people some of the time, and some of the people all the time, but you cannot fool all the people all the time.'
'Sir, my concern is not whether God is on our side; my greatest concern is to be on God's side, for God is always right.'
'If I were two-faced, would I be wearing this one?'

Regardless of whether he is either admired or despised, it is indisputable that he is always listed among the three top presidents in our nation's history. He only spent four of his fifty-six years as president. He was influenced in his earliest years by the ethics and traditions of Kentucky.

Mary Todd Lincoln

Lexington

U. S. First Lady

She was highly educated for her day and raised in an affluent family. She was the object of many suitors but chose the most unlikely among them. She was a gracious hostess with expensive tastes. She became the most controversial First Lady in the country's history.

Mary Ann Todd Lincoln was born on December 13, 1818, in Lexington, Kentucky. She was the fourth of seven children born to Robert Smith Todd and Eliza Ann Parker. Her father was a former soldier, merchant, lawyer, and member of the state legislature. They were among the socially elite in the community. A close neighbor to the family was Henry Clay, who visited in the home often. Mary grew up in a home filled with political interests and discussions.

Mary was six years old when her mother died in childbirth on July 4, 1825. Her father, within months, married Elizabeth Betsy Humphreys. The two would have nine additional children. Robert's in laws did not accept Betsy, and some of the children rebelled at her strong disciplinary actions. Mary was perhaps the most obstinate and vocal. Her disruptions in the large family most likely encouraged her father to send her away, at the age of fourteen, to several distinguished preparatory schools. She was first sent to the Shelby Female Academy in 1826. There she received a basic education studying "grammar, geography, arithmetic, poetry and literature." In 1832, she was sent to Madame Mentelle's Boarding School where she studied French, penmanship, dancing, and singing. In 1837, she returned to what was now called Dr. Ward's Academy, where she studied advanced cultural subjects. By 1839, she was a well-educated and opinionated young woman, unique for her day. She developed strong anti-slavery opinions.

At the age of twenty-one, she was an attractive young woman and the object of many suitors. Her older sister, Elizabeth, had married a wealthy young man, Ninian Wirt Edwards, and moved to Springfield, Illinois. Mary made frequent trips to visit them in Springfield. The affluent Springfield couple often hosted community gatherings in their home, especially to welcome Mary as their houseguest. Suitors were welcomed, and Mary was well courted by them. With Mary's charm, wit, and good looks, her brother-in-law, Ninian, said, "Mary could make a bishop forget his prayers." Among these suitors were two local attorneys, Stephen A. Douglas and Abraham Lincoln. Mary began to develop a relationship with Lincoln, sharing his political views, along with his sense of humor. They became engaged in January 1840 and developed a sometimes contentious relationship. At one point, they broke off the engagement. Finally, with the help of a mutual friend, the two were led back to each other, and on November 4, 1842, they were married in the parlor of the Edwards home in Springfield. She was twenty-three years old, and he was thirty-three years old.

The Edwards had concerns about the couple's "suitability" with their shared melancholy moods and differing social backgrounds. The Lincolns moved into a rented apartment before buying their Springfield home in 1844. They would have four boys born there. Mary was often left alone for months at a time while Lincoln was away on his circuit riding responsibilities. She was also a popular hostess for events, which helped her husband in political and social circles. The death of one of their children, Eddie, deeply affected Mary emotionally.

Mary was a great asset to Lincoln in his growing interest in politics. She improved his dress and appearance, summarized newspaper articles for him, shared political news, and began a letter-writing campaign for his support. During Lincoln's campaign for his Republican Party's presidential nomination in 1860, he had become a national figure due to his debates with then U. S. Senator Stephen A. Douglas. Newspapers carried detailed accounts of the debates, and Lincoln's speeches and often humorous stories were shared with the nation. Mary was a very vocal supporter of his views to save the Union and limit the spread of slavery. The couple waited in Springfield to hear the national convention's decision about the presidential nomination. Lincoln's friends and strategists at the convention began returning to Springfield and sharing news of a trend toward his selection. He finally received word by telegram, he reportedly ran home and said, "Mary, we are elected."

There were strong words of support for Lincoln coming from around the country. There were also stinging rebukes to him from Southern sympathizers, including Mary's family. Although Lincoln would forgive their attacks, Mary never forgave them.

The family moved into the White House after the election. Mary must have experienced mixed emotions when she saw the surroundings. It was a big house, well designed for her entertaining but in deplorable condition, dirty with very dated furniture. She was the first wife of a president to be called First Lady. Mary faced initial criticism as being an outsider from the locally elite residents. Mary and Abe were perceived as being unrefined Westerners. Soon after the Lincolns settled into the White House, their son Willie died. The experience was devastating for both parents but especially for Mary. She went into a long period of mourning.

Overcoming her grief, Mary immersed herself into improving the condition of the White House. She commenced on an expensive shopping spree for new furnishings. The cost was very high and created criticism from supporters and opponents, especially with the onset on war expenses and mounting casualties. Congress would pass several appropriation bills to offset some of the initial expenses. Lincoln was not pleased with Mary's actions. Mary even pursued Lincoln's financial supporters to cover the cost of her spending trips. Newspapers began to report her expenditures and made criticisms.

Mary had other duties and activities as the first lady. Besides hosting White House social events, she regularly visited hospitals filled with wounded soldiers. She cared for them and wrote letters for them. She accompanied Lincoln on his trips to visit the troops and became actively supportive of charitable events. In spite of her active life, she was often afflicted with migraine headaches and moments of returning bouts of grief. She even began to develop participation in spiritualism, claiming visitation of family and seeing ghosts in the White House. She had fits of temper that caused friction with the staff, leading Lincoln's personal secretary, John Hay, to refer to her as "the hellcat."

She was excited for Lincoln's re-election in 1864. There was even more celebration at the announcement of the war's end in April 1865. The celebration came to quick conclusion on the night of April 14, 1865. She sat next to her husband at Ford's Theater when he was shot by John Wilkes Booth. As Lincoln lay mortally wounded at a nearby boarding house, Mary became emotionally unhinged. No doubt the past experiences with her sons' deaths and her recognition of losing her husband came to the surface. Her hysteria caused Secretary of War Stanton to have her removed from the room where Lincoln lay. The next morning, she was allowed to enter the room and hold her husband's hand as he died. She closeted herself in a White House bedroom during his funeral service and trip to Springfield, Illinois, for burial. It would be several months before she actually left the White House.

Mary first moved to Chicago, staying with her son Tad. She had received condolence notes from people all around the world. One such note was from Queen Victoria, whose husband, Prince Albert, had died a few years earlier. Mary wrote back to her, "I have received the letter which Your Majesty has had the kindness to write. I am deeply grateful for this expression of tender sympathy, coming as they do, from a heart which from its own sorrow, can appreciate the intense grief I now endure." Mary began a campaign for Congress to allow her to receive a pension as the wife of a fallen soldier. A generous pension was given to her in 1870.

Mary traveled to Europe with Tad and stayed for several years before returning to the United States. Shortly after their return in July 1871, Tad died. Mary reacted with even greater compounded grief. She began to develop strange personal habits. Fearing poverty, she walked around in public with $56,000 in government bonds sewn in her petticoats. Family and friends noticed her erratic behavior.

Her oldest and only living son, Robert Todd Lincoln, took legal action to have her declared insane. At a much-criticized trial, on May 20, 1875, she was found insane and committed to an asylum, Belleview Place, in Batavia, Illinois. There were questions of Robert's ulterior motives, especially when a few months later Mary was successful in getting a retrial and found to be sane.

Mary left for a four-year trip to Europe, residing in Pau, France. She developed a number of physical injuries and returned to New York in 1881. She again petitioned Congress for an increase in her pension, which was approved. She returned to Springfield to live with her sister, Elizabeth. She died on July 16, 1882, at the age of sixty-two. She was buried beside her husband in the Oak Ridge Cemetery in Springfield, Illinois.

Much has been written about her mental condition and deep mood swings into depression. While those may have been a drain on her husband, she also provided much assistance in the rise of his career. She bore him four sons. She was a sounding board for many of his political decisions and actions. She was a faithful wife. Her early and unique educational opportunities in Kentucky provided her with the ability to offer her husband, and eventually the country, well-conceived ideas for the betterment of our country.

Adlai Stevenson I

Christian County

U. S. Vice President

He was the only U. S. vice presidential candidate to run with two different presidential candidates. He was the grandfather of the unsuccessful presidential candidate in 1952 and 1956. Although raised and educated in Kentucky, he would find political success in neighboring Illinois.

Adlai Ewing Stevenson was born on October 23, 1835, in Christian County, Kentucky. His parents were John Turner Stevenson and Eliza Ewing Stevenson. He came from an early Scottish immigrant family. The family was able, over time, to own large tracts of land in North Carolina and became very prominent. Young Stevenson was raised on the family tobacco farm worked by slaves in Kentucky. He attended public school in Blue Water, Kentucky. In 1850, the farm crop was destroyed by frost. In 1852, the family was forced to leave their failed farm. The slaves were freed, and the family moved to Bloomington, Illinois. His father found employment operating a sawmill. Stevenson briefly attended the local Illinois Wesleyan University. He returned to Danville, Kentucky, to attend Centre College. While there, he joined Phi Delta Theta fraternity. He also met fellow student Letitia Green. After graduation, due to his father's death, he returned to Illinois to run the sawmill.

In 1858, he was admitted to the bar at the age of twenty-three. He began to practice law at Metamora in Woodford County, Illinois. He became politically active supporting the Democratic Party, opposing Republican Abraham Lincoln in the 1858 election. His speeches often included "downhome Kentucky storytelling" that had great appeal with his audiences. In 1860, he was appointed master of chancery, assistant to the court of equity. The position likely exempted him from military service in the Civil War. In 1864, he was elected as district attorney.

In 1866, he married Letitia Green. They would have three daughters. In 1868, at the conclusion of his term as district attorney, he opened a law practice with his cousin, James S. Ewing, in Bloomington, Illinois. There, business prospered statewide, but his personal support of the Democratic Party created enmity with the locals. In 1874, Stevenson was nominated by his party for the U.S. Congress. Failing to gain local support, he won the district vote with 52 percent. In 1876, he lost a close re-election attempt, receiving 49.6 percent of the vote. In 1878, he was again successful in his race for Congress. He would lose close re-election bids in 1880 and 1882.

Even with his close elections, Stevenson was active in community. He was grandmaster of the Masonic Lodge; started a Democratic paper, the *Bloomington Daily Bulletin*; served as director of the People's Bank; and co-managed the McLean County Coal Company. In the 1884 national election, Stevenson campaigned for Democratic candidate Grover Cleveland. With Cleveland's victory, Stevenson was offered the position of assistant postmaster general of the United States. The post office at that time was politically controlled. Stevenson gained much political popularity in dismissing over 40,000 Republicans from their postal positions and replacing them with Democrats. Republican congressmen were angered. Toward the end of Cleveland's term, he nominated Stevenson to fill a vacancy at the U. S. Supreme Court. A Republican-controlled Senate, as revenge, refused to support Stevenson for the position. Stevenson returned to Bloomington to resume law practice at Stevenson and Ewing.

In 1892, the Democratic National Convention, meeting in Chicago, re-nominated Cleveland for president. With strong statewide support, Stevenson was selected as Cleveland's running mate. It was thought that Stevenson's Kentucky roots could influence voters in the Southern states to give their support. Stevenson and his wife traveled around the country campaigning for Cleveland, especially in the South. The team won the election. Stevenson was sworn in as the twenty-third vice president of the United States on March 4, 1893.

Stevenson's primary role as vice president was to preside over the Senate. He was admired by all for ruling "in a dignified, nonpartisan manner." He was a candidate for the presidential nomination at the 1896 national convention, but his support faded with the rise of William Jennings Bryan. Stevenson remained the active head of the Democratic Party and was considered again as presidential candidate in 1900. Bryan still had the popularity that won him the nomination, but Stevenson was nominated for vice president to bring balance to the ticket. Although losing to the Republican ticket of McKinley and Roosevelt, Stevenson earned the honor of being the only vice-presidential candidate to run with two presidential nominees.

Stevenson returned to Bloomington to continue his law practice. He ran unsuccessfully for governor in a close election in 1908. He died in Chicago, Illinois on June 14, 1914, at the age of seventy-eight. He was buried in the family plot in the Evergreen Cemetery in Bloomington, Illinois.

Stevenson remained philosophical about his life and political losses. He said, "Man is a strange animal, he doesn't like to read the handwriting on the wall until his back is up against it." He was an educated man blessed with his homespun stories learned from his Kentucky roots.

Zachary Taylor

Louisville

U. S. President

He was a military general and commanded some of the previously mentioned Kentucky innovators. Although not born in Kentucky, he received his early education and life lessons in Kentucky. He was the last Whig president and one of our shortest-term presidents.

Zachary Taylor was born on November 24, 1784, on a plantation in Orange County, Virginia. His parents were Richard Taylor and Mary Dabney Strother. He was the third of nine children. His father was a veteran of the Revolutionary War and a wealthy landowner. His mother was a well-educated woman, unusual for her time.

When their farmland became exhausted, the family moved to the new settlement in Louisville, Kentucky, on the Ohio River. It was the western frontier at the time and the family first lived in a small cabin, eventually building a larger brick house. The family had purchased about 10,000 acres and owned twenty-six slaves to farm the land. With public education just being created, Taylor received very little formal education. He learned from his mother and siblings when not working on the farmland. He received some tutoring and attended the Middleton Kentucky Academy. He was a bad speller, and his handwriting was very poor.

Ignoring any desire for college, Taylor joined the U. S. Army on May 3, 1808. He was commissioned as a first lieutenant of the Seventh Infantry Regiment and was assigned to very inferior camps in and near New Orleans. As with many other soldiers located there, he suffered from disease and returned to Louisville to recover. He would begin a distinguished forty-year career in the military. On June 20, 1810, he married a wealthy plantation owner's daughter, Margaret "Peggy" Mackall Smith. They would have six children. One daughter would marry Jefferson Davis, future Confederate president. In 1810, he was promoted to captain, while his limited military duty allowed him to increase his personal financial worth. He bought stock in a Louisville bank and purchased additional land, including a plantation and property in Mississippi. He became owner of over two hundred slaves.

In July 1811, he was assigned to Fort Knox in the Indiana Territory. With the beginning of the War of 1812, Taylor defended the attack on Fort Harrison in the Indiana Territory. It was the first victory of the war for the American forces. Taylor received recognition and high praise for his efforts. He continued his military exploits into the Illinois Territory with mixed results. He rejoined his family in Fort Knox before leaving to attack Indian and British forces. He established the northernmost U. S. outpost on the Mississippi River, Fort Johnson, near Warsaw, Illinois. When the war ended in 1815, his temporary rank of major was reduced to captain. He resigned the army, rejoining later after his new commission as major.

For the next two years, Taylor was in command of Fort Howard in Green Bay, Michigan Territory. In 1817, he returned to Louisville, Kentucky, to be with his family. In April 1819, he was promoted to the rank of lieutenant colonel. In 1821, he led his Seventh Infantry to Natchtoches, Louisiana, where he established Fort Jessup. In November 1819, he was transferred to Fort Robertson in Baton Rouge, Louisiana. Several years later, he bought a plantation near Baton Rouge and brought his family to their new location.

In May 1828, he was called back into temporary duty in the Michigan Territory. He returned home to Louisiana and his family. In April 1832, he was promoted to the rank of colonel commanding the First Infantry Regiment. He would lead his command to the West, fighting in the Black Hawk War. The war would be won by August 1832. In 1837, he was again assigned to lead his troops to Florida, fighting in the Seminole War. He would eventually assume command of all U. S.

forces in Florida, promoted to the rank of brigadier general. Requesting assignment relief, Taylor was able to travel around the country with his family, and he became interested in politics. In 1841, he was made commander of the Second Department of the Army's Western Division, stationed in Arkansas. During this period of relative calm, he oversaw his growing development of his properties.

In 1841, Taylor was sent to Fort Jessup in Louisiana. With the annexation of Texas in 1836, there was much concern of Mexican attacks to reclaim its lost territory. Taylor's previous nonpolitical involvement allowed him to be placed, over other higher-ranking officers, in command. Taylor was assigned command in Texas and established a base of operation in Corpus Christi. When the Mexican attacks began, Taylor's forces, though outnumbered, began a series of strategic victories. He was wounded during the conflict. He was noted for his humane treatment of all casualties, Mexican as well as American. His actions brought him to national attention and congressional accommodations. Being left with a smaller command, Taylor was seen as in a vulnerable position by Santa Anna's army. In February 1847, Taylor's outnumbered troops were attacked by Santa Anna. Casualties were high in both armies, but Taylor prevailed, and Santa Anna retreated in a final defeat of the war. He was later honored by both American and Mexican military societies. Taylor returned home in December 1847 to a hero's welcome in New Orleans and Baton Rouge. He completed his forty-year military service.

The election of 1848 was open to new candidates in both the Whig and Democratic parties. Taylor's independent attitudes made him acceptable to both parties' nomination for president. Taylor's war record had great appeal to Northerners, and his ownership of slaves had appeal to Southerners. He also had some political issue disagreements with both parties. Taylor finally acknowledged that "he had always been a Whig in principle, but did not consider himself a Jeffersonian-Democrat." At the 1848 Whig National Convention, he was selected as their nominee, winning over Henry Clay and Winfield Scott. He chose U.S. Representative leader Millard Fillmore for his vice-presidential running mate. In a three party race, Taylor and Fillmore won with 47.3 percent of the vote and 163 of the 290 electoral votes. He would be the last Whig to win the presidency and the last person from neither the Democratic nor Republican parties to win election. He was also the last president to own slaves while in office.

As president, Taylor maintained his independent stand on critical issues. He did not support the expansion of slavery into non-plantation areas. He was instrumental in creating the future Hay-Pauncefote Treaty of 1901, "giving the United States control over any canal created in Central America that connects the Pacific and Atlantic Oceans." Taylor also worked with Henry Clay and Daniel Webster to develop the Compromise of 1850, delaying secession of Southern states over the slavery issue. On July 4, 1850, Taylor attended holiday festivities during a fundraising event for the Washington Monument in Washington, D.C. He ate large amounts of raw fruit and consumed a lot of iced milk. He became severely ill over the next few days, as did several other cabinet members. It was speculated that the open city sewers contaminated the food. He died at 10:35 p.m. on July 9, 1850. He was sixty-five years old and just sixteen months into his term. He was temporarily interred for three months in the Public Vault of the Congressional Cemetery until his body was transferred to the Taylor Family plot on the original homestead site in Louisville, Kentucky.

In 1883, the Commonwealth of Kentucky placed a fifty-foot monument included with a life-sized statue of Taylor near his grave. Two adjacent plots of land were added to form a national cemetery named after him. Other honors named after him included Fort Taylor in Key West, Florida; counties named after him in Georgia, Iowa and Kentucky; highways named after him in Louisiana and Virginia, and a dormitory at Southeast Louisiana University. Later rumors of his assassination were dispelled by scientific examination of his remains.

As a military commander, Taylor traveled and lived all around the country. His early memories of the Kentucky frontier and his family led to his decision for a final resting place in the state.

Other Kentucky Innovators in Politics *(Executives)*

Wendell Hampton Ford • *Owensboro* • Governor, U. S. Senator
Richard M. Johnson • *Jefferson County* • U. S. Vice President
Tony Snow • *Berea* • U. S. Press Secretary
Ron Ziegler • *Covington* • U. S. Press Secretary

Chapter Six

Politics

(Legislative and Judicial)

Louis Brandeis

Louisville

Supreme Court Justice

He was known as the "people's lawyer." His immigrant family chose Kentucky as their state of choice. He graduated from Harvard Law School with the at that time the highest grade average in history. He was the first Jew appointed to the United States Supreme Court, serving for twenty-three years.

Louis Dembitz Brandeis was born on November 13, 1856, in Louisville, Kentucky. His parents, Adolph Barndeis and Frederika Dembitz, were immigrants from Prague, Bohemia. They fled Europe during the revolutionary activities of the 1840s and the growing attacks on Jews. His parents found the city of Louisville inviting with its location as a river town. Brandeis' childhood experienced the struggle of the Civil War. His family's abolitionist sentiments were not popular among the mostly Confederate sympathizers.

Brandeis grew up in a home very cultured for its day. His family had a great appreciation for the fine arts, books, and history. In the local school, Brandeis was interested in studying languages. He excelled as a student and graduated from Louisville Male High School at the age of fourteen, earning the highest academic honors. He continued his limited college education in Louisville. In 1872, expecting a national economic crisis, the Brandeis family moved back to Europe. Brandeis attended the Annenschule in Dresden, Saxony, again with high academic achievements. He began to direct his interest in the study of law at that time.

In 1875, the family returned to the United States. Brandeis enrolled at Harvard Law School at the age of eighteen. He became very active in discussions and mock trials. His father's business losses required him to earn funds in tutoring other law students. He began to experience the loss of his eyesight and chose to hire a fellow student to read aloud the textbooks and resource books. Even with his growing disability, Brandeis graduated as valedictorian, having achieved the highest grade point average at that time. A special resolution by the Harvard Corporation allowed him to graduate in 1877 with a Bachelor of Law degree, in spite of the fact that he was not yet twenty-one years old. He continued another year of study at Harvard until he was able, at the age of twenty-one, to begin his practice of law. He initially moved to St. Louis, Missouri, where, having been admitted to the Missouri bar, he joined a law firm. He did not feel challenged in being assigned to minor legal cases. When a Harvard friend, Samuel D. Warren, offered him a partnership in a new law firm in Boston, he quickly accepted. Warren's wealthy family was influential in Boston and helped to direct friends' and associates' legal business to the new firm.

While waiting for the new firm to develop, Brandeis worked as a law clerk for Horace Gray, the chief justice of the Massachusetts Supreme Court. He was later admitted to the Massachusetts bar without taking the required exam. The new firm was immediately successful, and Brandeis was able to be financially secure. He became involved in more progressive causes developing in American society. He had his first appearance before the U.S. Supreme Court in 1889 and impressed several of the justices. Brandeis also developed a personal philosophy leaning more toward legal advisor. He said "I would rather have clients than to be somebody's lawyer." Between 1889 and 1890, Brandeis and Warren wrote articles for the prestigious *Harvard Law Review*. The most significant was "The Right to Privacy," criticizing the use of published photographs without a subject's permission. The article had immediate influence in legal cases brought before the US Supreme Court.

In 1889, Warren resigned from the partnership to operate his deceased father's paper company. Brandeis added two other new partners. On March 23, 1891, Brandeis married Alice Goldmark of New York. They were married in a civil ceremony at her parents' home in New York City.

They would have two daughters. The couple did not live an ostentatious lifestyle. Although they did purchase a vacation home in Dedham, after his wife's failing health, Brandeis was very cautious in the family's expenses.

Brandeis became very active in the Progressive Movement. He was a leader against political corruption, the growing trend of monopolistic businesses, and what he deemed advertising manipulation of consumers. This led him to direct conflict with the new business moguls such as J. P. Morgan. He refused to accept payment for his representation in public interest causes. In 1908, Brandeis developed what became known as the Brandeis Brief. It was a scholarly defense of protection for workers' rights on the state level. He became an advocate for the public, earning the title of the "people's lawyer." In 1911, he wrote the book *The Opportunity and the Law.*

Brandeis became persuaded by Woodrow Wilson's philosophy and ideas about the unfair practices of business monopolies. He switched from his previous allegiance to Republican causes and enthusiastically joined the Democratic platform of Wilson. With Wilson's victory in 1912, the two men developed close communication of causes of important economic issues facing the country. He became Wilson's chief economic adviser. He developed the idea of the Sherman Anti-Trust Act and the Federal Trade Commission. These federal regulatory programs were threats to the leading entrepreneurs of the day.

In 1913, Wilson sought to place Brandeis in more authoritative positions. He suggested Brandeis as a member of his cabinet. There was strong reaction from the business community, and Brandeis wisely declined the offer. In 1914, Brandeis authored *Other People's Money and How Bankers Use It.* It also was not well received by the business community.

On January 28, 1916, President Wilson nominated Brandeis for a vacant seat on the U.S. Supreme Court. There was immediate strong opposition from political and business opponents. Prior to this time, the Senate quickly and simply voted for or against a president's nominee. But for the first time, opposition demanded public hearings before the Senate Judiciary Committee. The list of opponents and proponents required an unprecedented four months of public hearings. Besides the very obvious concerns of the business leaders, there was also a strong sentiment of anti-Semitism among political leaders. Finally, on June 5, 1916, Brandeis was approved with a Senate vote of forty-seven to twenty-two and began his twenty-three years of influential service on the US Supreme Court.

Brandeis was a strong supporter of President Franklin Roosevelt's New Deal policies. He also became an active supporter of the cause of Zionism, establishing a Jewish homeland.

During the twenty-three years, Brandeis made significant contributions on many important issues. Often siding with Justice Oliver Wendell Holmes, Brandies made decisions that have had influence on present-day issues. Among these are issues on freedom of speech, right of privacy, presidential limitations, and federal/state laws. His rulings are often used in current Supreme Court decisions today.

Brandeis retired from the Supreme Court on February 13, 1939. He continued active participation in the Zionism movement. On October 5, 1941, he died of a heart attack. In 1924, he began developing the law school and library at the University of Louisville. His professional papers are housed there. In 1948, Brandeis University began operation in Waltham, Massachusetts.

Brandeis' philosophy of the law was best expressed as "If we desire respect for the law, we must first make the law respectable." He also inspired President Truman's mantra, "The most important political office is that of private citizen." Brandeis also gave a haunting warning for our current political circumstances,

> Our government ... teaches the whole people by its example. If the government becomes the lawbreaker, it breeds contempt for the law; it invites every man to become a law unto himself; it invites anarchy.

Brandeis was described by current biographer, Jeffrey Rosen, as "the most farseeing, progressive justice of the 20th century." He noted that Brandeis understood the Constitution as "a living document to be constantly interpreted in light of the realities of the day." Brandeis recognized the states as the "laboratories of democracy."

It is a credit to Kentucky that the education and values developed by Brandeis in his early years brought fruition in national service for the advancement of civil liberties for Americans today. Although much of his life was spent away from the state, he continued to hold his state in high regard even in his final days.

Cassius Marcellus Clay

Clermont

Abolitionist

He was revered by some and vilified by others. He was described by some as a brilliant genius and by others as mentally unbalanced. His opinions were very much in the minority view of Kentucky in his day. Yet, he was very much ahead of his time in modern terms.

Cassius Marcellus Clay was born on October 19, 1810, near Richmond, Kentucky. He was one of the seven children born to General Green Clay and Sallie Lewis Clay. His father was a wealthy farmer with much land and many slaves. The family had a long history of active politicians. Young Clay was privileged to be able to attend Kentucky schools early in his life. He attended Madison Seminary, St. Joseph's College, Centre College in Danville, and Transylvania College in Lexington. He was able to attend Yale University, graduating in 1832. While at Yale, he was influenced by the speaking of abolitionist William Lloyd Garrison. While Clay respected the Abolitionist position, he was more comfortable with the emancipationist position, "favoring a gradual ending of slavery through legal means sanctioned by the Constitution."

Returning home after his experience at Yale, Clay worked on the family farm. In 1833, he married Mary Jane Warfield. They would have a marriage of forty-five years, producing ten children.

In 1835, Clay, relying on his family name more than his minority views, won election to the Kentucky state legislature, winning a second term in 1837. His promotion of ending slavery created dangerous enemies. During a public debate in 1843, he was shot in the chest by a pro-slavery assassin, Sam Brown. Although wounded, Clay was able to physically assault his attacker. There were also attempts to kidnap his children in order to stop Clay's speaking. One of his children, Cassius Marcellus Clay Jr. was reportedly fatally poisoned.

In 1844, he freed all his slaves and paid them wages for their continued work. In 1845, he started an anti-slavery newspaper, *True American*. An irate mob, called the Committee of Sixty, attacked his printing office and destroyed the publishing equipment. Clay moved the publication office to Cincinnati and continued the newspaper through 1846, when Clay was called to military service.

During he Mexican-American War there was a call for military volunteers from the nation in support of answering the Mexican military attacks on American-claimed territory. Clay was a captain in the Kentucky militia and led his troops to Mexico. The regiment was captured and taken as prisoners to Mexico City, where they remained until 1848.

In 1849, Clay began a campaign for governor. While giving a speech, he was attacked by pro-slavery activists, six Turner brothers. They beat and stabbed him, but he successfully fought them off, killing one. Clay was unsuccessful in his political bid for governor due to his anti-slavery views. In 1853, he donated land and financial support to Reverend William Fee to start Berea College, the first integrated college in the South.

With the Whig political party failing its supporters, Clay was an early founder of the new Republican Party in Kentucky. He was a friend and supporter of Abraham Lincoln. At the 1860 Republican Party National Convention, he was seriously considered for the vice president position. The ticket of Abraham Lincoln and Hannibal Hamblin won the election.

On March 28, 1861, President Lincoln appointed Clay as the U.S. ambassador to Russia. In Washington, D. C, while waiting for departure to St. Petersburg, the Civil War began. Early threats by Confederates were made on the capital city. Before Federal troops could be enlisted, Clay organized about 300 volunteers to protect the White House. They were called the "Clay Battalion." Relieved by the arrival of Federal troops, Lincoln honored him before Clay's departure with his family to Russia in 1861.

Clay was briefly recalled by President Lincoln to the United States in 1862 to assess the reaction in Kentucky and other border states to the impending Emancipation Proclamation. Clay was also able to give help to Lincoln in the final document. Clay returned to Russia and served as ambassador until 1869. It is speculated that Clay had some participation in the agreement of Russia sending naval vessels to the U.S. coasts as a warning to Britain and France not to intervene in the Civil War on the side of the Confederacy. He was instrumental in arranging the agreement selling Alaska to the United States.

Upon his return to Kentucky, he became very dissatisfied with President Grant's Reconstruction policies in the Southern states. He left the Republican Party and, in 1872, was active in forming the Liberal Republican revolt that nominated Horace Greely for president. He supported the Democratic candidates in the 1876 and 1880 elections. In 1884, he rejoined the Republican Party.

His personal life also experienced mixed loyalties. There were rumors of his various affairs. In 1878, after forty-five years of marriage, his wife divorced him, charging him with abandonment in marital infidelities. In 1894, at the age of eighty-four, he married Dora Richardson, the fifteen-year-old daughter of one of his sharecroppers. They would divorce within a year.

There were rumors of his failing mental capacities. He lived out the rest of his life at his home, called White Hall. On July 22, 1903, at the age of ninety-three, he died there of "general exhaustion." He was buried in the Richmond Cemetery.

Cassius Marcellus Clay had an important impact on the national conscience and made major contributions to the nation's establishment of equality for all. His idea of Berea College served as an inspiration for other such schools to be established throughout the country. His family home, White Hall, is kept by the Commonwealth of Kentucky as White Hall State Historic Shrine. One of his freed slaves honored him by naming his son Cassius M. Clay. That lineage progressed until a great-grandson was given that name in Louisville, Kentucky. As a heavyweight champion boxer, he would later change his name to Muhammad Ali.

Henry Clay
Lexington
Statesman

He was obstinate in his actions but was known as the "Great Compromiser." He was a shrewd politician with the longest tenure as elected Speaker of the House but lost three presidential elections. He justified his losses by famously saying, "I'd rather be right than President." Although born in another state, he chose Kentucky as his identified home.

Henry Clay was born on April 12, 1777, in Hanover County, Virginia, the seventh of nine children born to Reverend John Clay and Elizabeth Hudson Clay. His father was Baptist minister who owned twenty-two slaves, who assisted with the family tobacco farm. When Clay was four years old, his father died. Soon after the death, the British attacked the farm and house, leaving the widow and family in despair. Fortunately, Elizabeth married Captain Henry Watkins and he proved to be a good provider and advisor to the now additional seven children sixteen in all.

Clay attended the Old Field School and St. Paul's School in Hanover County. He was also tutored by Virginia jurist George Wythe, who introduced him to the study of law. In 1791, his family moved to Kentucky but arrangements were made for Clay to continue his studies in Richmond, Virginia, and join them later. In 1797, Clay was admitted to the bar. Sensing the growing competition in Virginia, Clay moved closer to Lexington, Kentucky, to be closer to his family. The family lived in Versailles.

After establishing his law practice, on April 11, 1799, he married Lucretia Hart in Lexington. They would have eleven children. Most of the children would live, suffering from childbirth complications, diseases, and battle injuries. He purchased a farm outside of Lexington and named it Ashland. He bred sheep, cattle, and racing horses. Clay began a successful law practice, earning a reputation as a legal scholar and courtroom orator. In 1803, Clay was elected to the Kentucky legislature, the first of seven terms. In 1805, Clay was appointed as a faculty member for Lexington's Transylvania College, the first university west of the Appalachian Mountains. He was sent to Washington, D. C., twice, in 1806 and 1810, to fill unexpired terms of U. S. Kentucky senators. Although his time there was brief, he made a strong positive impression on the legislators.

In 1811, he won election to the U. S. House of Representatives. He was elected there as the Speaker of the House, the youngest chosen to date, at the age of thirty-four. During his time as Speaker, Clay changed the largely ceremonial duties to more powerful duties of deciding committee appointments, setting the legislative agenda, and participating in debates on the House floor. He was strongly anti-Britain, perhaps influenced by early childhood memories. He led the quick passage of President Monroe's declaration of war against Britain, beginning the War of 1812.

He resigned from Congress on January 19, 1814, to go to Europe as part of a peace commission to end the war. The action led to the Treaty of Ghent, signed on December 24, 1814. While Clay was absent, Kentucky voters elected him to another term in the House. He was elected again as Speaker in 1815. With the slavery issue becoming more prominent in legislative matters. In 1816, Clay made his position known by becoming the president of the American Colonization Society, desiring to relocate slaves to Liberia. He also was a strong supporter of President Madison's legislative programs. He developed a program to help American manufacturing against the British competition, called the "The American System." This included the creation of tariffs on imported goods.

In the 1816 elections, Clay supported James Monroe. Upon Monroe's election, Clay sought the position of Secretary of State but was denied by Monroe. He became active in international affairs, supporting independence for Central and South American countries. He also supported and helped passage of the Monroe Doctrine. He was very critical of General Andrew Jackson's attacks in Florida without congressional approval. This led to a long and vicious feud between Clay and Jackson.

The slavery issue continued to become divisive as new states were petitioning to become part of the union. There was heated debate over whether these new states would be permitted to have slaves. Although some claim Clay originated the Missouri Compromise, it was the proposal of Jesse B. Thomas from Illinois in 1820. Clay was able to guide the legislation through Congress for approval. It allowed Missouri to be admitted as a slave state in 1821 but banned slavery north of the thirty-sixth parallel, later called the Mason-Dixon line.

1824 was a pivotal year for Clay. He had ambitions for the presidency in his party. He was hampered by illness. With other contenders, he failed to finish in the top three finalists: William Crawford, Andrew Jackson, and John Quincy Adams. With no one receiving majority votes, the race was sent to the House of Representatives. Clay was an influential Speaker of the House and, in spite of Jackson's favorite status, helped to select John Quincy Adams as president. Upon election, Adams appointed Clay as the coveted Secretary of State. Jackson accused the appointment of being a "corrupt bargain." The question is still debatable. Clay served as Secretary of State from 1825 until 1829.

In the 1828 elections, Clay's party changed their name to the to the "National Republicans." Andrew Jackson led a vindictive campaign for the presidency under the new "Democrat" party. Jackson won the election. While Adams was still president, Clay was offered a position on the U. S. Supreme Court. He declined the gracious offer and returned to his Kentucky farm, Ashland.

Angry at Jackson's political programs and legislation, Clay ran for a U. S. Senate seat in 1831. He won and returned to the Senate. He had much favored the more active legislative process in the House of Representatives but found the Senate more powerful in opposing Jackson's programs. He and Jackson would spar over many of Jackson's proposed ideas. After Jackson's 1832 presidential election victory over Clay, there was much negative reaction to Jackson's actions regarding the Treasury's use of local banking. Clay was able to pass a Senate censure of Jackson for his actions.

South Carolina, represented in the Senate by John C. Calhoun, was on a collision course with Jackson over increasing high tariffs. Calhoun wanted the states to be able to defy set national tariffs. Jackson threatened takeover of the state. Clay worked with Calhoun to create the Compromise Tariff of 1833, averting what could have begun a series of state secessions.

In the 1834, Jackson described Clay's party attacks and opponents mockingly as referred to as the "Whigs." The name stuck, and the National Republican party became known as the Whigs. Clay was distressed by the death of one of his daughters and chose not to run in the 1836 national election. Martin Van Buren's election was followed by the economic crisis, the Panic of 1837. The devastating effect on the national economy created dissatisfaction with the Democrats, and the Whigs saw hope in the 1840 national election. William Henry Harrison was chosen as the party candidate, and Clay had hoped for the vice presidency nomination. But again he failed, allowing a personal friend, John Tyler, to be Harrison's running mate. Clay gave strong support to his party's ticket, which won the election. Harrison offered Clay the Secretary of State position, but Clay declined. Harrison would die in office within a year.

The friendship between Clay and new President John Tyler soon fractured as Tyler began to adopt programs much to Clay's disapproval. Some of Clay's proposals were vetoed by Tyler, and some of Tyler's ideas were fought effectively in the Senate by Clay. He was again prompted to enter the presidential race in 1844. After some intra-party negotiations, Clay won the Whig party nomination. The Democrats, in a surprising move, nominated James K. Polk. The issue of Texas annexation, which Clay opposed and Polk supported, was a major influence on Polk's very close victory over Clay. Henry Clay Jr., Clay's son, was killed in the Mexican-American War while fighting in General Zachary Taylor's forces at the Battle of Buena Vista. After the election, Clay returned to his Kentucky law practice to help pay off campaign debts.

As the 1848 national election approached, Clay remained uncommitted. He was now seventy years old and suffering from the early stages of tuberculosis. His participation at the Whig National Convention caused many of his supporters to consider him for the nomination. His criticism of the anti-slavery Wilmot Proviso following the Mexican-American War disappointed supporters in the South and the North. He would lose the party's nomination to the war hero Zachary Taylor. Millard Fillmore was the vice-presidential candidate. The ticket won the election.

In 1849, Clay accepted his state's nomination for another term in the Senate. Becoming more concerned about federal influence over slavery and states' rights issues, Kentucky wanted representation by Clay's sound leadership. With the help of Illinois senator Stephen A. Douglas, Clay proposed a series of compromises. Rejected as a whole, the individual compromises garnered enough support for approval. The process became known as the Compromise of 1850. It would be Clay's legacy that he delayed a civil war for over a decade. He was not present for the final approval through Douglas' leadership. Clay had left to deal with his growing tuberculosis in Newport, Rhode Island. He eventually made his way to the National Hotel in Washington, D. C.

In 1851, Clay officially resigned from the U. S. Senate. He died on June 29, 1852, at the age of seventy-five. His body lay in state at the Capital rotunda, the first American given that honor. A train, viewed by many supporters for two weeks, took his body back to Kentucky. He was buried in the Lexington Cemetery, Lexington, Kentucky. In his will, he freed all his slaves.

He had a lasting impact on the history of the United States. He was a good representative for his home state of Kentucky. Senator Henry S. Foote of Mississippi stated, "had there been one such man in the Congress of the United States as Henry Clay in 1860–61 there would, I feel sure, have been no civil war." Abraham Lincoln described him as "my idea of a great man." At the beginning of the Civil War, Kentucky remained neutral, attributed largely to Clay's influence. In 1957, a Senate subcommittee selected the five greatest U. S. senators: Daniel Webster, John C. Calhoun, Robert La Follette, Robert A. Taft, and Henry Clay. Counties in sixteen states are named in his honor. His farm at Ashland, Kentucky is a museum today.

Very few men have held such honors for their contributions to our country. Although born a Virginian, Henry Clay immersed himself into the life and values of Kentucky. The state should be proud of contributing such a gift to our country.

Jefferson Davis

Fairview

Confederate Prȩsident

There was absolutely no desire to be president. He much preferred a military command. His support of secession came very reluctantly. His task was formidable with obvious disadvantages. He was charged with treason, having a bounty on his head. He was never tried, although he wanted a trial. He endured a humiliating capture and imprisonment. His later life was one of poverty with limited freedom.

Jefferson Finis Davis was born on June on June 3, 1808, in Fairview, Christian County, Kentucky. Coincidentally, he was born one hundred miles away from the Kentucky birthplace of Abraham Lincoln (and eight months earlier). He was the tenth and youngest child of Samuel Emory Davis and Jane Cook Davis. His father was an innkeeper. He was raised in a military family, with his father having fought in the American Revolutionary War and three older brothers who would fight in the War of 1812. At an early age, the Davis family moved to Wilkinson County, Mississippi, where they established a cotton farm, called the Rosemont Plantation. Young Davis attended the Wilkinson Academy in nearby Woodville. He was sent back to Kentucky, where he attended the Saint Thomas Catholic School in Washington County. He later attended Jefferson College in Washington and Transylvania University in Lexington,

Kentucky. In 1821, he returned to the Mississippi family farm. His father died on July 4, 1824.

An older brother, Joseph, became responsible for Davis' supervision. Joseph was an influential businessman and was able to get President James Monroe to appoint Davis to a position at the U. S. Military Academy at West Point. Davis graduated in 1828 and was assigned as a second lieutenant to the 1st Infantry Regiment in Wisconsin. He became involved in the Black Hawk War. When the tribal chief Black Hawk was captured, Davis was responsible for transporting him into captivity.

In March 1833, Davis was promoted to first lieutenant and transferred to the First Dragoons, a newly formed regiment under the command of future president, Zachary Taylor. Davis was his adjutant, the staff officer. Davis met and fell in love with Taylor's daughter, Sarah Knox, and asked her father for permission to marry. Taylor, not wanting his daughter to live the life of a military officer's wife, refused his permission. Davis responded by resigning from his military post in April 1835. He returned to civilian life back in Mississippi. Having been given adjoining land in Warren County by Joseph, Davis started a successful cotton farm called the Brierfield Plantation. As a civilian, he was able to bring Sarah to Kentucky, where the two were married on June 17, 1835, at her aunt's house near Louisville, Kentucky. He traveled south to visit his sister, Anna, in Louisiana. While there visiting, Davis and his new bride contracted malaria. After three months of marriage, Sarah died in September 15, 1835. Davis required several months of slow recovery.

Still very much in mourning, Davis traveled to restore his health. He visited Cuba, New York, and Washington, D.C., before returning to his farm in Mississippi. Still recovering from his experience with malaria and the loss of his wife, Davis became reclusive and devoted himself to improving his plantation and studying government and history. In 1836, he purchased increasing numbers of slaves to assist with operating and increasing the cotton farming. By 1840, he owned forty slaves.

Davis became active in local, state, and national politics, attending conventions and making impressive speeches supporting states' rights. On February 26, 1845, at the age of thirty-six, he married eighteen-year-old Varina Banks Howell. They would have six children. He was elected in December 1845 as a U. S. Representative. He continued to suffer illness from his malaria and complications from previous battle wounds.

In 1846, with the start of the Mexican-American War, Davis resigned from Congress and organized a volunteer military unit, the 155th Infantry Regiment. It was under the command of his former father-in-law, Zachary Taylor. Davis provided his troops with advanced rifles, and they distinguished themselves on the battlefield. Davis survived another battle injury. Taylor confessed to Davis, "My daughter, sir, was a better judge of men than I was." Davis also was acknowledged for his service by President James Polk.

In 1847, Mississippi Governor Brown appointed Davis to fill a vacant U. S. Senate seat. In January 1848, Davis was selected by the state legislature to serve the remaining two-year term. In 1850, he won re-election to a full Senate term. He was appointed chairman of the Committee on Military Affairs. Soon after his committee appointment, Davis resigned to run for the governor of Mississippi. He lost the election by less than 1,000 votes. He continued his political activities by campaigning for Democratic candidate, Franklin Pierce. With Pierce's victory, Davis was appointed Secretary of War in 1853. He was very productive in that role. He oversaw the increase in the size of the army, established a medical corps, improved rifle ammunition, and explored railroad routes to the West. In 1857, Davis left the federal position at the end of Pierce's term as president.

On March 4, 1857, he was re-elected to the U.S. Senate and re-appointed to the chairmanship of the Committee on Military Affairs. He was a strong supporter of states' rights but strongly opposed to the threats of secession. He continued to struggle with health problems while maintaining his reputation as an effective orator. He worked to promote acceptable compromises on the slavery issues. Unable to persuade Mississippi to continue a search for peaceful compromise, the state declared its secession in January 1861. Receiving word of the state's action, Davis resigned his Senate seat on January 21 with an emotional and memorable farewell address. Davis called it "the saddest day of my life." He would commit himself to the state's decision.

As expected, Davis was initially appointed as commander of the Mississippi forces. A few weeks later, he was notified of the convention of seceding states, held in Montgomery. Alabama, that he had been selected as the president of the Confederate States of America. On February 18, 1861, Davis accepted the position.

Davis faced immediate and continuing challenges in his position. His early attempts at dialogue with the Lincoln administration were denied because of the Confederacy's illegal actions. Davis faced difficulties on several fronts. First, he had a contentious relationship with his vice president, Thaddeus Stephens. Second, he had struggles determining the military command structure and authority. Third, his cabinet appointments were more representative of each seceding state than their personal ability. Fourth, he faced the overwhelming superiority of the Northern forces and supplies. With the number of states seceding, his difficulties increased.

Early military victories were offset by dwindling supplies. The growing inflation within the Confederacy was uncontrollable. Dissention within the military and cabinet led to accusations of favoritism by Davis. His most effective decision was placing all military command under General Robert E. Lee. The capital of the Confederacy was moved early on from Montgomery, Alabama, to Richmond, Virginia. With the limitation of men and supplies, Lee was forced to surrender in April 1865 at Appomattox. Lee's surrender did not include the end of the Confederacy. With Union forces nearing Richmond, Davis and the cabinet moved to south into Georgia and debated the continuation of the struggle. Following President Lincoln's assassination April 15, 1865, Union forces were quick to capture Confederate leaders assumed to have promoted the assassination. The Confederacy was officially dissolved on May 5, 1865. The leaders were charged with treason, and a reward was offered for their capture. On May 10, 1865, Davis was captured by pursuing Union forces near Irwinville, Georgia. He was imprisoned in inhumane conditions for two years at Fort Monroe, Virginia. His situation, being shackled in poor and unhealthy conditions, offended some in the North. Davis's wife and youngest daughter were allowed to visit him. Led by abolitionists such as Horace Greely, bail was posted, and Davis was freed. He wanted an actual trial, but it would never come.

Upon release, Davis went to Montreal, Canada, and joined with his wife and family. After improvements in his health, he traveled to Cuba and Europe in an unsuccessful search for respectable employment. On Christmas Day, 1868, President Andrew Johnson issued a presidential pardon and amnesty for those involved in the rebellion. The case against Davis was officially dismissed on February 15, 1869.

Davis faced financial difficulties. He did find work as president of the Carolina Life Insurance Company in Memphis, Tennessee. His ailing wife could not accompany him on his trips to secure employment. He left the position when the economic Panic of 1873 led to the company's merger. Davis began to find some support on giving speeches and writing articles throughout the late 1870s. In 1881, Davis completed his book, *The Rise and Fall of the Confederate Government*. It was a two-volume set that established some favorable views of the Confederate leader. He was well received on speaking tours, especially in the South. In October 1889, Davis wrote *A Short History of the Confederate States of America*.

On a trip to return to Brierfield Plantation, Davis became ill and refused medical assistance until reaching New Orleans. In a friend's home, he died on December 6, 1889. He was surrounded by his wife and family friends. His body was placed in state for several days in the New Orleans City Hall. He was interred in the Greenwood Cemetery. In 1893, he was reinterred at Hollywood Cemetery in Richmond, Virginia. That had been one of his final requests. On June 3, 1907, a life-sized statue and monument was dedicated with an audience of 125,000 spectators.

Many monuments, memorials, and historical sites were established throughout the South, including Fairview, Kentucky, in Davis' honor. His citizenship had never been officially restored. A movement in the 1970s led to U. S. Senate Joint Resolution 16 and its signing by Southern President Jimmy Carter on October 17, 1978, officially restoring his citizenship

Modern historians may view Jefferson Davis in a more favorable light as a reluctant Rebel leader who sought compromise on a national level. There is another movement that seeks to reassess the idea of the "noble cause" of the Southern revolt. This has led to the displacement of many Confederate memorials and statues throughout the country. While our country still confronts the meaning and consequences of the Civil War, the personal lives and sacrifices of both the North and South need to be remembered.

Alexander W. Doniphan

Mason County

Military

He was a hero in battle and in civilian life. The law came before his personal beliefs and the illegal request of his superiors. He was able to maintain a neutral status during the Civil War.

Alexander William Doniphan was born on July 9, 1808, near Maysville, Mason County, Kentucky. He was the youngest of ten children born to Joseph and Anne Smith Doniphan. His lineage included fighters in the Revolutionary War. His father was a successful farmer and served as the county sheriff. When young Doniphan was five years old, his father died. He was placed with an older brother, George, to live in Augusta, Bracken County, Kentucky.

In 1826, he graduated from Augusta College. He studied law under local attorney, Martin P. Marshall. He was admitted to the bar in 1830. Facing competition for the limited legal work needs, he moved to the newly admitted state of Missouri. After a brief period in Lexington, Missouri, he moved on to settle in Liberty, Missouri. He quickly earned a reputation as a good speaker and specialized as a defense attorney. In 1831, he joined the law practice with David Rice Atchison.

His big claim to fame came in 1833, when he and his law practice partners were asked to defend the Church of Jesus Christ of Latter Day Saints (Mormons). The growing religious group in Jackson County,

Missouri, became a source of controversy with the church's strong abolitionist views and suspicious religious practices. The group was forcibly expelled from the county and moved further north in the state. The governor of Missouri refused to provide protection for them, and local conflicts led to actual armed battles. In 1838, the Mormon War came to a head with the Battle of Crooked River. Missouri Governor Lilburn Boggs issued an executive order directing that the Mormons be "exterminated, or driven from the state."

Doniphan had joined a local militia group, the Liberty Blues in June 1836. He was given the rank of Brigadier General in the state militia. Governor Boggs ordered General Samuel Lucas to place the surrendered Mormon leader Joseph Smith and other leaders in custody in the local Caldwell County jail. Lucas initiated a military court martial trial and pronounced the church leaders guilty of treason. Lucas then ordered Doniphan to execute the prisoners. Defiantly, Doniphan refused to carry out the illegal order. He replied, "It is cold blooded murder. I will not obey your order. My brigade shall march to [the jail], in the morning, at 8 o'clock; and if you execute these men, I will hold you responsible before an earthly tribunal, so help me God." In December 1838, the prisoners were transferred to the Liberty jail, where Doniphan could help prepare their defense at the spring trial. Through unknown circumstances, the prisoners were allowed to escape and fled east across the Missouri River to Nauvoo, Hancock County, Illinois. Ever appreciative of Doniphan's assistance, Joseph and Emma Hale Smith named a son Alexander after Doniphan.

Doniphan was elected to the Missouri legislature as a Whig, representing Clay County in 1836, 1840, and 1854. He married Elizabeth Jane Thorton on December 21, 1837, in Liberty, Missouri. They would have two children.

In 1843, a notorious Mormon, Orin Porter Rockwell, was arrested after a failed attempt to assassinate Governor Boggs. Known as "the destroying angel of Mormondom," he was able to secure the services of Doniphan to defend him at trial. Doniphan successfully secured a dismissal of the charges, and a freed Rockwell returned to the new Mormon settlement in Utah. He surely shared his experiences with church leaders highlighting the services of Doniphan.

When the Mexican-American War started in 1846, Doniphan was elected colonel of his First Missouri Volunteers, under General Stephen

Watts Kearney's Army of the West. The army began a two-month march in June 1846, from Fort Leavenworth, Kansas, to Santa Fe, then into Mexico. After Mexican troops surrendered, Doniphan led his troops to march to California to put down a Native American uprising. After that, he led his troops back to Mexico, joining with General Zachary Taylor, to continue warfare. At the end of their enlistment period, Doniphan led his troops to New Orleans, where they traveled by steamboat back to St. Louis. He and his troops received a hero's welcome. His troops had achieved the longest military march in history since Alexander the Great, a total of nearly 5,500 miles.

In 1848, after the war, Doniphan returned to Liberty. He continued his law practice, returned to the state legislature, and helped establish William Jewell College in Liberty. He refused to accept offers to run for Congress. He faced the growing division within the country over slavery and state secession with moderate positions. He was a slave owner but strongly opposed secession. He attempted to keep Missouri neutral. He refused an offer of brigadier general for the Missouri State Guard. In 1863, in the midst of the Civil War, he moved with his family to St. Louis. He used his legal expertise to work with the Missouri Claims Commission, helping to process pension applications.

With the war's end, Doniphan and his semi-invalid wife moved to Richmond, Missouri. He practiced his law and started the Ray County Savings Bank. He was its president. His wife died in 1873. In 1878, he visited Salt Lake City, Utah. He received a hero's welcome for his services to the Mormon Church. Doniphan died on August 8, 1887, in Richmond. He was buried in Fairview Cemetery in Liberty, Missouri. A life-sized sculpture of Doniphan was created and stands outside the Ray County Courthouse in Richmond. Before World War I, Camp Doniphan was established next to Fort Sill, Oklahoma. William Jewell College named its most prestigious Senior Award in Doniphan's honor.

Although Alexander Doniphan did most of his service as a Missourian, he was trained, educated, and prepared for life's achievements in Kentucky. He continued the honored military traditions of his family and earned his unique place in history due to his love for the place of the law above all else.

John Marshall Harlan

Boyle County

Supreme Court Justice

He was known as the "Great Dissenter." He was named after early Supreme Court justice John Marshall. His naming may have been a premonition as he served on the U. S. Supreme Court for thirty-three years.

John Marshall Harlan was born on June 1, 1833, near Danville, Boyle County, Kentucky. His father was James Harlan, a slaveowner, lawyer, and politician. His mother was Elizabeth Davenport Harlan. His father served as U. S. Congressman from Kentucky from 1835-1839. He served as Kentucky Secretary of State from 1840-1844. He later served as state legislator from 1845-1851. These positions and his father's law practice prompted a family move to Frankfort, the state capitol.

Younger Harlan had several older brothers, likely including a then described mulatto half-brother, raised in the family home and tutored, against the tradition of the time. Harlan attended school in Frankfort and enrolled at Centre College. He was a fraternity member of Beta Theta Pi and graduated in 1850 with honors at the age of seventeen. In addition to studying law in his father's office, he also attended Transylvania University for two years. He was admitted to the Kentucky bar in 1853. He was later appointed as the state attorney general and served for eight years.

In 1856, he married Malvina French Shanklin, daughter of an Indiana businessman. The two enjoyed a long and happy marriage, producing three sons and three daughters. In 1858, he won election as county judge for Franklin County, Kentucky. In 1859, he lost a close election to the U. S. House of Representatives.

Harlan worked hard to keep Kentucky neutral in the approaching Civil War. He organized a volunteer Union company, the 10th Kentucky Infantry, as a lieutenant colonel. They saw action in the Western Theater. In February 1863, he received word of his father's death. He resigned his military service to return home to provide for the family. After his return home, he was nominated by the Union Party to be the Kentucky Attorney General. In 1863, he won an easy victory. He became increasingly opposed to President Lincoln's questionable executive authority. He campaigned for the unsuccessful Democratic candidate, George McClellan, in 1864. He lost a later effort for re-election as attorney general.

In 1870, Harlan moved to Louisville and established a law practice partnering with John E. Newman and later Benjamin Bristow. He switched allegiance to the Republican Party and worked to build the organization in Kentucky. He ran unsuccessfully for governor in 1871 and 1875. In the 1876 presidential election, he campaigned for the Republican Party nomination of Rutherford B. Hayes. After his victory, Hayes rewarded Harlan, age forty-four, with a nomination to fill a vacancy on the U.S. Supreme Court. His nomination was unanimously approved by Congress on November 29, 1877.

Although Harlan was honored with the high appointment, the financial situation of his family was often dire. He and his wife were trying to provide college educations for their children. He had to bring in supplemental income by agreeing to teach law at the Columbian Law School, later to become George Washington University.

Harlan's opinions on the Supreme Court were undoubtedly influenced by his experiences with a then labeled mulatto half-brother and his Christian fundamentalist background. He was an elder of the New York Avenue Presbyterian Church in Washington, D. C., and taught a men's Sunday School class throughout his tenure on the court.

During his thirty-three years on the Supreme Court, his record shows his having "authored 1,161 opinions, spoke for the Court 745 times and wrote 316 dissents." Many of his dissents were upheld by later Supreme Court decisions. His most famous dissent was regarding the

1896 *Plessy v. Ferguson* case. The court ruled in support of the "separate but equal" doctrine, allowing racial segregation on trains and other public facilities. Harlan was the lone dissenter. In his dissent, he wrote:

> In the view of the Constitution, in the eye of the law, there is in this country no superior, dominant, ruling class of citizens. There is no caste here. Our Constitution is color-blind and neither knows nor tolerates classes among citizens, in respect of civil rights. All citizens are equal under the law. The humblest is the peer of the most powerful. The law regards man as man and makes no account of his surroundings or of his color when his civil rights are guaranteed by the supreme law of the land are involved.

Interestingly, two years later, he would express strong warnings about the growing number of Chinese immigrants in the country.

In spite of the apparent inconsistency, Harland's dissent in the 1896 *Plessy v. Ferguson* case would be recognized and the majority opinion overturned in 1954 with the ruling of the *Brown v. Board of Education* case. Harlan was also an active dissenter in cases regarding individual and worker rights. On March 12, 1906, he donated a King James Version Bible to the Supreme Court. The "Harlan Bible" has been signed by every Supreme Court justice after taking the oath of office. His long and active life as a Supreme Court judge ended with his death on October 14, 1911. He was buried in Rock Creek Cemetery in Washington, D. C. His wife, Malvina, wrote a book about their life together, *Some Memories of a Long Life, 1854-1911*. His grandson, bearing his name, would join the Supreme Court in 1951.

Harlan's personal papers are stored at the University of Louisville and the Manuscript Division of the Library of Congress. There are several schools named in his honor in Illinois and Texas. During World War II, the naval ship, *SS John M. Harlan*, was named in his honor. His alma mater, Centre College, established the John Marshall Harlan Professorship in Government in 1994.

Far beyond the material memories of John Marshall Harlan is the legacy of legal opinions left for scholars and future judges to use in deliberations of constitutional guarantees for all American citizens. At the Boyle County Courthouse, in Danville, Kentucky, is State Historical

Marker #1606. Inscribed in memory of Harlan, it reads in part, "Harlan was a highly respected jurist because of his individualism, dedication, and courage. He dissented with vigor, often alone, on issues of civil rights, interstate commerce, and income tax. Many of his dissents became the law of the land." What a tribute for this citizen of Kentucky.

Fred Vinson

Louisa

Supreme Court Justice

He served his country admirably in all three national branches of government: legislative, executive, and judicial. He had a limited formal education and had a major impact on national law. He and President Harry Truman were personal friends.

Frederick Moore Vinson was born on January 22, 1890, in Louisa, Kentucky. His father was the Lawrence County jailer in their small town. Fred, as he was known, was born in a relatively nice brick home near the jail. When he was young, his father died, leaving his mother to find work for their support. Vinson worked at odd jobs for the neighbors after his school hours to help with the family's support. He attended the Kentucky Normal School and was at the top of his graduating class, studying law, from Centre College in Dansville, Kentucky. In 1911, he was admitted to the bar.

He was a popular young man and won election as the city's attorney serving until 1915. That year he began his own private practice of the law. In 1917, his law practice was put aside for his participation in World War I in the U. S. Army. In 1921, after the war, he was elected state attorney general. On January 24, 1924, he married Julia Roberta Dixon. They would have two sons. That same year, hoping to fill a congressional vacancy, Vinson was elected to represent his district as a Democrat in the U. S. House of Representatives. In the next seven elections, he won six times to continue his national legislative service. While in Congress he developed a personal friendship with a fellow Democratic representative from Missouri, Harry Truman. He supported many of Franklin Roosevelt's New Deal policies. Roosevelt appointed him to serve on the U.S. Court of Appeals for the District of Columbia. He was confirmed by the Senate on December 9, 1937. He was also designated by Supreme Court Justice Harlan Fiske Stone to serve as Chief Judge of the U. S. Emergency Court of Appeals. He served in that position until May 27, 1943.

With World War II in progress, he was appointed by Roosevelt to be director of the Office of Economic Stabilization. He also served as Federal Loan Administrator and director of War Mobilization and Reconversion. He helped in these capacities to fight inflation and keep the U. S. economy sound during and following the war. After Roosevelt's death, President Harry Truman appointed Vinson as Secretary of the Treasury on July 23, 1945. In that position, Vinson was instrumental in settling British debts from the Lend-Lease arrangements. He encouraged economic growth in the country through his tax cut provided in the Revenue Act of 1945. He also served as the first chairman of the board for the newly established International Bank for Reconstruction and Development and the International Monetary Fund. This provided important economic recovery for war-torn countries.

Vinson was a close associate of Truman's, often playing cards and socializing with him. It is very likely during these private times that Truman expressed his concern about the situation on the U. S. Supreme Court. It was deeply divided between battling egos and political divisions. In 1946, Truman appointed Vinson as Chief Justice of the U.S. Supreme Court. He was sworn in on June 24, 1946. He had the delicate job of settling inter-court disputes while dealing with important national issues.

Much criticism has been directed at Vinson's tenure at the Supreme Court. The unusually light court load and the cautious dealing with personality differences certainly played a part in the comparatively less productive period. Vinson also seemed to favor decisions for governmental authority as opposed to individual rights. Even so, he was a strong proponent of racial minority rights under the Fourteenth Amendment. He upheld the death penalty verdicts for the Rosenberg spies. He also sided with opposition of the government's takeover of the steel mills during the war. He wrote seventy-seven opinions for the court and wrote thirteen dissents

Vinson was still active on the court when, on September 8, 1953, he suffered a fatal heart attack at his Washington, D.C., home. Following a funeral service in the nation's capitol, he was buried in the Pine Hill Cemetery in Louisa, Kentucky. His papers are housed at the University of Kentucky in Lexington, Kentucky. His service to the country was unselfish and spread throughout all branches of the federal government. He served at a crucial time for the nation in World War II and sought to help the war-ravaged countries after the war. His education and training as a Kentuckian contributed assistance around the world.

Whitney Young Jr.
Lincoln Ridge
Civil Rights Activist

He was one of the most effective leaders of the civil rights movement on a national scale. He was an educator, organizational administrator, and personal advisor to several U. S. presidents. Kentucky shaped his educational and social experiences.

Whitney Moore Young Jr. was born on July 31, 1921, in Lincoln Ridge, Kentucky. He was a middle child born to Whitney Moore Young Sr. and Laura Young. His father was principal of the black preparatory school Lincoln Institute. He also served as president of the Kentucky Negro Education Association. His mother was a teacher at the school. She also became the first female postmistress in Kentucky and second in the United States, appointed by President Franklin Roosevelt in 1940.

Young Jr. received a good early education and enrolled at the Lincoln Institute when he was thirteen. He graduated as class valedictorian. He went to Kentucky State University, a black institution, where he received a Bachelor of Science degree in social work. He had early intentions of pursuing a medical career. He was a popular student, participated on the basketball team, and was elected as president of his senior class. He was a member of the Alpha Phi Alpha fraternity. He graduated in 1941.

Young studied engineering at Massachusetts Institute of Technology for two years and taught one year at a nearby school. With the outbreak of World War II, Young decided to join the U. S. Army. In 1944, he was sent to Europe and assigned to a road construction crew of black soldiers commanded by white officers. There was hostility between the races at apparent mistreatment of blacks. Young was able to intervene and serve as an effective buffer between the two races. He later explained, "It was my Army experience that decided me on getting into the race relations field after the war. Not just because I saw problems, but because I saw the potentials, too. I grew up with a basic belief in the inherent decency of human beings."

After the war, Young married his college sweetheart, Margaret Buckner. They would have two children. The couple moved to the University of Minnesota, where Young pursued a master's degree in social work, graduating in 1947. While there, he became involved with the local Urban League of St. Paul and, after graduation, served as the industrial relations secretary. In 1950, he was assigned as president of the Omaha, Nebraska, chapter of the National Urban League. Under his leadership, he was able to get blacks to work in previously "whites only" positions. The chapter tripled its paid membership. Young also was able to teach at the University of Nebraska and Creighton University.

In 1954, Young became the first dean of social work at Atlanta University. He became very involved in the city's social scene. He and his wife were the first black members to join the Unitarian Universalist Congregation of Atlanta. With the 1954 Supreme Court decision of *Brown v. Board of Education*, changes within Atlanta society needed mediation and guidance. Young, with other local civil rights leaders, such as Dr. Martin Luther King Jr., assisted where they could. He co-chaired the Atlanta Council on Human Relations. In 1960, he was awarded a Rockefeller Foundation grant allowing him to study for a postgraduate year at Harvard University. That year, he joined the National Association for the Advancement of Colored People. He became the president of the Georgia State branch.

In 1961, Young was selected as the Executive Director of the National Urban League. It was a challenging time for the Civil Rights Movement. The challenges of racial inequality were coming to national attention. With support of white businessmen and political leaders, Young was able to bring the more moderate organization into greater prominence.

From 1961 until 1965, the National Urban League grew from just 38 employees to over 1,600. Their annual budget increased in that period from $325,000 to over $6,100,000.

In 1963, Young led the organization to co-sponsor the March on Washington. Young also led the organization to establish innovative programs to improve black graduation rates through "Street Academy" and to solve community racial problems through "New Thrust." He made a bold proposal for a "Marshall Plan" for the country. He was able to give counsel to President Lyndon Johnson in incorporating some of the ideas into the "War on Poverty" program. He published two books, *To Be Equal* (1964) and *Beyond Racism* (1969). President Johnson honored Young with the Presidential Medal of Freedom, the highest civilian award. President Nixon offered Young a cabinet position that he turned down. He saw more benefit for his purposes through leadership in the independent civil rights organizations. In 1969, he served as president of the National Association of Social Workers. He was concerned by mounting national and international events. The Vietnam War was creating division within the nation and civil rights organizations. More militant organizations were growing impatient with the lack of progress for racial equality.

In March 1971, Young traveled to Lagos, Nigeria, to attend a conference. He went swimming with friends and suffered a heart attack. He died on March 11, 1971. President Nixon sent a plane to transport the body back to the United States. Young was buried in Kentucky, and at the ceremony, President Nixon gave his eulogy, stating, "he knew how to accomplish what other people were merely for." Young had earlier described own philosophy: "Support the strong, give courage to the timid, remind the indifferent, and warn the opposed."

His untimely death added to the many awards and honors given to him. Many schools were named after him. In Washington, D. C., the Whitney Young Memorial Bridge is named after him. The School of Social Work at Clark Atlanta University is named in his honor. The Whitney Young School of Honors and Liberal Studies was established at Kentucky State University. The Boy Scouts created the Whitney Young Jr. Service award. In 1974, the Los Angeles Urban League annual dinner began, which raises over $1,000,000 each year for the organization. His birthplace in Shelby County, Kentucky, is a designated National Historic Landmark.

The battle for racial inequality in our country is an ongoing process. With regular advances and reverses, our country needs many more Whitney Moore Young Jr.s today. It is one thing to acknowledge problems, but it is quite another thing to cooperate and work together to improve unfair situations. Kentucky should be proud to have given our nation such a conciliating innovator.

Other Kentucky Innovators in Politics *(Legislative and Judicial)*

Mitch McConnell • *Louisville* • U. S. Senator
Samuel Freeman Miller • *Richmond* • Supreme Court Justice
Carrie Nation • *Garrad County* • Prohibitionist
Rand Paul • *Bowling Green* • U. S. Senator
Stanley Foreman Reed • *Minerva* • Supreme Court Justice
Wiley Blount Rutledge • *Cloverport* • Supreme Court Justice

Chapter Seven

Sports

Muhammad Ali
Louisville
Boxing Champion

He was the three-time boxing heavyweight champion of the world and a controversial national figure. He is one of the most internationally recognized athletes. He was a strong human being that was debilitated in his last years by the effects of Parkinson's disease.

Cassius Marcellus Clay Jr. was born on January 17, 1942, in Louisville, Kentucky. His parents were Cassius Clay Sr. and Odessa Grady Clay. His father was a sign painter and muralist. His mother worked as a housecleaner and a cook. He had a younger brother. His mother raised him as a Baptist. He attended Central High School in Louisville. He was not a good student.

When he was twelve years old, his bicycle was stolen. When reporting the theft to police officer Joe E. Martin, Clay indicated his plan to beat up the offender. The officer, who coached at a gym, suggested that Clay learn to fight. Clay began regular training sessions in the gym. He was noticed for his good boxing skills. He had a unique and unorthodox style of boxing. He also became serious about keeping his body healthy with good eating habits and avoiding harmful, unhealthy habits. It was said that he trained for his dodging speed with his brother throwing rocks at him. In competition over the next two years, Clay won several state and national Golden Glove championships.

Clay grew up in a racially segregated community. He was personally disturbed by being forced to drink from "Colored Only" water fountains, and other forms of local discrimination. In 1955, he was deeply affected by the murder of Emmett Till, a black youth from Chicago. Till was visiting in Mississippi and accused of flirting with a local white woman. He was beaten and his badly mutilated body was later discovered. The photographs of his body displayed at his funeral service were fixed in Clay's mind.

Clay was encouraged to participate in the 1960 Olympic Games in Rome, Italy. Although he was physically prepared, he had hesitation because of his extreme fear of flying. After much persuasive counseling, he addressed his fears and flew to Rome. At the age of eighteen, he won his preliminary bouts and boxed in the light-heavyweight championship round on September 5, 1960. He beat his Polish opponent in a unanimous decision, winning a gold medal. He was treated with respect and had represented his country well. Upon his return, he went to a local Louisville café to eat and was told by a waitress, "We don't serve Negroes."

Having achieved the height of amateur boxing, Clay was ready to consider a professional career. Several things worked in his favor. First, he had the reputation for winning with his unique boxing style. Second, he was encouraged by other successful professional boxers to develop a means of calling attention to himself. Third, he was sponsored by a group of eleven white millionaires who signed him to a six-year contract. In typical Clay phraseology, he said, "They got the complexions and connections to give me good directions." He began training in Miami, Florida, under Angelo Dundee. While in Miami, Clay attended a Muslim mosque, led by Elijah Muhammad. He was influenced by the teachings of Nation of Islam.

He used his attention-getting words before his fights to describe his predicted round of victory and boxing style. He often used his familiar phrase that he was going to "Float like a butterfly, sting like a bee." Of his fight with Englishman Henry Cooper, he said, "This is no jive, Cooper will go in five." The growing audiences attending his fights often came to see the braggart lose.

His successes led to a heavyweight championship with Charles "Sonny" Liston. On February 25, 1964, the two men met. After the seventh round, Liston's battered body caused him to quit in defeat. Clay had won his first heavyweight championship. The next day, Clay astounded the nation by announcing his allegiance to the Nation of Islam, deemed a racist organization by many Americans. He also announced that he was changing what he called his "slave name" to his new given name, Muhammad Ali. Interestingly, the name Cassius Marcellus Clay came from an active abolitionist several generations earlier. Answering his critics, he explained his position, "Color doesn't make a man a devil. It's the heart and soul and mind that count. What's on the outside is only decoration."

Ali won every fight over the next three years. In the era of the Civil Rights Movement, he was viewed as a source of black pride and became a very popular sports figure. Everything changed dramatically in 1967. Like many American young men, Ali received his draft notice. The war in Vietnam required a large number of additional recruits. Ignoring other options, Ali simply refused to be drafted. He stated, "I ain't got nothing against them Vietcong." Adhering to religious beliefs, his decision at that time was highly unpopular with most of the American public. The reaction was severe. On April 28, 1967, he was stripped of his championship title. In June, the local court upheld his conviction of draft evasion. He immediately appealed, a process that took over three years before reaching the U. S. Supreme Court. During this prime time of athletic ability, Ali was not allowed to compete in the boxing ring. His contract with the millionaires' support had come to an end. He received income by speaking on college campuses. He was effective in his question-and-answer sessions after his usually memorized speeches. He was kept in the public view by national broadcaster Howard Cosell.

While his case was presented to the U. S. Supreme Court in late 1970, Ali was able to box in a highly publicized contest against Jerry Quarry in Atlanta. On October 26, 1970, Ali won in a quick knockout. The fight was viewed by many leaders of the Civil Rights Movement who supported Ali's stand on the war and religious freedom. The big event for Ali was what was called "The Fight" on March 8, 1971, in Madison Square Garden against the new champion, Joe Frazier. The fight, attended by celebrities such as Norman Mailer and Frank Sinatra, went the full fifteen rounds. Both fighters suffered significant physical damage, with Frazier winning the decision. Although Ali lost the fight, three months later he won a bigger fight when, on June 28, 1971, the Supreme Court unanimously reversed the lower court's decision and granted Ali his status as a conscientious objector.

A new champion, George Foreman, had defeated Frazier. An international audience viewed the historic Ali-Foreman fight in Kinshasa, Zaire, called the "Rumble in the Jungle." Using his famous rope-a-dope tactic, Ali knocked Foreman out in the eighth round. For the second time, he won the heavyweight championship of the world. Frazier, still bearing a personal grudge against Ali, faced him on October 1, 1975, in Manila, Philippines. The event was called the "Thrilla in Manila." Considered by many to be the greatest fight in history, both men received heavy blows, causing severe physical damage. Frazier's left eye was so swollen by the fifteenth round that his manager refused to let him continue. A victorious Ali announced his retirement the next day.

With the offers of millions of dollars, Ali was persuaded to come out of retirement to face a young Leon Spinks. On September 15, 1978, Ali faced Spinks in a fight that went the full fifteen rounds. Spinks was given the decision, and a surprised Ali gave up his championship title. A few months later, they met again in a rematch fight. This time after fifteen rounds, Ali was given the decision. It was the third time he had won the heavyweight world championship. Ali fought unsuccessfully on several other occasions with his past abilities noticeably in decline. On June 26, 1979, he announced his retirement. His career was legendary. He won fifty-six bouts (thirty-seven by knockouts) and lost only five.

The years of ferocious fighting had affected his body. In September 1984, he was hospitalized and diagnosed with Parkinson's disease. Over time, the disease would affect his speech and the control of his body. He continued to help international charities and sign autographs. He made product endorsements. On June 3, 2016, he died in a hospital in Phoenix, Arizona, at the age of seventy-four. After a memorial service, he was buried in his hometown of Louisville in the Cave Hill Cemetery.

During his career and after, Ali received numerous awards and honors. On December 10, 1974, Ali was invited to the White House by President Gerald Ford. A 1978 comic book featured Superman vs. Muhammad Ali. In the 1996, the Olympic Games in Atlanta, Georgia, were opened by Ali, with his fragile appearance, lighting the Olympic flame. In 1997, he received the Arthur Ashe Courage Award. In 1999, he was the first boxer to appear on a Wheaties box and named to the Kentucky Athletic Hall of Fame. On January 8, 2001, he was presented the Presidential Citizen's Medal by President Bill Clinton. In 2005, in a White House ceremony, he was presented the Medal of Freedom by

President George W. Bush. On December 19, 2005, the $60,000,000 nonprofit Muhammad Ali Center was opened in downtown Louisville.

Ali's personal family life included many marriages and children. In 1964, he married Sonji Roi. She refused to obey the Muslim expectations of a woman's role, and the marriage ended in divorce in 1966. In 1967, he married Belinda Boyd. She converted to Islam, and they had four children. During the next decade, Ali had several illicit affairs that produced other children. The marriage ended in 1977. That year, he married Veronica Porche, with whom he had had an earlier affair. They had two children. They were divorced in 1986. On November 19, 1986, Ali married longtime friend, Yolanda "Lonnie" Williams. They adopted a son. She would remain with Ali until his death.

Ali would be remembered for some of his more egotistical sayings, such as "My only fault is that I don't realize how great I am." He also said, "It's hard to be humble, when you're as great as I am." More insightful sayings also came from him, such as "Service to others is the rent you pay for your room here on earth." He also stated in a very personal moment, "I know where I am going and I know the truth, and I don't have to be what you want me to be. I'm free to be what I want." Muhammad Ali is one of the most recognizable international athletes in history. His life began in Kentucky and, at his choosing, buried in his hometown.

Jim Bunning

Southgate

Baseball/Politics

He was a professional baseball player, achieving major accomplishments and recognition. He was a state and national politician leaving an impact on important issues of the day. He left behind a reputation as a contentious advocate and competitor.

James Paul David Bunning was born October 10, 1923, in Covington, Kentucky, located near the Ohio River across from Cincinnati. His parents were Louis Aloysius Bunning and Gladys Best Bunning. He was the middle child of three boys. His father owned a ladder manufacturing company. The family observed a devout Catholic faith and practice. They encouraged a good education for their children. Before Bunning was two years old, the family moved to nearby Southgate, Kentucky. He attended St. Therese Grammar School. He attended St. Xavier High School in Cincinnati where he developed a love for and skills in sports—especially baseball. He was able to go to the Cincinnati Reds baseball games.

He graduated in 1949 and began attending Xavier University in Cincinnati, again playing on the baseball team. In the spring of his freshman year, the Detroit Tigers indicated an interest in signing Bunning. An unusual agreement was worked out with his family, which allowed Bunning to miss traditional spring training until he finished school. In the summers, he pitched for the Tigers' minor league teams with mediocre success. In 1952, he married his childhood sweetheart, Mary Theis. They would have nine children. In 1953, he graduated from Xavier University with a bachelor's degree in economics.

In Bunning's seventeen-year professional baseball career, he played for the Detroit Tigers, Philadelphia Phillies, Pittsburgh Pirates, and Los Angeles Dodgers. He amassed a record of 224 wins and 184 losses. He threw two no-hit games. His greatest accomplishment was on June 24, 1964 (Father's Day) when, as a Phillie, he pitched a perfect game, facing only twenty-seven batters. It was the first perfect game in the National League since 1880. He was only the second pitcher to accomplish 100 wins and 1,000 strikeouts in both the American and National Leagues. During his career, he made close friends, as well as despised enemies, for his advocacy for player rights. He also recovered from several baseball game injuries. He retired from baseball in 1971.

Following his retirement as a professional player, he spent several years as a coach and manager for major and minor league teams. He became part-owner of the Houston Astros, which proved to be unsuccessful. In 1977, he moved back to Fort Thomas, Kentucky. From there, he began to represent players as an agent. He also was encouraged to become active in local politics. He was elected that year as a city councilman for Fort Thomas. He was elected soon after as a Republican Kentucky state senator, serving as minority leader. It would be a launching pad for his progress to representing Kentucky on a national level.

In 1986, he was elected to the U. S. Congress, representing Kentucky's 4th District. He was elected for five more two-year terms without any serious opposition. He was noted as a staunch Republican conservative. He was a strong defender of the Social Security system. His strong Roman Catholic beliefs made him a vociferous opponent to abortion rights. In 1996, the Baseball Hall of Fame announced his selection, after fifteen years of nominations. Upon the official announcement, the House of Representatives gave him a standing ovation. In 1998, he ran for the U. S. Senate. In a very close contest, he won by less than 1 percent of the final vote.

His career in the U. S. Senate was marked by legislative accomplishments, especially those regarding national economic issues. He was a powerful voice, often crude and boisterous. He won his share of opposition, even within his own party. He won a controversial reelection in

2004, filled with Bunning's uncomplimentary, personal accusations, sometimes referred to as "slinging rhetorical fastballs," against his opponents. With his reelection secure, Bunning became even more contentious with fiery speeches on the U. S. Senate floor, denouncing Democratic leadership and programs. Some even began to question his mental abilities. In 2008, it was reported that his Jim Bunning Foundation was spending less than twenty-nine percent of its income on actual charities. He was reported to have had a salary of $180,000.

As he approached the 2010 elections, he was assumed to pursue a third Senate term. But there was strong opposition from within his party's leadership, primarily from fellow Kentucky senator, Mitch McConnell. He was accused of being too old and out-of-touch with Kentucky interests. In July 2009, he attacked his opponents, saying, "Over the past year, some of the leaders of the Republican Party in the Senate have done everything in their power to dry up my fundraising." On July 17, he announced his involuntary decision not to run for a third term. His finished his final year in the Senate with a historic individual and unpopular attack on the strongly supported extension of unemployment benefits, even though the unemployment rate at that time was near ten percent. In retaliation against his party's leadership, he campaigned for Rand Paul, who was not the party favorite, to replace him in the Senate. Rand Paul won the election. In December 2010, in his farewell speech in the U. S. Senate, Bunning said,

> I have been booed by 60,000 fans at Yankee stadium standing alone on the pitcher's mound, so I have never really cared if I stood alone here in Congress as long as I stood by my beliefs and many values. I have also thought that being able to throw a curve ball never was a bad skill for a politician to have.

Bunning spent his final days traveling around the country attending baseball shows and signing autographs. He suffered a stroke in October 2016. On May 26, 2017, he died in Edgewood, Kentucky, at the age of eighty-five. At the time of his death, he left behind his wife of sixty years, nine children, thirty-five grandchildren, and seven great-grandchildren. His funeral service was held at Cathedral Basilica of the Assumption in Covington, Kentucky. He was buried in St. Stephens Cemetery in Fort Thomas, Kentucky.

Jim Bunning was a highly regarded professional baseball player. He achieved significant records in the major leagues and left an important legacy for players' rights. In 2017, Major League Baseball Players Association director Tony Clark said, "That responsibility of leaving the game better for those who follow remains in place today, fifty-one years later. All players—past, present and future—will forever owe Jim a debt of gratitude."

Bunning was also a representative for Kentucky in government service for nearly a quarter century. He sought to protect his state and maintain his personal and religious values. He was a devoted family man. He was controversial at times but was respected for his strong stands.

Earle Combs
Pebworth
Baseball Player/Manager

He was the leadoff batter for the New York Yankees, playing center field. His twelve-year career batting average was .325, playing only for the Yankees. His teammates comprised the famous group known as "Murderers' Row." In the age of the Roaring Twenties, he was a unique person admired by his fellow Yankees, the fans, and the press. He was nicknamed the "Kentucky Colonel."

Earle Bryan Combs was born on May 14, 1899, in Pebworth, Owsley County, Kentucky. He was one of the six children born to James J. Combs and Nannie Brandenburg Combs. His father was a farmer. After his early childhood education and helping on the family farm, Combs attended Eastern Kentucky Normal School. He was active in the sports programs and stood out playing baseball. He prepared for a teaching career after college graduation. He began teaching in one-room schoolhouses back in Owsley County, Kentucky. In 1921, he married high school sweetheart Ruth McCullom. They would have three sons. During the summers, he played baseball for local teams. In 1922, while playing in Lexington for a semi-pro team, he was noticed by a scout for the Louisville Colonels of the American Association. He had a high batting average, and his speed allowed him to make risky stolen bases. He was offered a contract paying more than his teaching salary. He signed the contract, ending his teaching career.

After an acknowledged, poorly played first game, he was encouraged by his manager and teammates. His play improved immediately. In 1924, he was bought by the New York Yankees in a bidding war. He proved to be well worth the investment. In his rookie year, he was hitting .400 and doing well in centerfield. On June 15, at a game in Cleveland, he slid into home plate and broke his ankle. He missed the rest of the season.

The next season, Combs was assigned the leadoff batting position. He was able to place the hit ball in the outfield gaps allowing him to specialize in triples. Accomplishing his goal to get on base, he was told to wait for the sluggers to bring him in. Fortunately for the Yankees, the sluggers following Combs were notables: Babe Ruth and Lou Gehrig. By 1927, the Yankees had developed into the decidedly best team in major league baseball. That year, Babe Ruth hit his record 60 home runs and Combs had a record 231 hits. The Yankees would go on to win three of the four World Series games they played.

Compared to his teammates, who were often boisterous off the field, Combs was a consistent man on and off the field. He never smoked or swore and was openly unashamed of his regular practice of Bible reading. Unlike his famous teammates, he was available and friendly with the press. The fans loved him, especially those behind him in center field. Babe Ruth said of him,

> Combs was more than a grand ballplayer. He was a first-class gentleman. No one ever accused him of being out on a drinking party and you'd laugh at the words he used for cussing. Often he'd sit in his room and read the Bible, for he came from a strict mountaineer family. But Earle was all man, and a great competitor.

The Yankees would go on to win the World Series in 1928 and 1932. Combs was a main contributor with his high batting average. If there was one weakness in his game, it was his throwing from center field. He was a weak thrower and never developed the strong arm he desired. His managers all said, "If you had nine Combs on your ball club, you could go to bed every night and sleep like a baby."

In July 1934, tragedy struck Combs. Chasing a fly ball in center field, he crashed into the wall. He fractured his skull, injured his shoulder and knee. He was rushed to the hospital, where he remained in critical condition. He surprisingly willed himself into a slow recovery over several months, vowing to return to the Yankees. In 1935, he began the season playing eighty-nine games before receiving another serious injury, a broken collarbone. He was finally forced to retire as an active player at the age of thirty-six.

The Yankee administration, well aware of his mental skills and insight, hired him as a full-time coach. They assigned him to train a new rookie they had hired named Joe DiMaggio. Combs helped to develop him into a great fielder and hitter. Over the next few years, with changes in management, Combs left the Yankees and coached for the St. Louis Browns, Boston Red Sox, and Philadelphia Phillies. In 1954, he retired and returned to his 400-acre Kentucky farm in Madison County. In 1955, he was appointed as the Kentucky State banking commissioner, serving until 1959. He then served on the Eastern Kentucky University's Board of regents, serving until 1975. He was known to have privately given finances to some needy students to help with their tuition and living expenses. After a long illness, he died on July 21, 1976, at the age of seventy-seven, in Richmond, Kentucky. He left behind his wife of fifty-five years, three sons, and twelve grandchildren. He was buried in the Richmond Cemetery.

In 1970, Combs was honored by his fellow baseball players by his induction into the Baseball Hall of Fame. Reacting to the honor, Combs replied, "I thought the Hall of Fame was for superstars, not just average players like me." In 2006, he was inducted as a charter member in the Eastern Kentucky Athletics Hall of Fame.

He was called the "Kentucky Colonel" by his teammates. (This was before Harlan Sanders' fame). He was given the title for his gentlemanly attitude and actions, reflecting his upbringing in the refined culture of the Kentucky hills.

Denny Crum
Louisville
Basketball

He was a star college basketball player. Although not born in Kentucky, he would always be associated with the state due to his national titles and victories as a college coach. He was also recognized for his victories as a coach in international competitions. He was given the nickname "Cool Hand Luke." He was also called "Mr. March" for his many appearances as a coach in the NCAA March Madness national college tournament.

Denzel Edwin "Denny" Crum was born on March 2, 1937, in San Fernando, California. Little is known of his childhood and early education. In 1954, he attended and played basketball at Los Angeles Pierce College. He was named the conference player of the year. In 1956, he transferred to the University of California in Los Angeles (UCLA). His first year, playing under head coach John Wooden, he received the school's Irv Pohlmeyer Trophy. He later received the Bruin Bench "Most Improved Player" award. He graduated in 1958.

Crum stayed on at UCLA as the freshman basketball coach for two years. In 1960, he returned to Pierce College, first as assistant and later as head basketball coach. In 1968, he returned to UCLA as an assistant coach and recruiter for John Wooden. He helped the team in achieving three national titles.

In 1971, he was hired as head coach for the Cardinals at the University of Louisville. He would remain there for a long tenure of thirty years. After a first year of training and coaching, Crum led the school's team to the 1972 NCAA Final Four playoffs. He was defeated in the semi-final by UCLA, his former mentor John Wooden's team. Crum would lead the school to five other NCAA Final Four appearances (1975, 1980, 1982, 1983, and 1986). In 1977, he coached the U.S.A. basketball team to a gold medal in the World University Games.

His first NCAA national championship came in 1980. That year he was named as national coach of the year. He would earn that honor again in 1983 and 1986. His second NCAA championship was won in 1986.

As a coach, Crum developed some positive and negative traits. His in-game coaching allowed his teams to score quickly after timeouts, with effective play calling. On the negative side was a record of poor college graduation rates for his players, well below the national average. In 1990, Crum was selected to the UCLA Hall of Fame. In 1994, he was inducted into the Naismith Memorial Basketball Hall of Fame.

In 2001, on his sixty-fourth birthday, Denny Crum announced his retirement. He still had two years left on his contract, but circumstances seemed to suggest it was the best time. The young team had several losing seasons, and the school had not been able to return to the NCAA Final Four since 1986. There were reports that the administration was anxious to hire Rick Pitino as his replacement. In 2002, he was honored with the Legends of Coaching award by John R. Wooten Award committee. In 2007, the University of Louisville named their home basketball court in his honor. In 2010, he was inducted into the Pierce College Athletic Hall of Fame.

After retirement, Crum was still active in the sports world as a sports radio co-host. In 2004, he broadcasted from Louisville and his co-host Joe B. Hall broadcasted from Lexington. He continued his popular sports show until late 2014.

As with his early childhood experiences, Crum has been very private about his personal life. In 1951, he married Joyce Elaine Lunsford. They had two children. After a divorce, on February 11, 1977, he married Joyce Phillips. They had one child. After another divorce, on June 9, 2001, he married Susan Sweeney, a local television news reporter in Louisville. They had no children and remain married today.

Crum maintains an active lifestyle, spending time at his hunting ranch in Idaho. He plays professional poker and breeds horses. He founded the Denny Crum Scholarship Foundation, Inc.

Crum's career was impressive with 674 wins in his coaching years. He still has a friendly relationship with many of his past players and assistant coaches. He continues his support and interest in the University of Louisville. Although born in California, Crum continues to find his home and life in Kentucky.

Paul Hornung

Louisville

Football

He was a star professional football player and a famed sports broadcaster. He gave up an invitation to play for the University of Louisville under then-coach Bear Bryant to join the strong football program at Notre Dame. He lived a playboy lifestyle that at times conflicted with the strict leadership of Green Bay Packer coach, Vince Lombardi.

Paul Vernon Hornung was born on December 23, 1935, in Louisville, Kentucky. His parents divorced when he was just four years old. He was mostly raised by his mother in a devout Catholic home. Early in his life, he loved football, often playing in neighborhood games after his school team's practice. At the Flaget High School in Louisville, Hornung excelled in all sports. He lettered in each of his four years in basketball, baseball, and football. In 1953, he was named Kentucky's Most Valuable High School Football Player. Upon graduation, he was besieged by many colleges offering him generous scholarships. Influenced by his mother's encouragement, Hornung selected the prominent Catholic school, Notre Dame. The school had a strong successful program that also appealed to Hornung.

As an underclassman, Hornung had to wait to earn his coveted spot as starting quarterback. He began playing as a halfback and as a safety.

He adapted to the positions well, ending the 1955 season ranked fourth in the nation in total offense. He was identified by the local sportswriters as the "Golden Boy." He was a six-footer with blond hair and very attractive. There were numerous stories about his escapades with college girls. In his senior year, he was finally given the position of starting quarterback. Although the team failed to perform up to its standard, Hornung continued his strong offensive statistics. In 1956, Hornung was honored with the Heisman Trophy Award for that year's best college football player in the nation. He is the only Heisman winner from a team with a losing year's record. He graduated that year from Notre Dame with a degree in business, a challenging task with his sports obligations and social activities.

In 1957, as expected, Hornung was the first choice in the National Football League draft. The worst team in professional football the previous year was the Green Bay Packers. Hornung's was limited in his play as a halfback and a field goal kicker. In 1958, he was ready and wanted to be traded. His life changed with the new head coach, Vince Lombardi. Lombardi recognized the talents that Hornung possessed and gave him more playing time. Hornung led his league in scoring from 1959 through 1961. In 1961, he set the then-record for total points scored in a season with 176 points.

He was a member of the Army Reserve and was called for duty in 1961 with the Cold War threat. He was able to get some weekend passes from his duty in Fort Riley, Kansas. A special pass was arranged by President John F. Kennedy to allow Hornung to play in the National League Championship game against the New York Giants. He was named that year as the league's Most Valuable Player. Lombardi's friendship with Kennedy might have had some influence. Hornung's presence gave the team a real boost before the game. Teammate Henry Jordan said, "When Paul got that leave from the Army and walked into that locker room, you could just feel the confidence growing in that room." Hornung's scores insured a decisive victory for the Packers and earned him the Most Valuable Player Award. Hornung commented "This is the greatest day of my life."

Things went sour for him in 1962. Hornung and some other professional players were caught up in a gambling scandal that was brought to the attention of NFL Commissioner Pete Rozelle. After an investigation, Hornung acknowledged his guilt and, in the spring of 1963, was suspended indefinitely from professional football. Most likely with Lombardi's intervention, even after Horning had initially lied to him, the ban was lifted in the spring of 1964. Hornung promised Lombardi to have nothing to do with any gambling, even avoiding his annual attendance at his beloved Kentucky Derby.

In 1965, he helped lead the team to its league championship. In one December game that season against the Baltimore Colts, he scored a team record five touchdowns. He again led his team to a third league championship. In 1966, Hornung suffered a pinched nerve that sidelined him much of the season. He was unable to play in the first Super Bowl game in 1966, when his team beat the Kansas City Chiefs. With Hornung's limited physical abilities, he was traded to the New Orleans Saints. But before he could even finish spring training, his pinched nerve forced him into retirement. He ended his pro football career with 3,711 rushing yards and 72 touchdowns.

In his retirement, Hornung became a respected sports broadcaster. He also found time to make major successful investments in real properties in and around Louisville. His private life, viewed by many as a ladies' man was reinforced early in his career with the Packers when coach Lombardi asked him if he wanted to be a football player or a playboy. Hornung answered, "A playboy!" He married in 1967, divorced, and married again in 1980.

Hornung received numerous awards and honors. In 1985, he was elected to the College Football Hall of Fame. The next year, he was inducted into the Pro Football Hall of Fame. In 1990, he was inducted into the Wisconsin Athletic Hall of Fame. The top high school player in Kentucky is annually given the Paul Hornung Award. Since 2010, the nation's best college football player of the NCAA is given an award in Hornung's honor.

There has been some recent criticism of Hornung's worthiness to be included in the Halls of Fame. Vince Lombardi would later describe his feeling about Hornung,

> You have to know what Hornung means to this team. I have heard and read that he is not a great runner or a great passer or a great field-goal kicker, but he led the league in scoring for three seasons. In the middle of the field he may be only slightly better than an average ballplayer, but inside the

> twenty-yard line he is one of the greatest I have ever seen. He smells that goal line.

Such high praise from one of the best football coaches in history.

Paul Hornung began his life in Kentucky. He received his early education living with a single parent. He excelled in sports. Although he would find his professional career far away from Kentucky, he would return to his home state to find fulfillment in retirement.

Pee Wee Reese
Ekron
Baseball

He had a decent record as a professional baseball player, but his fame was built on personal relationships. He was of average size, but his nickname came from his expertise in marbles competition. He was immortalized as one of *The Boys of Summer*.

Harold Henry Reese was born on July 23, 1918, in Ekron, Meade County, Kentucky. He was raised on the family farm by parents Carl Marion Reese and Emma Allen Reese. When he was seven years old, the family moved to Louisville, Kentucky. Before he was twelve years old, he was runner-up to the *Louisville Courier-Journal* pee wee marble championship. (A pee wee was a small marble.) He also developed an early love for baseball.

He attended Louisville Manual High School. He was on the school's baseball team but did not get to play actively until his senior year. He was also involved in helping with family finances by delivering newspapers and selling box lunches. He graduated from high school in 1936. He found work at several jobs but was most productive as a cable splicer for a local telephone company. His work climbing up and down telephone poles helped his physical development. He found time to play baseball with the New Covenant Presbyterian Church team. He greatly improved his fielding and batting skills. He became the team spark plug and caught the attention of local semi-pro teams. In 1937, his baseball team won the Louisville city championship. The local Louisville Colonels of the American Association signed him to a professional contract. His consistently improving play as a shortstop led to another nickname, "The Little Colonel."

The team was purchased by the Boston Red Sox as a farm club. The player-manager was Joe Cronin, who played as the team's shortstop. Feeling threatened by Reese's abilities, on July 18, 1939, he allowed Reese to be sold to the Brooklyn Dodgers. Reese's first reaction to the surprising trade was one of horror. The Dodgers had the dubious reputation as the worst fielding team in professional baseball.

Coincidentally, the player-manager for the Dodgers was Leo Durocher, who also played as the team's shortstop. Analyzing Reese's skills and the team's needs, Durocher willingly gave up his player position to allow the rookie to replace him. It was a fortunate move for Reese, who found himself under the personal tutelage of Durocher in spring training. Reese made his professional baseball debut for the Dodgers on April 23, 1940. He made an unimpressive debut on the field. But under Durocher's continued coaching, he improved, becoming a good fielder and a great base runner.

Tragedy came to him on June 1, 1940, when, while batting, he was hit in the head by a pitch. He was knocked unconscious and carried to the Illinois Masonic Hospital. He spent several weeks there recuperating. He returned to the field on June 21. He continued to make major contributions to the Dodger's victories and greatly improved team fielding. Tragedy again struck on August 15, 1940, when sliding into second base, he broke his heel. He was out for the season.

In 1941, he began the season playing with a brace on his ankle. He was not back to normal batting and fielding, but the Dodgers did go on to win the National League pennant for the first time since 1920. In 1942, during spring training, Reese married Dorothy "Dottie" Walton, his hometown sweetheart on March 29 at the First Presbyterian Church in Daytona Beach. The two would have a son and a daughter in a long marriage of fifty-seven years.

Reese improved his batting average and fielding during the 1942 season. At the end of the season, like many other players, Reese enlisted in the U. S. military to fight in World War II. He enlisted in the U.

S. Navy with the Seabees, a construction battalion. He served in the Pacific Theater for three years. On his return home, he heard about the Dodgers signing a black baseball player, an infielder named Jackie Robinson. Reese had some concern that he might eventually be replaced by Robinson.

During the 1946 season, Reese dramatically improved in his batting average and field play, perhaps motivated by the threat of Robinson, then in minor league training. In 1947, Robinson was called up to the major leagues and assigned to play first base for the Dodgers. When Reese met Robinson, it was the first time in his life that Reese had shaken hands with an African American. Reese came from the segregated South and had never had any association with African Americans. Earlier, when some of his teammates had a petition to boycott Robinson being on the team, Reese had refused to sign with them. Perhaps it was through his father's early teachings or his religious beliefs, but Reese purposely chose to become friends with Robinson. They traveled together on the road, and Reese gave Robinson encouragement in the face of the racial opposition by fans and other players.

On the team's first road trip in Cincinnati, the fans and Reds' players were excessively abusive in heckling Robinson. Reese walked across the field and approached Robinson. Reese talked with him giving encouragement, while putting his arm on Robinson's shoulder. The simple act was enough to quiet the fans and opposing players. It symbolized a white man's acceptance and support of a black team member. When asked later why Reese did what he did, he answered, "I was just trying to make the world a little better. That's what you're supposed to do with your life, isn't it?" Reese's action earned him even greater respect among his teammates and fans.

Robinson had been switched to play second base for the Dodgers. This allowed the pair to develop one of the most effective double-play teams ever. In 1949, Reese was named as the team captain by Branch Rickey, the team's president and manager. He told Reese, "You're not only the logical choice, you are the only possible choice, the players all respect you." It wasn't only the players who had great respect for Reese. The local fans started Reese fan clubs, and he made time to spend with the kids—signing autographs and answering their questions. On July 22, 1955, Pee Wee Reese night was held at Ebbets Field. It was just before his thirty-seventh birthday. Pre-game presentations were made with many substantial gifts. Reese, asked to say a few words, told the crowd, "When I came to Brooklyn in 1940, I was a scared kid. To tell you the truth, I'm twice as scared right now."

For several years, the Dodgers had won the National League pennants but lost in the World Series to their rival New York Yankees. Finally, in 1955, the Dodgers defeated the Yankees to win the World Series. Reese had contributed to their league championship and the World Series victory.

In 1956, Reese injured his back in spring training. He saw limited play in the regular season and even less play in the 1957 season. In 1958, the Dodgers moved from Brooklyn to Los Angeles. Reese traveled with them, but on December 18, 1958, he retired as a player and was hired by the Dodgers as a coach. The team was able to win the World Series again in 1959.

After the 1959 season, Reese retired from the Dodgers and began a career in television baseball broadcasting, serving as color man. He worked for CBS and NBC over a ten-year period. Afterward, he spent several years broadcasting Cincinnati Reds and Montreal Expos baseball games. In 1972, he returned to Kentucky, working for the Hillerich & Bradsby Company, which made the Louisville Slugger baseball bats. He worked as their public relations representative.

Reese suffered physically his last few years. He dealt victoriously with prostate cancer. In March 1997, he was diagnosed with lung cancer. After a successful surgery to remove a tumor, he began radiation treatments. During that time, he also experienced a broken hip. On August 15, 1999, he died at his Louisville home. He left behind his wife, two children, three grandchildren, and two great-grandchildren. His funeral was held at Southeast Christian Church in Louisville. There were over two thousand people in attendance. He was buried in Resthaven Memorial Cemetery in Louisville.

At his funeral service, a most memorable eulogy was given by Joe Black, a black Dodger pitcher. He said,

> Pee Wee helped make my boyhood dream come true to play in the majors, the World Series. When Pee Wee reached to Jackie, all of us in the Negro League smiled and said it was the first time a white guy had accepted us. When I finally got up to Brooklyn, I went to see Pee Wee and said, 'Black

> people love you. When you touched Jackie, you touched all of us.' With Pee Wee, it was No. 1 on his uniform and No. 1 in our hearts.

In his sixteen years in his major league career, Reese played in 2,166 games, with 2,170 hits, 126 home runs, and 885 runs batted in. He ended with a batting average of .269, an on-base percentage of .366, and a fielding average of .962. In 1984, he was inducted into the National Baseball Hall of Fame. Undoubtedly, the greatest lasting tribute is a statue on Coney Island, just outside of the old Brooklyn Dodger stadium. It is a statue of two men, one with arm around the other's shoulder. It immortalizes the event when a white Kentuckian encouraged a black man from California in front of a hostile crowd on a professional ballfield.

Pee Wee Reese exemplified the values and virtues of a Kentucky true gentleman. He served as a model for all people to embrace the opportunities to encourage all people in achieving their dreams.

Darrell Waltrip
Owensboro
NASCAR Driver

"You either loved him or hated him." During his races, there were fans expressing strong support and boos from other fans. He initially enjoyed creating controversy, as it drew crowds, lucrative sponsors, and media attention. He would change his lifestyle and racing style, winning a stronger fanbase, especially after winning racing seasons. After his racing career, he used his media time as a popular sports commentator to campaign for driver safety and support.

Darrell Lee Waltrip was born on February 5, 1947, in Owensboro, Kentucky. He was the oldest of three sons. Little is known of his formal educational experience. By the age of twelve, he was interested in go-karts. With his father's encouragement and assistance, he began to change his interest to stock car racing. When he was sixteen, he entered his first race. Undeterred by wrecking in that first race, he continued to race at the Kentucky Motor Speedway. His racing improvements led to victories and notoriety. He would find widespread success and recognition on the Fairgrounds Speedway in Nashville, Tennessee. He won two track championships there in 1970 and 1973.

On August 15, 1969, he married Stephanie "Stevie" Radar. They would have two children.

In Nashville, he was asked to do radio promotions for the upcoming races. His good communication skills entertained the listeners with trash talk about his competitors. Attendance at the racetrack improved, and he became a popular figure. His radio success led to a friendship with Ralph Emory, a popular television host in Nashville. Throughout the 1970s and 1980s, the two men formed a close media bond. Waltrip also became a sought-after speaker.

Waltrip started his National Association of Stock Car Auto Racing (NASCAR) career on May 7, 1972, in the Winston Cup 500 at Talladega, Alabama. His race car was sponsored by Terminal Transport of Owensboro, Kentucky. He faced challenging opposition among the experienced and popular racers. It would be three years before Waltrip won his first Winston Cup race on his hometown racetrack on May 10, 1975. That year, he signed a contract to compete for the DiGard racing team.

He was a fierce competitor for DiGard, noted for his aggressive racing style. He faced criticism for his apparent recklessness and dissatisfaction with his contract arrangement. NASCAR was experiencing growing popularity on a national level, and audiences seemed to both be drawn to and against such active drivers.

In 1981, Waltrip ended his contract agreement with DiGard and signed up with the Junior Johnson racing team. He was very successful due to numerous wins and a growing fanbase. On February 20, 1983, at the Daytona 500, Waltrip had a serious crash. He was taken by ambulance to the Halifax Medical Center for treatment. While in recovery, he heard from fans with whom he was very unpopular. He realized that it was time for him to change some of his more negative attitudes and actions. One factor may have been his becoming a Christian that year and beginning to learn what that commitment meant to him. The next year, Waltrip resumed his winning record. During 1981 through 1986, he would win three national championships and forty-three NASCAR Winston Cup races for the Junior Johnson team.

In 1987, Waltrip joined with the Hedrick racing team. Hedrick had helped Waltrip open a Honda dealership in Franklin, Tennessee, a few years earlier. His series of victories would decline over the next few years, and he would suffer other serious injuries. He was voted by NASCAR fans as the "Most Popular Driver" in 1985 and 1990.

In 1991, Waltrip, with financial backing and an expert crew, created his own racing team. After several racing victories, Waltrip suffered another serious injury at the Daytona International Speedway. For the next six years, Waltrip continued to compete in seasons but was challenged by financial obligations as the owner of his own racing team.

In 1997, Waltrip, needing finances, sold his team to the Tim Beverly team. Waltrip saw limited racing and successes over the next three years. He had his farewell tour in 2000, having his final race on November 19 in the Napa 500 at the Atlanta Motor Speedway.

Waltrip's past media experiences led to a contract with Fox television network to broadcast NASCAR events. It would be the beginning of a long relationship, continuing to the present. At the 2001 Daytona 500, he was elated, announcing the victory of his younger brother, Michael. The victory was overshadowed by the tragic crash and death of famed racer Dale Earnhardt. Earnhardt had been a past fierce competitor on the track against Waltrip. But there was a kinship that caused Waltrip giving the invocation at Earnhardt's funeral service.

After his own injuries and Earnhardt's death, Waltrip became a leading voice for mandatory racing car driver safety issues. While he continued in his broadcasting career, he also became involved in other interests. He expanded his automobile franchise ownerships in Franklin, Tennessee. He worked as consultant for several racing film productions. He was the voice of "Darrell Cartrip" in several of the Disney *Cars* movies.

Waltrip received many honors and awards. In 2000, he received the Bill France Award of Excellence for his lifetime achievements. In 2003, he was inducted into the national Motorsports Hall of Fame. In 2005, he was inducted into the International Motorsports Hall of Fame. In 2012, he was inducted into the NASCAR Hall of Fame. In February 2015, at the National Prayer Breakfast in Washington, D. C., he gave the keynote address and shared his personal testimony.

In 1987, Waltrip established the Motor Racing Outreach NASCAR ministry and continues to serve as chairman. In 2004, he wrote his autobiography, *DW: A Lifetime Going Around in Circles.*

Waltrip had a career record of eighty-four NASCAR wins. He is ranked among the top five all-time recordholders. His influence has spread fan beyond the racetracks into the media and entertainment areas of life. His Christian influence has also had an impact on others. He was able to move from one of the most hated drivers to one of the most popular drivers within an active career. His Kentucky roots enabled him to develop into the racing legend he is today.

Other Kentucky Innovators in Sports

Bill Arnsparger • *Paris* • Football Coach
Gay Brewer • *Lexington* • Pro Golfer
Steve Cauthen • *Covington* • Horse Racing jockey
Chris Collingsworth • *Fort Thomas* • Football, Announcer
Gregory Kaidanov • *Lexington* • Chess Grand Master
Mary T. Meagher • *Louisville* • Olympic Swimmer
Phil Simms • *Lebanon* • Football, Announcer

Chapter Eight

Others

Roy Bean
Mason County
Judge

He had the most unusual preparation for becoming an official judge. Throughout most of his life, he could not stay in one place very long because of murders, debts, or affairs. His judicial rulings were the source of legends in the Old West.

Phantly Roy Bean Jr. was born in 1825 in Mason County, Kentucky. He was the youngest of five children born to Phantly Roy Bean Sr. and Anna Henderson Gore Bean. The family lived in poverty, and the older children left home as early as they could. Bean Jr. was constantly in trouble at home and in the community as a child and youth. By the age of fifteen, he left Kentucky with an older brother.

They joined a wagon train going west to New Mexico and crossed the Rio Grande River, settling in Chihuahua, Mexico. The two brothers opened a trading post. Bean was a handsome young man and had great appeal with the women. Getting into a heated argument with a Scottish customer, Bean challenged him to a duel, which was illegal at that time. On horseback, Bean shot the Scotsman in the right arm, and on February 24, 1852, both men were arrested for illegal dueling. While in custody, Bean was visited by some of his female companions. One of them smuggled a knife into Bean's cell, which he used to dig a hole in the wall. He escaped and traveled to San Gabriel, California.

Another brother owned a saloon there, and Bean helped him in the operation. In November 1852, his brother was killed, and Bean took over the saloon. Before long, Bean killed a Mexican official in an argument over a woman. He was taken by the official's friends and lynched from a tree. The rope stretched and slipped. Bean, who had been left to die, was rescued by the woman, who had hidden nearby. He had a permanent rope burn and stiff neck for the rest of his life. He left and traveled to Mesilla, Dona County, New Mexico where his older brother now was sheriff. In 1861, the brothers operated a saloon and store in Pinos Altos, New Mexico. During the Civil War, Bean favored the Confederacy. He moved to San Antonio and smuggled supplies from British ships to the nearby troops. On October 28, 1866, he married eighteen-year-old Virginia Chavez. After the first year, Bean was arrested for aggravated assault on his wife. In spite of the stormy marriage, they would have four children. The family settled in a poor area near San Antonio that became known as Beanville.

Bean began operating a saloon that served the incoming railroad workers. He also was involved in trading stolen goods. In 1880, sensing an opportunity for greater profits, Bean sold his business and left his wife and children to go farther west to where over 8,000 railroads workers lived in a tent city. With the money he received from his sold business, he made some provision for care of his children and purchased supplies for his new business. By the spring of 1882, he had established himself in Vinegaroon, near the Pecos River. He built a small tent saloon. The area was over 200 miles from any law enforcement center. The growing illegal activities within the workers' community caught the attention of a Texas Ranger. He received permission to establish a justice of the peace for the community. Bean quickly offered his services. On August 2, 1882, Bean was appointed justice of the peace in the newly organized Precinct 6 in Pecos County.

Bean set up his court activities in his tent saloon. The bar patrons served as jury members and were expected to buy drinks during recesses. It was noted that his first official act as "judge" was to "shoot up the saloon shack of a Jewish competitor." His only source of official law was one book, an 1879 edition of the *Revised Statutes of Texas*. He ignored any later editions and resources. It is not clear how closely he followed this one source.

Some of his rulings were highly creative and sometimes made in desperation. Since there was no jail, penalties were usually made in the form of fines, usually what the person had in his possession. All fines went to directly Bean, not to any other authority. When an Irishman killed a

Chinese laborer and was charged with murder, Bean ruled "homicide was the killing of a human being; however, he could find no law against killing a Chinaman." The case was dismissed. When a corpse was discovered and the man had a concealed weapon on his body, Bean charged the dead man a twenty dollar fine for carrying a concealed weapon, ten dollars in court costs, and ten dollars in burial fees. That was all the man had on his person, and Bean took the forty dollars.

Bean advertised himself as "the only law west of the Pecos." He traveled at times by mule to investigate crime settings. When the railroad workers moved farther west, Bean decided to follow the camp. With business profits and growing law income, Bean set up a new saloon/court on the railroad right-of-way in a community he called Langtry. The saloon/court was named the Jersey Lilly. Bean had an imaginary love affair with a photo of British singer Lilly Langtry. With his finances secure, he sent for his wife and children to join him. Bean won re-election in 1884. After defeat in 1886, a new precinct was created, and Bean was appointed as justice of the peace. He continued winning elections until 1896.

He was becoming a well-known figure from the Old West and entertained notable train travelers, adding to his local popular image. He found time and resources to help the poor in his community, no doubt recalling his time living in poverty. On March 16, 1903, after a heavy night of drinking, Bean died in San Antonio. He was buried at the Whitehead Memorial Museum in Del Rio.

Judge Roy Bean became the subject of several motion pictures, television shows, and books. In 1965, an Official Texas Historical Marker was erected in Del Rio honoring his life. Although his reputation was built elsewhere, he began his life as a Kentuckian.

Daniel Boone

Boonesboro

U. S. Explorer

He was the greatest American frontiersman. He was a family man. He was captured by American Indians. He was cheated out of his property by a state, as well as by the federal government. He found his final peace and freedom in the early wilderness of Missouri, but he left his permanent mark on the state of Kentucky.

Daniel Boone was born in a log cabin on November 2, 1734, near Reading, Pennsylvania. His father, Squire Boone Sr., was a blacksmith and weaver. His mother, Sarah Morgan, had recently emigrated from England before meeting and marrying Squire Boone Sr. Boone was the sixth of eleven children born to the couple. He had little formal education, but he received a basic education from his Aunt Sarah. His life skill education came from his father, who acquainted him with surviving in the wilderness. Boone got his first rifle at the age of twelve and quickly developed successful hunting skills. Boone also learned wagoner skills from his father.

At age fifteen, Boone moved with his family to Rowan County, North Carolina. Eager to avoid large settlements and having an interest in exploring the wilderness, the Boones made numerous moves to new locations. Boone set up his own hunting business. With the encroaching French and Indian War in 1755, Boone joined with General Edward Braddock as a wagoner. He met a lifelong friend, John Finley, who shared tales of the great wilderness in Kentucky with Boone. While Braddock attempted to capture Fort Duquesne, the company was attacked by an ambush of French and Indians. Boone escaped on horseback.

On August 14, 1756, Boone married his Irish sweetheart, Rebecca Bryan. They settled in North Carolina and started a family resulting in ten children. Boone felt that he now had all that a man needed: "a good gun, a good horse, and a good wife." But ever the adventurer, Boone began a trek west to the mysterious wilderness of Kentucky.

In 1767, Boone, with several other adventurers, set out for Kentucky. He was the first to lead an expedition to explore Eastern Kentucky and found that the hunting met his expectations. Two years later, he was joined by his friend John Finley and two others to explore farther west in Kentucky. They cleared a 300-mile path through the Cumberland Gap that became the main highway for future travelers. Boone encountered Indians, having both friendly and hostile experiences.

He returned home and was hired by Richard Henderson and the Transylvania Company to lead a small group of settlers to colonize Kentucky. He reached the site of what became Boonesborough in April 1775. He returned home to bring his family to the new settlement. Forts were constructed for protection from the Indians who were unhappy with the uninvited neighbors. Boone was given the rank of major in the local militia. In July 1776, his daughter Jemima was captured by the Shawnee and Cherokee tribes. He was able to rescue her. Boone took the settlers' money to invest in speculative land permits but was robbed on his trip to make the purchases. The settlers were angry with him, and he promised to repay them. It would take many years, but he did keep his promise.

In 1778, Boone himself was captured by the Shawnee tribe. The chief adopted Boone as his son, and Boone was told of the tribe's plans to attack and destroy Boonesborough. Fearing for his family's welfare, Boone escaped and traveled alone 160 miles back to Boonesborough to warn the settlement. His family had returned to North Carolina, and the attack was successfully defended. Boone traveled to his family and returned with them to Kentucky in 1780. Boone became a lieutenant colonel of Fayette County, a legislative assistant and sheriff.

There were continued engagements with hostile Indians. In 1782, at the "Battle of Blue Licks," Boone's two sons fought along with him. One son was killed and the other seriously wounded. In 1786, Boone moved with his family to Maysville, Kentucky. He continued as an elected state legislator. In the state's survey of land ownership, Boone's lands were called into question. A court ruled against him, and much of Boone's land investments were lost. Angry at how the state had treated him as the early explorer and trailblazer, Boone left Kentucky.

In 1788, Boone and his family settled in what is now Point Pleasant, West Virginia. In 1789, he was appointed lieutenant colonel of Kanawha County and served as a legislative delegate in 1791. Growing dissatisfied with politics and the increasing number of neighbors, Boone was ready to head west once again.

In 1795, Boone and family moved to the Spanish territory that would become Missouri. The Spanish government appointed him commandant of the Femme Osage district along with a grant of 8,000 acres. He continued hunting and enjoyed the beauty and challenges of the new wilderness. The Spanish-held lands had been passed on to Napoleon in France. In 1803, the United States bought what was called the Louisiana Purchase. The territory of Missouri was now in federal hands and ownership. When land surveys were made, it was determined again that Boone had no legal claim to the lands granted to him by the Spanish. After an appeal was made, Boone was granted 850 acres.

In 1810, Boone returned briefly to Kentucky to pay off his outstanding debts to the early settlers of Boonesborough. He had received some income from books he wrote about his wilderness experiences. He was left with only fifty cents. He returned home and spent several years of peaceful life, enjoying hunting. In 1813, his wife, Rebecca, died. Boone would spend the rest of his life in his son's home in St. Charles, Missouri.

He died on September 26, 1820, at the age of eighty-six. He was buried next to his wife, west of Defiance, Missouri, on a hilltop overlooking the Missouri River. In 1845, Boone's family had the bodies exhumed for reburial in Frankfort, Kentucky, just a few miles from the fort of Boonesborough. Substantiated rumors abound that Boone was buried at his wife's feet and they dug up the grave next to her, leaving Boone still buried in Missouri.

Since his death, many books have been written about Daniel Boone. These have added to the myths and legends about the undisputed greatest woodsman in American history. He found his final peace and rest in the early wilderness of Missouri. He would leave an important mark on the history of the settlement of Kentucky.

Jim Bowie
Logan County
Military

Myths and legends have glorified the man from Kentucky who became identified as the Texas hero of the Alamo. Few legitimate sources provide an accurate paper trail of his life and experiences. While some parts of a legend carry some degree of truth, there is also much of his life not shared in those legends.

James "Jim" Bowie was born about April 10, 1796, in Logan County, Kentucky. He was the ninth of ten children born to Reason (Rezin) Bowie and Elve Ap-Catesby Jones (Johns) Bowie. His father was a successful livestock farmer and a slave owner. When Bowie was four years old, the family sold their Kentucky property and ventured west to the Spanish Missouri territory in what is now New Madrid. The next year, they moved again to Spanish Louisiana territory. After they pledged allegiance to the Spanish government, they eventually settled on purchasing 640 acres in Opelousas. The children helped with the farming responsibilities. They also received an informal education providing an adequate knowledge of writing and speaking English and Spanish. They also received education in survival skills, learning to hunt, fish, and use firearms and other weapons.

The plantation grew, and the family became the biggest slave owners in the area with twenty slaves. Bowie worked as a log floater, taking lumber to markets. He had grown into a strong young man with a reputation for skills in hunting and fishing. After the beginning of the War of 1812, Bowie and a brother joined a local military unit. On their way to New Orleans to join with Andrew Jackson's forces, the war ended and no action was seen. Bowie settled in Rapides Parish and resumed work floating lumber. He also began a quasi-legal business of slave trading. In 1818, he worked with the pirate Jean Lafitte in buying captured slaves and selling them at market for a profit. He and his brothers made over $65,000 and quit the slave trading business.

In 1825, the brothers bought the Acadia Plantation near Thibodaux, Terrebonne Parish. They raised livestock and grew sugar cane. They also later created the first steam mill in Louisiana to grind sugar cane. In 1827, Bowie had arguments with local officials that developed into a gunfight and eventually physical combat. Bowie effectively used a special knife to win the dispute, in what became known as the "Sandbar Fight." His reputation as a superior knife fighter spurred the popular description of his "Bowie knife." The best evidence of the knife's origin traces back to a blacksmith in Arkansas who fashioned it according to the instructions of Bowie or Bowie's older brother.

He became engaged to Cecelia Wells in Alexandria. She died on September 7, 1829, two weeks before their scheduled wedding. Bowie actually spent little time at their plantation, traveling to Arkansas and Mississippi and even to the East Coast. On February 12, 1831, the brothers sold their highly successful plantation with eighty-two slaves, as well as other land speculations, to Natchez investors for $90,000. Bowie had already left for Mexican Texas by 1830. In February of that year, Bowie took an oath of allegiance to Mexico, required for land buyers. He also was baptized into the Roman Catholic Church, another requirement for businessmen in the territory.

With ample funds, he traveled freely throughout the territory, gambling and at times accumulating debts. He settled in Saltillo, the state capital. As a citizen, he was able to purchase a land grant for 4,428 acres. He also persuaded more than a dozen other local citizens to make the same purchases and sell them to him. That practice would be outlawed three years later. He moved to San Antonio, then called Bextar, where he became connected with a prominent family, the Veramendis. The father was the vice governor of the province. On April 25, 1831, he married their daughter, Ursula. They would have two children. In spite of his boasted riches, the couple eventually lived in the residential palace with her parents.

Mexico, fearing U. S. expansion interest, began a series of discriminatory laws against American settlers, who were called Anglos. In 1832, the local commander required all residents to surrender their arms. Bowie served in part of an armed rebellion in the Battle of Nacogdoches that resulted in the Mexican forces being defeated. He then served as a delegate to the Convention of 1833, requesting statehood for Texas.

A few months later, a cholera epidemic swept through Texas. Bowie's wife and children died, and he suffered from a case of yellow fever. The loss of his family was devastating for Bowie, and he began a life of heavy drinking and was described as "careless in his dress."

In 1835, the Mexican authorities ordered the arrest of all Texans in the territory. The Texans began a call for war and large numbers of Mexican troops entered the Texas territory. The actual revolution began on October 2, 1835. Stephen F. Austin had formed a militia, the Texas Army, to counter the Mexican forces. Bowie was appointed as a colonel in the volunteer militia. Several battles ensued, with the outnumbered Texans holding their positions. After a victory in the Battle of Concepcion, one of Bowie's troops offered praise for their commander, "…as a born leader, never needlessly spending a bullet or imperiling a life, who repeatedly admonished.... 'Keep under cover boys, and reserve your fire; we haven't a man to spare.'"

On November 3, 1835, Texas declared itself an independent state. Having no official commission, Bowie enlisted in the army as a private. His request to create a volunteer militia did not receive command approval. Bowie played important roles in the military skirmishes with the Mexican forces. He received orders from General Sam Houston to go to San Antonio to evaluate the situation with the local fortification, known as the Alamo. He was given authority to destroy the fortification, preventing it from being used by the Mexicans who were en route. The local commander was Colonel James C. Neill.

On January 19, 1836, Bowie arrived with thirty men who joined the seventy-eight men already stationed. The men were poorly equipped for war, and requests were made for supplies. On February 3, Lieutenant William B. Travis, a past associate of Bowie's, soon arrived with thirty men. David Crockett arrived on February 8 with twelve men. O'Neill gave his command to Travis and left. Tension developed between

Travis and Bowie for leadership. A vote of the troops gave support for Bowie. After Bowie's drunken celebration, an agreement as worked out for Bowie to command the volunteers and for Travis to command the regulars.

On February 23, it was learned that Mexican troops totaling 1,500 were nearing San Antonio. The request of the Mexicans for surrender terms were refused by Bowie. The next day, Bowie contracted a disease "of a peculiar nature" and was confined to a cot. The problem most likely resulted from years of heavy drinking complicated by pneumonia or tuberculosis. Travis was placed in charge of all troops.

On March 6, 1836, with advanced warnings, the Mexicans attacked the Alamo before dawn. The overwhelming number of the Mexican forces captured the fortress and all 188 soldiers were killed. Bowie was shot while defending himself in his cot. After the battle, Santa Anna separated the bodies of Bowie, Travis, and Crockett from the corpses. The other soldiers were buried. The three leaders, out of respect, were burned on a funeral pyre. Sometime later, the remaining ashes were gathered and interred at the Cathedral of San Fernando.

The myths and legends of Jim Bowie grew and developed into heroic folklore. His life was featured in magazines, books, motion pictures, and television series. A city and county in Texas are named after him. Even though Bowie left memorable imprints in Louisiana and Texas, his life began in Kentucky.

Kit Carson

Madison County

U. S. Explorer

He was a frontiersman, soldier, Western guide, trapper, and Indian agent. Although born in Kentucky, his time later in Missouri was productive and instrumental in his career. He achieved national acclaim and was the subject of numerous magazine stories, books, and movies.

Christopher Houston "Kit" Carson was born on Christmas Eve 1809, in a log cabin in Madison County, Kentucky. He was born two months premature, which may have affected his physical growth. He was the sixth of ten children to Lindsey Carson and Rebecca Robinson Carson. His father was a soldier in the American Revolutionary War and a wilderness farmer. In 1810, the family moved west to Howard County, Missouri, and bought land from Daniel Boone's family in Boone's Lick, near the Missouri River. Young Carson would grow up in a community faced with the challenges of the frontier wilderness. He was able to play with friendly Native Indian children and learned to fear the hostile local Native Indians. He learned the skills of hunting and trapping from his father.

In 1818, when Carson was just nine years old, his father died when a burning branch fell on him. As one of the older children still at home, Carson assumed responsibility to try to provide for the family needs. He said, "I jumped to my rifle and threw down my spelling book." He never received a basic education and could neither read nor write. It was a cause of much embarrassment throughout his life.

Carson's mother remarried, and differences developed between Carson and his stepfather. In 1824, at the age of fourteen, Carson was apprenticed to a saddlemaker in the village of Franklin, Missouri. His other brothers had traveled on west, following the Santa Fe Trail through the Rocky Mountains. Sitting still, cutting leather, and mending harnesses were not exciting to Carson. Two years later, in August 1826, he ran away. As required by law, the saddlemaker had to publicly report the runaway apprentice. An advertisement was printed in the October 6, 1826 edition of the *Missouri Intelligencer,*

> Notice is hereby given to all persons, that Christopher Carson, a boy about 16 years old, small of his age, but thick-set; light hair, ran away from the subscriber, living in Franklin, Howard County, Missouri, to whom he had been bound to learn the saddler's trade, on or about the first of September last. All persons are notified not to harbor, support or assist said boy under penalty of law. One cent reward will be given to any person who will bring back said boy.

Carson had quickly fled far from Missouri. He joined with a caravan of merchants, Bent's wagon train, heading west to Santa Fe, New Mexico. He worked as a laborer, tending to the needs of the accompanying herds. He settled in Taos, New Mexico, which was a headquarters for fur-trapping expeditions throughout the area. Carson joined with them and learned valuable lessons in wilderness living. Carson was "five foot four and 135 pounds of solid muscle." He worked for the Ewing Young trappers traveling in Arizona and California. He also worked for Jim Bridger's Hudson Bay Company. In addition, he worked as a hunter for William Bent at Bent's Fort. He also lived among several Indian tribes. He was married twice to Indian women, one Arapahoe and the other Cheyenne. Neither marriage lasted, but they resulted in the birth of two daughters. Carson took a steamboat to St. Louis, Missouri, to take one of his daughters to a convent for schooling. In spite of his lack of formal education, he was a quick to learn and became fluent in Spanish, French, and several Indian languages. He had a working vocabulary of Apache, Arapahoe, Blackfoot, Cheyenne, Comanche, Crow, Navaho,

Paiute, Shoshone, and Ute. He also could communicate in the universal Indian Sign Language.

In 1842, on one of his trips back to St. Louis to visit his daughter, he met the explorer John C. Fremont. Fremont had come to the city looking for a guide on his mapping trip to the Wind River in Wyoming, in the Far West. Carson convinced Fremont of his knowledge of the land and his ability to translate languages that would be encountered. The two men would become good friends and business associates for the next several years. The first expedition took them through the southern pass of the Rocky Mountains. In 1843, the second expedition took them to the Great Salt Lake area in Utah and even farther west to Fort Vancouver in the Pacific Northwest. In 1845–46, another expedition led them to California and Oregon. Fremont made regular reports back to Washington, D.C., with glowing comments about Carson and his valuable wilderness skills. Carson became a popular national figure when the reports were printed for the American public. Ten thousand copies of Fremont's reports became the *Pioneer's Guide for the Oregon Trail.*

In 1843, Carson married his third wife, Maria Josefa Jaramillo, the daughter of a prominent Taos family. He purchased a home in Taos where his family lived while Carson continued his travels. They would eventually have eight children.

In 1846, skirmishes with the Mexican troops in the Southwest led to military combat. Carson was asked by Fremont to assist General Stephen W. Kearny in New Mexico. They engaged in battle against Mexican forces near San Pasqual, California. Kearny's troops were overwhelmed, and Carson, with two others, managed to escape from the surrounding forces. They traveled to find reinforcements and led them back to rescue Kearny's troops. They would win further battles in San Diego, San Gabriel, and Los Angeles. Carson's heroic efforts were reported to President James Polk, who appointed him lieutenant in the mounted rifle regiment. The appointment was later rejected by a defiant U. S. Senate.

In 1849, Carson returned to Taos and began life as a farmer and occasional scout for the military. Concerned about fair treatment for the Indians, Carson became an agent in the Office of Indian Affairs and later served as a superintendent of Indian Affairs for the Colorado Territory. He became most active in working for the Utes and the Jicarilla Apaches. He saw the encroaching white settlements' effect on the Indian population and advocated for the creation of reservations to protect the

Indian interests. In 1858, Dr. De Witt C. Peters wrote a book, *The Life and Adventure of Kit Carson, the Nestor of the Rocky Mountains*. This added to the popularity and legends about Carson.

In 1861, with the beginning of the Civil War, Carson left his position with Indian Affairs and was appointed a lieutenant colonel leading the First New Mexico Volunteer regiment. From 1861 to 1865, he fought invading Confederate soldiers, as well as rebelling Indian tribes. One of his assignments was to relocate the Navajos to Bosque Redondo, a reservation located near Fort Sumner, New Mexico, by "any means necessary." The tribe was forced to march 300 miles in a journey known as the Long Walk. It was a sorrowful experience, with hundreds of Navajos losing their lives.

In 1865, he was appointed as brigadier general of volunteers. He left the army in 1867. He returned home to Taos, hoping to expand his ranching enterprise. His wife, Josefa, died on April 23, 1868, from complications after giving birth to their eighth child. Devastated, Carson was taken to Fort Lyon, Colorado, where he died one month later on May 23, 1868, from an abdominal aortic aneurysm. Carson and his wife were eventually taken to Taos, New Mexico, for burial together in what became known as the Kit Carson Cemetery.

His house in Taos would become a museum. Carson's autobiography, *Kit Carson's Own Story*, was published in 1927. Carson City, the capital of Nevada, was named in his honor.

Kit Carson, although a famed frontiersman and trapper, was also an accomplished soldier. His kind nature is also acknowledged in his innovative concern with the welfare of Native Americans. His early life experiences in Daniel Boone's wilderness territory provided needed life skills. Kentucky can proudly claim his place of origin.

William J. Crowe Jr.

La Grange

Military

He played a significant role in reducing tensions during the cold war with Russia in the 1980s. He served his country with distinction in several U. S. wars. His diplomatic prowess helped in strengthening foreign alliances. He served several US presidents in both political parties. He achieved national and international respect from military leaders.

William James Crowe Jr. was born on January 2, 1925, in La Grange, Kentucky. His father, after having served in the U. S. Navy in World War I, became a lawyer with a "predictable routine" that his son found boring. At the beginning of the national Great Depression, the family moved to Oklahoma City, Oklahoma. Crowe attended Classen High School and then the University of Oklahoma.

Inspired by his father's military experiences and his own desire to travel and see the world, Crowe joined the U. S. Navy. In 1946, at the end of World War II, Crowe was admitted to an accelerated training program at the U. S. Naval Academy. He graduated in 1947.

Crowe began his active duty at sea aboard the USS *Carmick*. In 1948, he completed his submarine schooling and two years later qualified in operating diesel submarines. In the early 1950s, he served as flag lieutenant and aide to the Commander of the U. S. Atlantic Fleet Submarine

Force, located in New London, Connecticut. He was promoted to lieutenant in 1952. In 1954, he served as Assistant to the Naval Aide to President Dwight D. Eisenhower. That same year he married Shirley Grennell. They would have three children. He attended night classes at George Washington University. He took advantage of a full-time naval graduate program and, in 1956, received a master's degree in personnel administration.

After graduation, Crowe was assigned as Executive Officer of the USS *Wahoo* based in Honolulu, Hawaii. In 1958, he was promoted to lieutenant commander, serving as the personal aide to the Deputy Chief of Naval Operations for Plans, Policy and Operations. In 1960, he was given his first command on the USS *Trout*, the newest diesel submarine based in Charleston, South Carolina. In 1962, he was promoted to commander and selected to study as a graduate student in social sciences. In 1965, he received his master's and doctoral degrees from Princeton University.

Crowe returned to active submarine duty, serving as Chief of Staff to the Commander of the Submarine Squadron in San Diego, California. He was then promoted to Commander of Division 31, focusing on antisubmarine activities. In 1967, he was promoted to captain, and as part of the Plans and Policy Office, he became actively involved in the USS *Pueblo* capture in January 1968.

In 1970, at the age of forty-four, Crowe volunteered for service in Vietnam. He became the Senior Advisor to the Vietnamese Riverine Force in the Mekong Delta. In 1973, having returned to the U. S., he was promoted to rear admiral. He returned to the Pentagon and served in the Strategic Plans, Policy and Nuclear System Division. In June 1976, he took over command of the Middle East Force, based in Bahrain, in the Persian Gulf. The next year, he was promoted to vice admiral. In May 1980, he received his fourth star, and Admiral Crowe assumed the role of Commander in Chief of Allied Forces and Southern Europe and later as Commander in Chief of U. S. Naval Forces, Europe. In 1983, he was appointed as Commander in Chief of the Pacific Command. He caught the attention of President Ronald Reagan and Secretary of Defense Casper Weinberger.

On October 1, 1985, he became the eleventh Chairman of the Joint Chiefs of Staff. New legislative enactments gave him additional powers and control over the military services and direct advisor to the president.

Crowe faced some immediate national and international challenges. There was much inter-service rivalry that called for careful settlements and political considerations. Internationally, the country faced new challenges of terrorism and the height of the Cold War with the Soviet Union. Regarding terrorism, Palestinians hijacked ships, Americans were killed in airport attacks, and Libyan leader Muammar Qaddafi threatened control of international waterways. Crowe advised appropriate military responses, resulting in the massive attacks on Libya.

Crowe expressed strong disagreement with President Reagan on the 1986 limitations agreed to with Soviet leader Mikhail Gorbachev. Representing the thinking of the Joint Chiefs, Crowe expressed his concern that the proposal was "completely unacceptable" regarding U.S. security. After further executive discussions, the proposal was not completed. In 1987, Crowe initiated his own discussion with his Soviet counterpart to reduce the threat of an accidental nuclear war. Those discussions led to an official agreement signed by Reagan and Gorbachev that reduced the tensions of the ongoing Cold War. Much credit was given to Crowe for his actions.

After four years, Crowe decided against continuing in the role of Chairman of the Joint Chiefs. He retired on September 30, 1989, replaced by Army General Colin Powell. Crowe returned the University of Oklahoma and founded the William J. Crowe chair in geopolitics. In 1990, he was the first recipient of the Distinguished Sea Service Award of the Naval Order of the United States.

In the 1992 presidential race, he surprised everyone with his support of Bill Clinton. In 1993, he wrote his memoirs, *The Line of Fire: From Washington to the Gulf, the Politics and Battles of the New Military*. That year President Clinton appointed him chairman of the President's Foreign Intelligence Advisory Board. In 1994, he was appointed the U. S. Ambassador to the Court of St. James. He served there until 1997. He used his pleasant personality and good humor to represent well the U. S.'s interests.

Upon his return to the United States, he served as a corporate advisor and on several educational boards. He continued his teaching at several institutions, as well as political service advising responses to international terrorist activities. He received four Defense Distinguished Medals and other international awards. In 2000, he was awarded the Presidential Medal of Freedom. He continued to make political news in

2004, when he joined over twenty other military commanders declaring that President George W. Bush "did not understand the world and was unable to handle in either style or substance the responsibilities of global leadership."

Admiral James Crowe died of a heart condition on October 18, 2007, at Bethesda Naval Hospital in Maryland. He was eighty-two years old. His funeral service was held at the U. S. Naval Academy with Bill Clinton as speaker. He was buried in the U.S. Naval Academy Cemetery. He is the only deceased former Chairman of the Joint Chiefs not to be buried at Arlington National Cemetery.

In 2008, Crowe was honored with an established fellowship in his name at the University of Kentucky's Patterson School of Diplomacy and International Commerce. In 2009, the International Programs Center at the University of Oklahoma established the Admiral William J. Crowe Jr. Award. He was also awarded doctor of law (LL.D) honorary degrees from national and international universities. Although achieving his life accomplishments around the world, he would begin his journey in Kentucky.

Patty and Mildred Hill

Louisville

"Happy Birthday"

They created the third-most recognized song in the English language. They loved children but never married and had their own. They were acknowledged for their pioneering work in early childhood education. They did not live to see the true popularity or financial benefits of their simple song.

Mildred Jane Hill and Patty Smith Hill were two of the six children born to Reverend William Wallace and Martha Smith Hill. Mildred was born on June 27, 1859, in Louisville, Kentucky. Patty was born on March 27, 1868, in Anchorage, Kentucky. In 1861, their father became director of the Bellewood Female Academy in Anchorage, Kentucky. Their mother served as a teacher at the school. Both parents were committed to provide quality education for their children. Their mother broke social tradition by educating slave children.

Mildred developed an early interest in music. She studied music from her father and other tutors. She went on to study music in Louisville and Chicago. She became a composer, teacher, and performer. She had a special interest in what was called at that time "Negro Music." In 1896, she wrote a chapter entitled "History of Music in Louisville" as part of J. Stoddard Johnston's book *Memorial History of Louisville*.

Patty took a broader educational path to her career. In 1887, she was valedictorian of her class at the Louisville Collegiate Institute. She became a faculty member of Columbia University's Teacher College in

New York. She had a special interest in early childhood education. She was president of the National Education Association. She established and directed the Louisville Free Kindergarten Association. Both sisters were recognized at the Chicago World's Fair for their work in "progressive education programs."

Both sisters contributed to what would become the popular "Happy Birthday" song. It was originally "Good Morning, to You." It was used in the classroom for teachers to greet their students each morning. Mildred composed the simple melody, and Patty wrote the words. The song first appeared in an 1893 songbook, *Song Stories For The Kindergarten*. An optional third verse was added with the "Happy Birthday" lyrics. It was first published in 1922. The song grew in popularity and was used by many schools around the country.

Mildred died in Chicago, Illinois, on June 5, 1916. Patty died in New York City on May 25, 1946. Both sisters were buried in Cave Hill Cemetery in Louisville, Kentucky. They were posthumously inducted into the Songwriters Hall of Fame on June 12, 1996.

In 1935, the song was copyrighted under the Clayton F. Summy Company. The law at that time allowed the private use of the song, but any use in a public medium required paying a royalty of $1,500 to $5,000. The copyright was eventually sold to Warner Brothers. Both sisters' estates would later receive compensation, but the sisters did not see any of the financial benefits.

In 2013, a lawsuit was filed questioning the extended copyright. The song had been sung in 143 movies, numerous television shows and public ads and translated into eighteen languages. It brought in over $2,000,000 a year in revenue, part of which was used for a children's education organization requested earlier by the sisters. In September 2015, Judge George H. King ruled that the extended copyright was invalid and the song was to be considered in the public domain. A settlement was made in December 2015, with Warner Brothers returning over $14,000,000 to past payees of the royalties.

A Happy Birthday Park was created in Louisville, Kentucky, to honor the sisters for the song, as well as their innovative emphasis on the importance of early childhood education. A local bridge under consideration was named after them. Kentucky can be proud of the legacy of these two women and their international impact. The state would be recognized for this major contribution.

Charles Manson
Ashland
Criminal

Kentucky should be happy that at least one of its citizens left the state. Born into a rough family background, he became a skilled criminal, usually breaking federal laws and spending over half of his early years incarcerated. He would become infamous as the leader of a "family" that committed horrific crimes that caught the national attention.

Charles Milles Manson was born on November 12, 1934, in the General Hospital in Cincinnati, Ohio. His mother was an unmarried sixteen-year-old named Kathleen Maddox, who had a relationship with Colonel Walker Henderson Scott Sr. of Ashland, Kentucky. His birth record indicates his name as "no name Maddox." Several months before his birth, Kathleen married William Eugene Manson of West Virginia. The marriage was for the purpose of giving Charles a surname. His mother continued a wild life, going on extended drinking sprees with her brother, Luther. While William Manson held down a job in a dry-cleaning shop, Charles was often left with babysitters in West Virginia, Ohio, and Kentucky. The couple divorced on April 30, 1937.

In 1939, Kathleen, Luther, and his girlfriend, Julia Vickers, were arrested trying to rob a wealthy new acquaintance. All were sentenced to prison. Charles was placed in the home of an aunt and uncle in West

Virginia. His mother was paroled in 1942, and the eight-year-old son was happily reunited with her. For several years, they lived in hotel rooms while his mother continued drinking and living with so-called "uncles" many nights. The family moved to Charleston, West Virginia, where his mother's lifestyle continued. Manson began to develop his own lifestyle of truancy and petty crimes. By 1947, his mother unsuccessfully tried to place Manson in a foster home. The court intervened and placed him in the Gibault School for Boys in Terre Haute, Indiana. After ten months, receiving no help, Manson ran away and returned to his mother. Manson lived in a rented apartment and supported himself in Charleston through community burglaries. He was caught and sentenced to Boys Town in Omaha, Nebraska. In just a few days, he teamed up with another resident, stole a car and firearms, and traveled east across the country on a crime spree involving a series of armed robberies. At the age of thirteen, Manson was caught and sent to the Indiana Boys School. He faced physical abuse and, for defense, developed what he called his "insane game." He acted out convulsions and screaming to scare off any attackers.

In 1951, after several years of continued abuse, Manson, with two other residents, escaped the Boys Home and headed west in a stolen car, committing robberies along the way. They had now committed a federal offense, the Dyer Act, in driving a stolen car across state lines. He was sent to the National Training School for Boys in Washington, D. C. Manson underwent his first professional psychiatric examination. He was illiterate and declared antisocial, "quite unable to accept any kind of authoritative direction." But Charles had learned to "work" his doctors and persuaded them to recommend a transfer to the Natural Bridge Camp, a minimum-security institution. Just before a scheduled parole hearing in 1952, Manson raped an inmate at knifepoint. He was then transferred to the federal reformatory in Petersburg, Florida, where he continued to commit homosexual offenses. Transferred again to a maximum-security institution in Chillicothe, Ohio, Manson now adopted a period of good behavior, which led to his early release in May 1954. He moved in with his aunt and uncle in West Virginia.

In January 1955, he married Rosalie Jean Willis. Manson worked at various odd jobs to support his now-pregnant wife. In October, he moved his family to Los Angeles in a stolen car. After his eventual arrest and failing to appear at his hearing, he was sentenced to three years' imprisonment at Terminal Island, San Pedro, California. During that time, his son, Charles Manson Jr. was born. His wife would later live with another man, causing Manson to try to escape after stealing another car. He received five years' parole in September 1958, the same year the couple was divorced. Rosalie remarried and had custody of Charles Jr.

After a series of pimping for young prostitutes across state lines, he was arrested in Laredo, Texas, in violation of the Mann Act. He was returned to Los Angeles. After a period of court appeals, in June 1966, Manson was sent to the U. S. Penitentiary at McNeil Island, Washington. He became obsessed with music, motivated by the success of the Beatles. He wrote many songs and held to the possibility of being discovered and becoming famous. He was released in March 1967. He had spent over half of his thirty-two years in punitive institutions. He had requested to remain in prison as it had "become his home." His request was denied.

After his release, Manson moved to Los Angeles and then San Francisco. Over the next few years he developed a communal cult group of followers, known as the Manson Family. Mind control and widespread drug use allowed for Manson's domination of the group's behavior. This eventually led to the crime of the decade. On August 9, 1969, Manson directed a select team of followers to attack the home of actress Sharon Tate. She, her unborn child, and four friends were cruelly murdered. The next day another attack was made by a different team on the home of Leno and Rosemary LaBianca.

On April 22, 1971, a string of other crimes led to the arrest of Manson and the team of murderers. They were convicted of seven counts of first-degree murder in a sensationalized trial of national interest. California had abolished the death penalty, and life sentences were given with the possibility of parole. Mason used his time in prison to create more music and became a popular figure with the growing anti-establishment younger generation of the 1970s. He had various altercations in prison that led to his placement in the Pelican Bay State Prison.

He became a popular television star with recorded appearances on various talk shows. He also continued to violate prison rules. On November 19, 2017, he died in confinement after unsuccessful treatment for gastrointestinal bleeding. His cause of death was cardiac arrest and colon cancer. His remains and estate were declared the property of his grandson, Jason Freeman.

Charles Manson's directed murders in 1969 were considered by many historians as the final crisis of the 1960s. The decade had witnessed assassinations, murders, and international atrocities. His life continues to be a source of cult worship around the world. Kentucky is fortunate that that which was spawned in Kentucky never found roots.

Mary Towles Sasseen
Henderson
Mother's Day

She was the originator for the "Mother's Day" movement. Her love for education and children were characteristics of her generous and kind nature. Sadly, after marriage, she died in childbirth. Others would carry her crusade to fruition in a national observance of "Mother's Day."

Mary Towles Sasseen was born on March 5, 1860, in Henderson, Kentucky. Little is known of her early life, except her love for her mother. In September 1885, she began teaching at Center Street School in Henderson. During her third year of teaching, she was able to create a program celebrating motherhood. She chose to celebrate the day on April 20, her mother's birthday. She began a campaign to introduce the recognition-of-mothers program around the country.

In 1893, Sasseen published her thirty-two page *Mother's Day Celebration* pamphlet. In the pamphlet, she described the activity as follows: "By a Mother's Day, I mean a day on which parents shall be invited to the school and a programme presented, the recitations being on the subject of mother, the songs referring to home." She traveled extensively and spread her ideas at the educational meetings she attended. She was able to establish programs in New York, Ohio, Indiana, and Colorado. In 1899, she unsuccessfully sought political service as the Democratic nominee for Superintendent of Public Instruction in Kentucky.

In the early 1900s, Sasseen was forced to give up teaching because of poor health. She maintained her life's goal of getting Mother's Day recognized nationally beginning in Boston, Brooklyn, and Little Rock. On September 28, 1904, she married Judge William Marshall Wilson, from Pensacola, Florida. Two years later, in 1906, she would unfortunately die in childbirth. She was buried in the Henderson Cemetery.

In West Virginia on May 10, 1907, a woman by the name of Anna Marie Jarvis held a celebration at a local church to honor her own mother's memory and all other mothers. She announced plans to campaign for a national observance of mothers on the second Sunday in each May. After a long campaign that had gained interest, President Woodrow Wilson officially proclaimed the second Sunday in May as a national observance of Mother's Day in 1914.

To clarify the originator of the special day, the Kentucky legislature passed a resolution acknowledging Sasseen as the "originator of the idea of Mother's Day celebration" in 1926. In the Henderson Cemetery, a marker was erected by the county historical society. It is inscribed "Mary Towles Sasseen in 1887 founded Mother's Day."

Mary Towles Sasseen had an unselfish life goal that she never saw fulfilled nationally in her lifetime. Others would take up the campaign to bring her dream to fruition. But the idea of recognizing the importance of our mothers was begun in a quiet town of Kentucky.

Other Kentucky Innovators

Joseph Holt • *Breckinridge County* • Union Army General
Robert S. James • *Logan County* • Clergyman
Gene Robinson • *Lexington* • Gay Clergyman

Conclusion

It is important to have a combined, written record with historical documentation of the lives and contributions of these accomplished individuals. It is also important for current and future generations to find the motivation for becoming part of a future list of Kentucky innovators.

State leaders—political and educational—need to be aware of the necessary elements to continue to make Kentucky a state of fertile soil, able to produce more aspiring innovators. Our youth need examples that can challenge them to see their own potential in developing lives that can contribute to the benefit of all people. Our country needs the continued leadership that Kentucky has provided for the last two centuries.

Hopefully, more attention and resources can be given within the state to enable these innovators to develop new ideas to improve the state and her citizens. New innovations can help the state to prosper economically. New industries can start, grow, and create that productive atmosphere vital to a state's future.

Resources and References

Chapter One

George Clooney
Websites
imdb.com/name/nm0000123/bio
usatoday.com/story/life/2017/08/22/george-amal-clooney
wikipedia.org/wiki/George_Clooney
Photo Credit
https://www.facebook.com/WhiteHouse/photos/pcb.10155095309249238/10155095259989238/?type=3&theater#.

Johnny Depp
Books
Blitz, Michael and Krasniewicz, Louise. *Johnny Depp: A Biography*. Westport, CT; Greenwood Press, 2007.
Meilke, Denis. *Johnny Depp: A Kind of Illusion*. Richmond: Reynolds & Hearn, 2007.
Websites
celebritychest.info/10-facts-about-johnny-depp/
imdb.com/name/nm0000136/bio
rottentomatoes.com/celebrity/johnny_depp/
tmz.com/person/johnny-depp/
wikipedia.org/wiki/Johnny_Depp
Photo Credit
https://www.flickr.com/photos/sharongraphics/5581027450/

Irene Dunne
Books
Gehring, Wes D. *Irene Dunne: First Lady of Hollywood*. Lanham, MD: Scarecrow Press, 2006.
Websites
biography.com/people/Irene-dunne-38885#!
imdb.com/name.nm0002050/
meredy.com/irenedunne/
nytimes.com/1990/09/06/obituaries/irene-dunne
rottentomatoes.com/celebrity/Irene_dunne/
wikipedia.org/wiki/Irene_Dunne
wikiquote.org/Irene-Dunne
Photo Credit
https://taptaptappy-203.tumblr.com/post/164169054934/classic-hollywood-glam-irene-dunne

D. W. Griffith
Books
Barry, Iris and Bowser, Eileen. *D. W. Griffith: American Film Master*. New York: Garland, 1985.
Brown, Karl. *Adventures with D. W. Griffith*. New York: Da Capo Press, 1968.
Drew, William M. *D. W. Griffith's Intolerance: Its Genesis and Its Vision*. Jefferson, NJ: McFarland & Company, 1986.
Henderson, Robert M. *D. W. Griffith: His Life and Work*. New York: Oxford University Press, 1972. ISBN 019501541X
Schickel, Richard. *D. W. Griffith: An American Life*. New York: Simon and Schuster, 1984. ISBN 0671225960
Websites
imdb.com/name/nm0000428/bio
newworldencyclopedia.org/entry/D._W._Griffith

pbs.org/wnet/americanmasters/d-w-griffith-about-d-w-griffith/621/
sensesofcinema.com/2006/great-directors/griffith/
wikipedia.org/wiki/D._W._Griffith

Photo Credit

www.loc.gov

Florence Henderson

Websites

biography.com/people/Florence-henderson-9542153#!
imdb.com/name/nm0001341/
washingtonpost.com/local/obituaries/florence-henderson
wikipedia.org/wiki/Florence_Henderson

Photo Credit

https://commons.wikimedia.org/wiki/File:Carol_Brady.png

Ashley Judd

Books

Dickerson, James L. *Ashley Judd: Crying on the Inside.* Schrimer Trade Books, 2002.

Websites

contactmusic.com/Ashley-judd
imdb.com/name/nm0000171/
wikipedia/org/wiki/Ashley_Judd

Photo Credit

http://www.defenseimagery.mil; VIRIN: 090118-N-4794M-1216

Jennifer Lawrence

Websites

imdb.com/name/nm2225369/bio
jenniferlawrencefoundation.com/about/
jenniferlawrence.us/
wikipedia.org/wiki/Jennifer_Lawrence

Photo Credit

https://www.flickr.com/photos/nasahqphoto/26197229180/

Patricia Neal

Websites

biography.com/people/patricia-neal-39134#!
imdb.com/name/nm0623658/
nytimes.com/2010/08/09/movies/09neal.html
tcm.com/tcmdb/person/139424%7C121098/Patricia-Neal/
wikipedia/org/wiki/Patricia_Neal

Photo Credit

https://www.imdb.com/name/nm0623658/

Diane Sawyer

Websites

ans-wer.com/biography/diane-sawyer-biography.html
biography.com/people/diane-sawyer-9472787
britannica.com/biography/Diane-Sawyer
everipedia.org/wiki/Diane-Sayer/
hollyoodlife.com/diane-sawyer/
imdb.com/name/nm0768151/

Photo Credit

https://catalog.archives.gov/id/7268194

William Shatner

Books

Shatner, William. *Get A Life!* New York: Simon and Schuster, 1999.
Shatner, William and Fisher, David. *Up Till Now: The Autobiography*, New York: St. Martin's Press, 2008.
Shatner, William and Fisher, David. *Leonard: My Fifty-Year Friendship with a Remarkable Man.* New York: Thomas Dunne Books, St. Martin's Press, 2016.

Websites
biography.com/people/william-shatner-9480789
brainyquote.com/authors/william_shatner
tvguide.com/celebrities/william-shatner/bio/179280/
wikipedia.org/wiki/William_Shatner
Photo Credit
https://d26horl2n8pviu.cloudfront.net/link_data_pictures/images/000/274/718/shared_link/1200px-William_Shatner_by_Gage_Skidmore_2.jpg?1521717591

Chuck Woolery
Websites
allmusic.com/artist/chuck-woolery-mn0001266077/biography
everipedia.org/wiki/Chuck-Woolery/
imdb.com/name/nm0941103/bio
nndb.com/people/378/000022312/
tv.com/people/chuck-woolery/
tvbanter.net/2015/01/you-wanted-to-know-about-chuck-woolery.html
wikipedia.org/wiki/Chuck_Woolery
wikipicky.com/tv-celebrity/chuck-woolery-wiki-bio
Photo Credit
https://wikipicky.com/tv-celebrity/chuck-woolery-wiki-bio

Chapter Two

Rosemary Clooney
Books
Clooney, Rosemary. *This for Remembrance: the Autobiography of Rosemary Clooney, an Irish-American Singer*. Playboy Press, 1977.
Clooney, Rosemary. *Girl Singer: An Autobiography*. Doubleday, 1999.
Websites
biography.com/ people/rosemary-clooney-9251425
imdb.com/name/nm0167041/
notablebiographies.com/sup/Supplement-Ca-Fi/Clooney-Rosemary.html
rosemaryclooney.com/biography.html
thefamouspeople.com/profiles/rosemary-clooney-6518.php
who2.com/bio/rosemary-clooney/
wikipedia.org/wiki/Rosemary_Clooney
Photo Credit
https://en.wikipedia.org/wiki/File:Rosemary_Clooney_1954.jpg

Don and Phil Everly
Websites
allmusic.com/artists/phil-everly-mn0000847960/biography
biography.com/people/don-everly-21422445
cnn.com/2014/01/03/showbiz/singer-phil-everly-dies/index.html
imdb.com/name/nm0263616/bio
rollingstone.com/music/artists/the-everly-brothers/biography
en.wikipedia.org/wiki/The_Everly_Brothers
Photo Credit
https://commons.wikimedia.org/wiki/File:Everly_Brothers_1970.JPG

Red Foley
Books
Brown, Maxine. *Looking Back to See: A Country Music Memoir*. Fayetteville: University of Arkansas Press, 2005.
Websites
alancackett.com/red-foley-biography
imdb.com/name/nm0284215/bio
last.fm/music/Red+Foley
nndb.com/people/247/000051094/
wikipedia.org/wiki/Red-Foley
Photo Credit
https://commons.wikimedia.org/wiki/File:Red_Foley_Billboard_2.jpg

Lionel Hampton
<u>*Books*</u>
Jackson,Jeffrey H. *Music and History: Bridging the Disciplines.* University of Mississippi Press, 2005.
<u>*Websites*</u>
biography.com/people/lionel-hampton-9327170
blackthen.com/lionel-hampton/
britannica.com/biography/Lionel-Hampton
en.wikipedia.org/wiki/Lionel_Hampton
imdb.com/name/nm0359019/bio
nndb.com/people/764/000026686/
<u>*Photo Credit*</u>
https://en.wikipedia.org/wiki/Lionel_Hampton#/media/File:Lionel_Hampton_1948.jpg

Larnelle Harris
<u>*Websites*</u>
cbn.com/music/larnelle-harris
wikipedia.org/wiki/Larnelle_Harris
<u>*Photo Credit*</u>
https://en.wikipedia.org/wiki/File:Larnellelivesolo.jpg

Naomi Judd
<u>*Books*</u>
Judd, Naomi. *Love Can Build A Bridge.*
Judd, Naomi. *Naomi's Guide to Aging Gracefully: Facts, Myths and Good News for Boomers.*
<u>*Websites*</u>
abcnews.go.com/Entertainment/naomi-judd-story?id=43988719
biography.com/people/naomi-judd-16450335
imdb.com/name/nm0005072
usmagazine.com/celebrity-moms/news/20141311/
wikipedia.org/wiki/Naomi_Judd
<u>*Photo Credit*</u>
https://en.wikipedia.org/wiki/File:Naomi_Judd_AHA.jpg

Wynonna Judd
<u>*Books*</u>
Judd, Wynonna. *Coming Home to Myself.* 2005.
Judd, Wynonna. *Restless Heart.* 2011.
<u>*Websites*</u>
biography.com/people/wynonna-judd-17191536
en.wikipedia.org/wiki/Wynonna_Judd
imdb.com/name/nm1024568/
<u>*Photo Credit*</u>
https://en.wikipedia.org/wiki/File:Wynonna_Judd_in_Kansas.png

Loretta Lynn
<u>*Books*</u>
Lynn, Loretta. *Coal Miner's Daughter.* 1976.
Lynn, Loretta. *Still Woman Enough.* 2002.
Lynn, Loretta. *You're Cookin' It Country.* 2004.
<u>*Websites*</u>
allmusic.com/artist/Loretta-lynn-mn0000234325/biography
en.wikipedia.org/wiki/Loretta_Lynn
imdb.com/name/nm0528750/bio
littlethings.com/loretta-lynn-facts/
lorettalynn/com/bio
who2.com/bio/loretta-lynn/
<u>*Photo Credit*</u>
https://www.soundslikenashville.com/wp-content/uploads/2016/04/loretta-lynn_Loretta_Lynn-681x1024.jpg

Bill Monroe
Books
Smith, Richard D. *Can't You Hear Me Callin': The Life of Bill Monroe, Father of Bluegrass.* Hardcover: Little, Brown and Company, 2014.
Teachout, Terry. *Kentucky Trobadour: A Biography of Bill Monroe and The Bluegrass Music He Invented.* 2001.
Rosenberg, Neil V. and Wolfe, Charles K. *The Music of Bill Monroe.* University of Illinois Press. ISBN 9-252-03121-0
Websites
axs.com/10-best-bill-monroe-songs-56034
billmonroe.com/bill-monroe-bio
biography.com/people/bill-monroe-21369943
brainyquote.com/authors/bill_monroe
en.wikipedia.org/wiki/Bill_Monroe
imdb.com/name/nm05988463/
npr.org/2011/09/12/140366232/
Photo Credit
https://media.npr.org/assets/img/2011/09/12/billmonroe_wide-2bbe2769a88cb3f3e9aaf41aea77e79918563574-s1600-c85.webp

Dottie Rambo
Websites
britannica.com/biography/Dottie-Rambo
dottierambo.net/about
en.wikipedia.org/wiki/Dottie_Rambo
imdb.com/name/nm2157478/
legacy.com/obituaries/kentucky/obituary,aspx?pid=109586974
theguardian.com/music/2008/may/20/obituaries.usa
thoughtco.com/southern-gospel-legend-dottie-rambo-dies-709659
Photo Credit
https://www.learnreligions.com/southern-gospel-legend-dottie-rambo-dies-709659

Mary Travers
Websites
biography.com/people/mary-travers-485970
en.wikipedia.org/wiki/Mary_Travers
telegraph.co.uk/culture/music/worldfolkandjazz/6201272/Obituary-Mary-Travers-of-Peter-Paul-and-Mary.html
Photo Credit
https://commons.wikimedia.org/wiki/File:Peter_Paul_and_Mary_1970_Crop.JPG

Merle Travis
Websites
alancackett.com/merle-travis-biography
britannica.com/biography/Merle-Travis
en.wikipedia.org/eiki/Merle_Travis
imdb.com/name/nm0871419/bio
nndb.com/people/763/000047622/
Photo Credit
https://www.npr.org/2012/03/29/149560865/merle-travis-a-traditional-ballads-ever-loving-light

Chapter Three

John James Audubon
Books
Audubon, John James. *Audubon and His Journals, Volumes 1 and 2.* Charles Scribner and Sons, 1897.
---. *Selected Journals and Other Writings.* Penguin Nature Classics, 1996.
Blaugrund, Annette. *John James Audubon.* New York: Abrams, 1999.
Burroughs, John. *John James Audubon.* Woodstock, NY: Overlook Press, 1987.
Chancellor, John. *Audubon: A Biography.* New York: Viking Press, 1978.

Ford, Alice. *John James Audubon: A Biography*. New York: Abbeville Press, 1986.
Herrick, Francis Hobart. *Audubon the Naturalist: A History of his Life and Time*. New York: D. Appleton and Company, 1917.
Rhodes, Richard. *John James Audubon: The Making of an American*. New York: Alfred A. Knopf, 2004.
Streshinsky, Shirley. *Audubon: Life and Art in the American Wilderness*. New York: Villard Books, 1993.

Websites

audubon.org/content/john-james-audubon
biography.com/people/john-james-audubon-9192248
brainyquote.com/authors/john_james_audubon
en.wikipedia.org/wiki/John_James_Audubon
notablebiographies.com/An-Ba/Audubon-John-James.html
parks.ky.gov/parks/recreationparks/john-james/
pbs.org/net/americanmasters/john-james-audubon-drawn-from-nature/106/
newworldencyclopedia.org/entry/John_James_Audubonthefamouspeople.com/profiles/john-james-audubon-354.php

Photo Credit

http://www.whitehouseresearch.org/assetbank-whha/action/viewAsset?id=94

Ben M. Bogard

Books

Bogard, Ben. *Pillars of Orthodoxy*. Louisville, KY: Baptist Press, 1900.
Bogard, Ben and Jackson, Doss Nathan. *Evolution: Unscientific and UnScriptural*. 1926.
Pratt, J. Kristian. *The Father of Modern Landmarkism: The Life of Ben M. Bogard*. Mercer University Press, 2013

Websites

conservapdia.com/Ben_M._Bogard
encyclopediaofarkansas.net/encyclopedia/entry-detail.aspx?entryID=1593
enwikipedia.org.wiki/Ben_M._Bogard
everipedia.org/wiki/Ben_ M._Bogard
mupress.org/The-Father-of-Landmarkism-The-Life-of-Ben-M.-Bogard-P780.aspx
spokeo.com/Ben-Bogard/Famous-Missionary

Photo Credit

https://encyclopediaofarkansas.net/media/dr-benjamin-marcus-bogard-7311/

Edgar Cayce

Books

Cayce, Edgar Evans. *Edgar Cayce on Atlantis*. New York: Hawthorn, 1968. ISBN 0-312-96153-7
Cayce, Hugh Lynn. *The Outer Limits of Edgar Cayce's Power*, 2004.
Cerminara, Gina. *Many Mansions: The Edgar Cayce Story on Reincarnation*. Signet Books, 1950. ISBN 0-451-16817-8
Hartzell, Harmon. *Edgar Cayce: A Seer out of Season*. London: Aquarian Press, 1990.
Kirkpatrick, SidneyD.. *An American Prophet*. Riverhead Books, 2000. ISBN 1-57322-139-2
Kittler, Glenn D. *Edgar Cayce on the Dead Sea Scrolls*. Warner Books, 1970. ISBN 0-446-90035-4
Puryear, Herbert B. *The Edgar Cayce Primer: Discovering The Path to Self-Transformation*. New York: Bantam Books, 1982. ISBN 0-553-25278-X
Stearn, Jess. *The Sleeping Prophet*. Bantan Books, 1967. ISBN 0-553-26085-5
Surgue, Thomas. *There Is a River*. Virginia Beach, VA: A. R. E. Press, 1942. ISBN 0-8476-8001-0
Todeschi, Kevin. *Edgar Cayce on the Akashic Records*. 1968. ISBN 978-0-87604-401-8

Websites

edgarcayce.org/edgar-cayce/his-life/
en.wikipedia.org/wiki/Edgar_Cayce
in5d.com/top-10-edgar-cayce-predictions/
in5d.com/top-10-edgar-cayce-prophecies.html
near-death.com/paranormal/edgar-cayce.html

Photo Credit

https://en.wikipedia.org/wiki/Edgar_Cayce

Thomas D. Clark

Books

Clark, Thomas D. *The Beginning of the L & N.* 1933.
Clark, Thomas D. *A History of Kentucky.* New York: Prentice Hall, 1937.
Clark, Thomas D. *Kentucky, Land of Contrast.* New York: Harper & Row, 1968.

Websites

en.wikipedia.org/wiki/Thomas_D._Clark
explorekyhistory.gov/items/show/152
goodreads.com/author/show/70728.Thomas_D._Clark
historians.org/publications-and-directories/perspectives
nytimes.com/2005/06/30/us/thomas-clark-101-chronicler-of-the-history-dies.html
revolvy.com/topic/Thomas+D.+Clark

Photo Credit

https://www.historians.org/Images/Perspectives/October%202005/clark.jpg

Mordecai Ham

Websites

azquotes.com/author/44785-Mordecai_Ham
believersweb.org/view.cfm?ID=126
canecreekchurch.org/what-s-your-legacy/15-mordecai-ham
christianity.com/church/church-history/timeline/1801-1900/mordecai-ham-outspoken-evangelist-11630588.html
en.wikipedia.org/wiki/Mordecai_Ham
higherpraise.com/preachers/ham.html
sluiceboxedadventures.com/rearguard5_ham.html
tribune.org/mordecai-ham/

Photo Credit

https://www.sbcevangelist.org/images/MordacaiHam.jpg?width=200&height=auto&shrink=

Duncan Hines

Books

Hatchett, Louis. *Duncan Hines: The Man Behind the Cake Mix.* Macon, GA: Mercer University Press, 2001.

Websites

en.wikipedia.org/wiki/Duncan_Hines
npr.org/sections/thesalt/2017/03/26/520866833/duncan-hines-the-original-road-warrior-who-shaped-restaurant-history
slate.com/articles/arts/books/2014/05/louis_hatchett_s_biography_of_duncan_hines_reviewed.html
visitbgky.com/duncanhines/

Photo Credit

https://compote.slate.com/images/eb15aa75-a268-4801-9b91-60c6af34f26f.jpg?width=1600

Harlan Hubbard

Books

Berry, Wendell. *Harlan Hubbard: Life and Work.* Lexington, KY: University Press of Kentucky, 1990. ISBN 0-8131-1725-9
Hubbard, Harlan. *Shantyboat in the Bayous.* 1990.
Wallis, Don. *Harlan Hubbard and the River: A Visionary Life.* Yellow Springs, OH: OYO Press, 1989. ISBN)-9622336-0-9

Websites

en.ikipedia.org.com/story/news/local/ft-thomas/2016/08/29/hubbard-studio-listed-nationalhistoricregister/89563336
dcwi.com/hubbard/bio.html
en.wikipedia.prg/wiki/Harlan_Hubbard
passtheword.ky.gov (oral interviews with Harlan and Anna Hubbard)

Photo Credit

https://www.google.com/search?q=harlan+hubbard&client=firefox-b-1-d&source=lnms&tbm=isch&sa=X&ved=2ahUKEwjL0KGt487nAhXtT98KHZyzDvgQ_AUoAnoECBIQBA&biw=1405&bih=903#imgrc=kwGSSn4cKaNX9M

Robert Penn Warren
Books
Millichap, Joseph R. *Robert Penn Warren after Audubon: The Work of Aging and the Quest for Transcendence in His Later Poetry*. Louisiana State University Press, 2009. ISBN 978-0-8071-3456-6
Websites
cliffnotes.com/literature/a/all-the-kings-men/ikipe-penn-warren-biographt
en.wikipedia.org/wiki/Robert_Penn_Warren
goodreads.com/authors/show/3736.Robert_Penn_Warren
loc.gov/rr/program/bib/warren/
imdb.com/name/nm0913014/bio?ref_=nm_ov_bio_sm
poets.org/poetsorg/poet/Robert-penn-warren
Photo Credit
https://commons.wikimedia.org/wiki/File:Robert_Penn_Warren.jpg

Chapter Four

James Gilbert Baker
Websites
en.wikipedia.org/wiki/James_Gilbert_Baker
nap.edu/read/11912/chapter/3#7
aas.org/obituaries/james-gilbert-baker-1914-2005
Photo Credit
http://www.peterson.af.mil/hqafspc/history/baker.htm

Stephen Bishop
Books
Brucker, Roger. *Grand and Gloomy: Stephen Bishop at Mammoth Cave*. 2009
Lyons, Joey Medley. *Making Their Mark: The Signature of Slavery at Mommoth Cave.*
Mitchell, Elizabeth. *Journey to the Bottomless Pit: The Story of Stephen Bishop & Mammoth Cave*. 2004.
Websites
en.wikipedia.org/wiki/Stephen_Bishop_(cave_explorer)
kyforky.com/Stephen-bishop/
nps.gov/maca/learn/historyculture/black-history.html
rogerbrucker.com/ggp.html
uky.edu/kaae
Photo Credit
https://upload.wikimedia.org/wikipedia/commons/4/47/James_Gilbert_Baker.png

George Devol
Websites
en.wikipedia.org.com/biography/George-C-Devol
en.wikipedia.org/wiki/George_Devol
famousbirthdays.com/people/ikipe-devol.html
nytimes.com/2011/08/16/business/ikipe-devol-developer-of-robot=arm-dies-at-99.html
spectrum.ieee.org/automaton/industrial-robots/ikipe-devol-a-life-devoted-to-invention-and-robots
theatlantic.com/technology/archive/2011/08/unimate-the-story-of-george-devol-and-the-first-robotic-arm/243716/
washingtonpost.com/local/obituaries/ikipe-c-devol-9
Photo Credit
https://www.invent.org/inductees/george-devo

Larry Flynt
Books
Flynt. Larry and Ross, Kenneth. *An Unseemly Man: My Life as A Pornographer, Pundit and Social Outcast*, 1996. ISBN 0-7871-1143-0
Websites
celebritynetworth.com/richest-businessmen/ceos/larry-flynt-net-worth
en.wikipedia.org/wiki/Larry_Flynt
imdb.com/name/nm0283658/
nndb.com/people/415/000022349/

Photo Credit
https://en.wikipedia.org/wiki/File:Larry_Flynt_2009.jpg

Benjamin Holladay
Books
Clark, Arthur C. and Frederick, JV. *The Stagecoach King*. 1940.
Holladay, Alvis Milton. *The Holladay Family*. 1994.
Websites
en.wikipedia.org/wiki/Ben_Holladay
en.wikipedia.org/wiki/Overland_Trail
wyomingtalesand trails.com/stagelines.html
Photo Credit
https://en.wikipedia.org/wiki/File:Ben_Holladay,_City_Founder_(Beaverton,_Oregon_Historical_Photo_Gallery)_(233).jpg

G. Scott Hubbard
Websites
aa.stanford.edu/people/g-scott-hubbard
ca.wikipedia.org/wiki/G. Scott_Hubbard
commons.erau.edu/space-congress-bios-2016/26/
en.wikipedia.org/wiki/G._Scott_Hubbard
everipedia.org/wiki/G._Scott_Hubbard/
planetary.org/about/board-of-directorsscott-hubbard.html
profiles.stanford.edu/g-scott-hubbard
revolvy.com/man/index.php?s=G.%20Scott%20Hubbard&item_type=topic
speakerpedia.com/speakerts/g-scott-hubbard
wsj.com/articles/g-scott-hubbard-on-the-future-of-space-exploration-1404756170
Photo Credit
https://www.nasa.gov/centers/ames/images/content/73329main_hubbar.jpg

Casey Jones
Books
Jones, Massena F. *The Choo-Choo Stopped at Vaughan*. Quail Ridge Press.
Lee, Fred J. *Casey Jones*. Kingsport, Tennessee: Southern Publishers, 1939.
Websites
biography.com/people/casey-jones-9357038
en.wikipedia.org/wiki/Casey_Jones
taco.com/roots/caseyjones.html
time.com/3828342/casey-jones-wife/
Photo Credit
https://commons.wikimedia.org/wiki/File:Casey_Jones.jpg

William Lipscomb
Books
Hargattai, Istvan. *Candid Science III: More Conversations with Famous Scientists*. UK: Imperial College Press, 2003.
Websites
en.wikipedia.org/wiki/William_Lipscomb
improbable.com/2011/04/15/bill-lipscomb-is-gone
newsharvard.edu/gazette/story/2011/04/illiam-lipscomb-dies-at 91/
nobelprize.org/nobel_prizes/chemistry/laureates/1976/lipscomb-bio.html
nytimes.com/2011/04/16/us/16lipscomb.html
thefamouspeople.com/profiles/William-lipscomb-7532.php
Photo Credit
https://en.wikipedia.org/wiki/File:William_n_lipscomb_jr.jpg

Garrett Morgan
Books
Georiady, Nicholas P. *Garrett A. Morgan: American Negro Inventor*. Franklin Publishers, 1969
Haber, Louis. *Black Pioneers of Science and Invention*. Harcourt, Brace & World, 1970
Websites
biography.com/people/garrett-morgan-9414691

blackinventor.com/garrett-morgan/
black-inventor.com/Garrett-Morgan.asp
encyclopedia.com/people/history/historians-miscellaneous-biographies/garrett-morgan
en.wikipedia.org/wiki/Garrett_Morgan
history.com/this-day-in-history/garrett-morgan-patents-three traffic-signal
pbs.org/wgbh/theymadeamerica/whomade/morgan_hi.html
Photo Credit
https://en.wikipedia.org/wiki/File:Garrett_Morgan.gif

Thomas Hunt Morgan
Books
Allen, Garland E. *Thomas Hunt Morgan: The Man and His Science.* Princeton University Press, 1978. ISBN 0-691-08200-6
Kohler, Robert E. *Lords of the Fly: Drosophila Genetics and The Experimental Life.* University of Chicago Press, 1994. ISBN 0-226-45063-5
Shine, Ian B. and Wrobel, Sylvia. *Thomas Hunt Morgan: Pioneer of Genetics.* University Press of Kentucky, 1976. ISBN 0-8131-0095-X
Sturtevant, A. H. and Muller, H. J. and Bridges, C. B. *The Mechanism of Mendelian Heredity.* New York, 1914.
Websites
britannica.com/biography/Thomas-Hunt-Morgan
dnaftb.org/10/bio.html
encyclopedia.com/people/science-and-technology/genetics-and-genetic-engineering-biographies/thomas hunt-morgan
en.wikipedia.org/wiki/Thomas_Hunt_Morgan
famousscientists.org/Thomas-hunt-morgan
genomenewsnetwork.org/resources/timeline/1910_Morgan.php
nature.com/scitable/topicpage/Thomas-hunt-morgan-the-fruit-fly-scientist-6579789
nobelprize.org/nobel_prizes/medicine/laureates/1933/morgan bio-html
Other
Sturtevant, A. H. *Thomas Hunt Morgan, 1866-1945, A Biographical Memoir.* Washington, D. C.: National Academy of Sciences, 1959
Photo Credit
http://wwwihm.nlm.nih.gov/

Harlan Sanders
Books
Ozersky, Josh. *Colonel Sanders and the American Dream.* University of Texas Press, 2012. ISBN 978-0-292-74285-7
Pearce, John. *The Colonel.* 1982. ISBN 0-385-18122-1
Sanders, Harland. *The Incredible Colonel.* Illinois: Creation House, 1974. ISBN 978-0-88419-053-0
Websites
astrumpeople.com/colonel-harland-sanders-biography-inspring-history-of-kfc/
content.time.com/nation/article/0,8599,2019218,00.html
en.wikipedia.org/wiki/Colonel_Sanders
facebook.com/notes/jesus-is-coming-soon/colonel-harland-sanders
geni.com/people/Harland-David-Sanders-Colonel-Sanders-Sanders-/6000000008501379464
history.com/news/hungry-history/8-things-you-may-not-kno-about-the-real-colonel-sanders
imdb.com/name/nm0761571/
thebalance.com/colonel-sanders-bio-kentucky-fried-chicken-story-1350966
thefamouspeople.com/profiles/colonel-sanders-3728.php
theverge.com/2016/7/5/12096466/colonel-sanders-kfc-meme-life-story
Photo Credit
https://imagesvc.meredithcorp.io/v3/mm/image?url=https:%2F%2Fstatic.onecms.io%2Fwp-content%2Fuploads%2Fsites%2F6%2F2018%2F01%2Fgettyimages-72431338-2000.jpg

Philip A. Sharp
Websites
britannica.com/biography/Phillip-A-Sharp

en.wikipedia.org/wiki/Phillip_Allen_Sharp
ki.mit.edu/people/faculty/sharp
nobelprize.org/nobel_prizes/medicine/laureates/1993/sharp-bio.html
thefamouspeople.com/profiles/phillip-allen-sharp-7671.php

Photo Credit

https://upload.wikimedia.org/wikipedia/commons/thumb/e/e0/Phillip_Sharp_HD2007_with_Winthrop_Sears_Medal.jpg/440px-Phillip_Sharp_HD2007_with_Winthrop_Sears_Medal.jpg

Nathan Stubblefield

Books

Lochte, Bob. *Kentucky Farmer Invents Wireless Telephone! But Was It Radio? Facts and Folklore About Nathan Stubblefield*. 2001 ISBN 0-9712511-9-3

Websites

anomalyinfo.com/Stories/1892-1928-stubblefields-wireless
borderlandsciences.org/journal/vol/51/no3/Vassiltatos_on_Stubblefield_Earth_Energy.htm
earlyradioistory.us/1902ken.html
en.wikipedia.org/wiki/Nathan_Stubblefield
explorekyhistory.gov/items/show/489
rense.com/general96/stubble.html
wfmu.org/LCD/GreatDJ/Stubble.html

Photo Credit

http://en.wikipedia.org/wiki/Special:FilePath/Nathan_b_stubblefield.jpg

John T. Thompson

Websites

britannica.com/technology/Thompson-submachine-gun
en.wikipedia.org/wiki/John_T._Thompson
explorekyhistory.gov/items/show/540?tour=35%index=23
goordnance.army.mil/hof/1990/1992/thompson.html
nfatoys.com/tsmg/web/genthomp.html

Photo Credit

https://commons.wikimedia.org/wiki/File:JohnTaliaferroThompson.jpg

W. T. Young

Websites

archive.boston.com/news/globe/obituaries/articles/2004/01/26/wt_young_made_fortune_in_peanut_butter_thoroughbreds/
en.wikipedia.org/wiki/William_T._Young
horse-races.net/library/obit-young.html
libraries.uky.edu/WTYL

Other

Schmitz, David. "Overbrook Master," *The Blood-Horse*, January 24, 2004

Photo Credit

http://www.uky.edu/PR/News/Archives/2004/Jan2004/040113_wt_young_dies.htm

Chapter Five

Alben Barkley

Books

Barkley, Alben W. *That Reminds Me*. (autobiography) Garden City, NY: Doubleday, 1954.
Barkley, Jane. *I Married the Veep*. (memoir) New York City: Vanguard, 1958.
Libbey, James K. *Dear Alben: Mr. Barkley of Kentucky*. Lexington, KY: The University Press of Kentucky, 1979.

Websites

biography.com/people/alben-w-barley-9199285
bioguide.congress.gov/scripts/biodisplay.pl?index=B000145
britannica.com/biography/Alben—Barkley
conserapedia.com/Alben_Barkley
courier-journal.com/story/opinion/columnists/2016/04/28/comment-great-death-alben-barkley/83651798/
en.wikipedia.org/wiki/Alben_W._Barkley

famousbirthdays.com/people/alben-barkley.html
trumanlibrary.org/trivia/vicepres.html
Photo Credit
https://en.wikipedia.org/wiki/File:Alben_Barkley,_Vice-President.jpg

John Breckinridge
Books
Davis, William C. *Breckinridge: Statesman, Soldier, Symbol.* Lexington, KY: The University Press of Kentucky, 2010.
Eicher, John H. and Eicher, David J. *Civil War High Commands.* Stanford, CA: Stanford University Press, 2001.
Heck, Frank H. *Proud Kentuckian: John C. Breckinridge, 1821-1875.* Lexington, KY: The University Press of Kentucky, 1976.
Websites
britannica.com/biography/John-C-Breckinridge
levelandcivilarroundtable.com/articles/biography/breckinridge.html
en.wikipedia.org/wiki/John_C._Breckinridge
history.com/topics/john-c-breckinridge
neh.gov/humanities/2011/novemberdecember/feature/the-manwho-came-in-second
nndb.com/people/557/000050407/
Photo Credit
https://en.wikipedia.org/wiki/File:John_C_Breckinridge-04775-restored.jpg

A. B. "Happy" Chandler
Books
Chandler, Harry and Trimble, Vance H. *Heroes, Plain Folks, and Skunks: The Life and Times of Happy Chandler: An Autobiography.* Chicago: Bonus Books, 1989.
Harrison, Lowell H. and Klotter, James C. *A New History of Kentucky.* Lexington, KY: The University Press of Kentucky, 1997.
Mann, Arthur. *Baseball Confidential: Secret History of the War Among Chandler, Durocher, MacPhail, and Rickey.* New York: McKay, 1951.
Marshall, William. *Baseball's Pivotal Era: 1945-1951.* Lexington, KY: The University Press of Kentucky, 1999.
Websites
bioguide.congress.gov/scripts/biodisplay.pl?index=C000290
brettuminger.wordpress.com/2011/12/13/a-bchandlers-life/
britannica.com/biography/Happy-Chandler
en.wikipedia.org/wiki/Happy_Chandler
muse.jhu.edu/article/401836
nytimes.com/1991/06/16/obituaries/AB-happy-chandler-92-dies-led-baseball-during-integration.html
quotes-inspirational.com/by/happy-chandler/
sabr.org/node/33749
sportsecyclopedia.com/mib/comish/happy.html
Photo Credit
https://upload.wikimedia.org/wikipedia/commons/thumb/4/44/Happy_Chandler_-_Harris_and_Ewing_Crop.jpg/440px-Happy_Chandler_-_Harris_and_Ewing_Crop.jpg

Abraham Lincoln
Books
Bruns, Roger. *Abraham Lincoln.* New York: Chelsea House, 1986.
Flood, Charles Bracelen. *Lincoln at the Gates of History.* New York: Simon & Schuster, 2010.
Goodwin, Doris Kearns. *Team of Rivals.*
Donald, David Herbert. *Lincoln.* New York: Touchstone, 1995.
Jacobs, William Jay. *Lincoln.* New York: Scribner's, 1991.
Judson, Karen. *Abraham Lincoln.* New York: Enslow, 1998.
Miller, William Lee. *Lincoln's Virtues: An Ethical Biography.* New York: Alfred A. Knopf, 2002.
Oates, Stephen B. *With Malice Toward None: A Life of Abraham Lincoln.* New York: Harper Perennial, 1994.
Sandburg, Carl. *Abraham Lincoln: The Prairie Years and the War Years.* New York: Harcourt, Brace, 1954.
Vidal, Gore. *Lincoln.*

Websites

brainyquote.com/authors/us-presidents/abraham-lincoln
civilwar.org/learn/biographies/abraham-lincoln
history.com/topics/us-presidents/abraham-lincoln
historynet.com/abraham-lincoln
notablebiographies.com/Ki-Lo/Lincoln-Abraham.html

Photo Credit

https://upload.wikimedia.org/wikipedia/commons/thumb/a/ab/Abraham_Lincoln_O-77_matte_collodion_print.jpg/930px-Abraham_Lincoln_O-77_matte_collodion_print.jpg?20201120053800

Mary Todd Lincoln

Books

Baker, Jean H. *Mary Todd Lincoln: A Biography*. New York: W. W. Norton & Company, 1987. ISBN 033393024369

Clinton, Catherine. *Mrs. Lincoln: A Life*. New York: Harper Collins, 2010.

Donald, David Herbert. *Lincoln*. New York: Touchstone, 1995.

Emerson, Jason. *The Madness of Mary Lincoln*. Carbondale, Illinois: Southern Illinois University Press, 2007. ISBN 978-08093-2771-3

McDermott, Stacy Pratt. *Mary Lincoln: Southern Girl, Northern Woman*. New York: Routledge.

Packard, Jerold M. *The Lincolns in the White House: Four Years That Shattered a Family*. New York: St. Martin's Press, 2013. ISBN0312313020

Randall, Ruth Painter. *Mary Lincoln: Biography of a Marriage*. Little, Brown & Co., 1953.

Williams, Frank J. and Burkhimer, Michael. *The Mary Lincoln Enigma: Historians on America's Most Controversial First Lady*. Carbondale, IL: Southern Illinois University Press, 2012.

Websites

cnn.com/2016/07/06/health/mary-todd-lincoln-pernicious-anemia/index.html
en.wikipedia.org/wiki/Mary_Todd_Lincoln
firstladies.org/biographies/firstladies.aspx?biography=17
historynet.com/mary-todd-lincoln
thoughtco.com/mary-todd-lincoln-1773489

Photo Credit

https://www.loc.gov/item/2004664342/

Adlai Stevenson I

Books

Baker, Jean H. *The Stevensons: A Biography of an American Family*. New York City: W. W. Norton & Company, 1997. ISBN 978-039335981

Websites

en.wikipedia.org/wiki/Adlai_Stevenson_I
study.com/academy/lessons/vice-president-adlai-steveson-biography-facts-quotes.html
thefamouspeople.com/profiles/adlai-e-stevenson-3503.php

Photo Credit

https://upload.wikimedia.org/wikipedia/commons/thumb/5/57/Adlai_Stevenson_I_by_Saroney_c1892.jpg/440px-Adlai_Stevenson_I_by_Saroney_c1892.jpg

Zachary Taylor

Books

Bauer, K. Jack. *Zachary Taylor: Soldier, Planter, Statesman of the Old Southwest*. Baton Rouge. LA: Louisiana State University Press, 1985. ISBN 978-0-8071-1237-3

Dyer, Brainerd. *Zachary Taylor*. Baton Rouge. LA: Louisiana State University Press, 1946.

Hamilton, Holman. *Zachary Taylor: Soldier of the Republic (vol.1)*. Indianapolis, IN: Bobbs-Merrill Company, 1941.

---. *Zachary Taylor: Soldier in the White House (vol.2)*. Indianapolis, IN: Bobbs-Merrill Company, 1951.

McKinley, Silas B. and Bent, Silas. *Old Rough and Ready: The Life and Times of Zachary Taylor*. New York: Vanguard Press, 1946.

Websites

britannica.com/biography/Zachary-Taylor
en.wikipedia.org/wiki/Zachary_Taylor

history.com/topics/us-presidents/zachary-taylor
thefamouspeople.com/Zachary-taylor-154.php
thoughtco.com/Zachary-taylor-12th-president-the-united-states-105525
totallyhistory.com/zachary-taylor/
us-presidents.insidegov.com/l/33/Zachary-Taylor
whitehouse.gov/about-the-white-house/presidents/zachary-taylor/

Photo Credit

https://en.wikipedia.org/wiki/File:Zachary_Taylor_restored_and_cropped.jpg

Chapter Six

Louis Brandeis

Books

Brandeis, Louis. *Other People's Money and How the Bankers Use It*. New York: Stokes, 1914.
Dawson, Nelson L. *Brandeis and America*. Lexington, Kentucky: University Press of Kentucky, 1989.
Fraenkel, Osmond K. *The Curse of Bigness. Miscellaneous Papers of Louis Brandeis*. New York: The Viking Press, 1934.
Frankfurter, Felix. *Mr. Justice Brandeis*. New Haven: Yale University Press, 1932.
Freedman, Suzanne. *Louis Brandeis: The People's Justice*. Springfield, NJ: enslow, 1996.
Goldman, Solomon. *The Words of Justice Brandeis*. New York: Henry Schuman, 1953.
Mason, Thomas A. *Brandeis: A Free Man's Life*. Viking Press, 1946.
Strum, Philippa. *Louis D. Brandeis: Justice for the People*. Harvard University Press, 1984.
Urofsky, Melvin I. *Louis D. Brandeis and the Progressive Tradition*. 1981.
Urofsky, Melvin I. *Louis D. Brandeis: A Life*. New York: Pantheon, 2009. ISBN 0-375-42366-4

Websites

biography.com/people/louis-brandeis-39048
brainyquote.com/authors/louis_d_brandeis
brandeis.edu/legacyfund/bio.html
britannica.com/biography/Louis-Brandeis
en.wikipedia.org/wiki/Louis_Brandeis
en.wikiquote.org/wiki/Louis_Brandeis
notablebiographies.com/Br-Ca/Brandeis-Louis.html
npr.org/2016/06/07/481076322/

Photo Credit

https://upload.wikimedia.org/wikipedia/commons/thumb/a/a6/Brandeisl.jpg/440px-Brandeisl.jpg

Cassius Marcellus Clay

Books

Clay, Cassius Marcellus. *The Life, Memoirs, Writings, and Speeches of Cassius Marcellus Clay showing his Conduct in the Overthrow of American Slavery, the Salvation of the Union and the Restoration of the Autonomy of the States*. Cincinnati, OH: J. Fletcher Brennan & Co., 1886.
Ellison, Betty Boles. *A Man Seen But Once: Cassius Marcellus Clay*. AuthorHouse, 2005.
Kiel, Richard and Wallace, Pamela. *"Kentucky Lion": The True Story of Cassius Clay*. Morrison Mcnae Publishing, 2007.
McQueen, Keven. *Cassius M. Clay: Freedom's Champion*. Turner Publishing Company, 2001.
Richardson, H. Edward. *Cassius Marcellus Clay: Firebrand of Freedom*. Lexington, KY: University Press of Kentucky, 1976.
Robertson, James Rood. *A Kentuckian at the Court of the Tsars*. Berea, KY. 1976.

Websites

biography.com/people/cassius-marcellus-clay-9250370
britannica.com/biography/Cassius-Marcellus-Clay
en.wikipedia.org/wiki/Cassius_Marcellus_Clay_(politician)
madisonhistoryky.org/Cassius_Clay.php
nndb.com/people/817/000107496/
richardiel.com/clay.html

Photo Credit

https://en.wikipedia.org/wiki/File:Cassius_Marcellus_Clay.jpg

Henry Clay

<u>*Books*</u>

Baxter, Maurice G. *Henry Clay and the American System.* 1995.
Eaton, Clement. *Henry Clay and the Art of American Politics.* Boston, MA: Little, Brown and Company, 1957.
Heidler, David S. *Henry Clay: The Essential American.*
Hensley, Jerry. *Henry Clay: Compromise and Ambition.* Outskirts Press, 2013.
Mayo, Bernard. *Henry Clay, Spokeman of the West.* 1937.
Remini, Robert V. *Henry Clay: Statesman for the Union.* New York: W. W. Norton Co., 1991.
Unger, Harlow Giles. *Henry Clay: America's Greatest Statesman.* Da Capo, 2015.

<u>*Websites*</u>

bioguide.congress.gov/scripts/biodisplay.pl?index=C000482
britiannica.com/biography/Henry-Clay
en.wikipedia.org/wiki/Henry_Clay
history.com/topics/henry-clay
let.rug.nl/usa/biographies/henry-clay/
u-s-history.com/pages/h321.html

<u>*Photo Credit*</u>

https://upload.wikimedia.org/wikipedia/commons/thumb/c/c9/Henry_Clay_1848_restored.jpg/440px-Henry_Clay_1848_restored.jpg

Jefferson Davis

<u>*Books*</u>

Allen, Felicity. *Jefferson Davis: Unconquerable Heart.* Columbia: University of Missouri Press, 1999. ISBN 9780826212191
Ballard, Michael B. *A Long Shadow: Jefferson Davis and the Final Days of the Confederacy.* Jackson: University of Mississippi Press, 1986. ISBN 9780820319414
Cashin, Joan E. *First Lady of the Confederacy: Varina Davis's Civil War.* Belknap Press of Harvard University Press, 2006.
Collins, Donald E. *The Death and Resurrection of Jefferson Davis.* Lanham, MD: Roman & Littlefield Publishers, 2005. ISBN 9780742543041
Cooper, William J. *Jefferson Davis, American.* Knopf Doubleday Publishing Group, 2000. ISBN 978-0-3077-7264-0
Davis, Jefferson. *The Rise and Fall of the Confederate Government, Volumes 1 & 2.* New York: D. Appleton and Company, 1881.
Eaton, Clement. *Jefferson Davis.* New York: The Free Press, 1977.
Hattaway, Herman and Beringer, Richard E. *Jefferson Davis: Confederate President.* Lawrence: University of Kansas Press, 2001.
Patrick, Rembert W. *Jefferson Davis and His Cabinet.* Baton Rouge: Louisiana State University Press, 1944.
Potter, Robert. *Jefferson Davis: Confederate President.* Steck-Vaughn Company, 1994
Stoker, Hudson. *Jefferson Davis, Volumes I-III,* New York: Harcourt, Brace & Company, 1955, 1959, 1964.

<u>*Websites*</u>

biography.com/people/Jefferson-davis-9267899
britannica.com/biography/Jefferson-Davis
civilwarhome.com/divisbio.html
en.wikipedia.org/wiki/Jefferson_Davis
encyclopediavirginia.org/Davis_Jefferson_1808-1889
history.com/topics/American-civil-war/jefferson-davis
history.com/news/10-things-you-may-not-know-about-jefferson-davis
parks.ky.gov/parks/historicsites/Jefferson-davis

<u>*Photo Credit*</u>

https://upload.wikimedia.org/wikipedia/commons/thumb/1/10/President-Jefferson-Davis.jpg/440px-President-Jefferson-Davis.jpg

Alexander W. Doniphan

<u>*Books*</u>

Dawson III, Joseph G. *Doniphan's Epic March: The 1st Missouri Volunteers in the Mexican War.* Lawrence, KS: University of Kansas Press, 1999. ISBN 978-0-7006-0956-7
Hamele, Ottamar. *When Destiny Called: A Story of the Doniphan Expedition in the Mexican War.* San Antonio, TX: Naylor Co., 1948. [REF F553.6 Hi77]

Lanius, Roger D. *Alexander William Doniphan: Portrait of a Missouri Moderate.* Columbia, MO: University of Missouri Press, 1997. ISBN 978-0-8262-1132-3
Robinson, Jacob S. *A Journal of the Santa Fe Expedition under Colonel Doniphan.* Princeton: Princeton University Press, 1932. [REFF553.6 R563j IN CASE]

Websites
en.wikipedia.org/wiki/Alexander_William_Doniphan
explorekyhistory.gov/items/show/202
josephsmithpapers.org/person/alexander-william-doniphan
revolvy.com/main/index.php?s=Alexander%20Doniphan
shsmo.org/historicmissourians/name/d/doniphan

Photo Credit
https://www.josephsmithpapers.org/bc-jsp/content/jsp/images/content/library/images/450x600/per583---H2-page-282 59_Doniphan.jpg

John Marshall Harlan

Books
Beth, Loren P. *John Marshall Harlan: The Last Whig.* Lexington, KY: University Press of Kentucky, 1992. ISBN 0-8131-1778-X
Harlan, Malvina. *Some Memories of a Long Life, 1854-1911.* New York: Modern Library, 2002
Latham, Frank B. *The Great Dissenter: Supreme Court Justice John Marshall Harlan, 1833-1911.* New York: Cowles Book Company, 1970
Przbyszewski, Linda. *The Republic According to John Marshall Harlan.* Chapel Hill, NC: University of North Carolina Press. 1999. ISBN 0-8078-4789-5

Websites
biography.com/people/john-marshall-harlan-9328814
britannica.com/biography/John-Marshall-Harlan-United-States-jurist-1833-1911
en.wikipedia.org/wiki/John_Marshall_Harlan
explorkyhistory.gov/items/show/107
legal-dictionary.thefreedictionary.com/John+Marshall+Harlan
supremecourthistory.org/timeline_harlan_1877_1911.html

Photo Credit
https://upload.wikimedia.org/wikipedia/commons/thumb/0/0f/JudgeJMHarlan.jpg/440px-JudgeJMHarlan.jpg

Fred Vinson

Books
Pritchett, C. Herman. *Civil Liberties and the Vinson Court.* University of Chicago Press, 1969. ISBN 0-226-68443-1
St. Clair, James E. and Gugin, Linda C. *Chief Justice Fred M. Vinson of Kentucky: A Political Biography.* Lexington, KY: University Press of Kentucky, 2002. ISBN 978-0-8131-2247-2

Websites
biography.com/people/fred-vinson-40076
bioguide.congress.gov/scripts/biodisplay.pl?index=V000106
britannica.com/biography/Fred-M-Vinson
en.wikipedia.org/iki/Fred_M._Vinson
shapell.org/manuscript/Truman-supreme-court-justice-vinson

Photo Credit
www.loc.gov

Whitney Young Jr.

Books
Dickerson, Dennis. *Militant Mediator.* 1998.
Weiss, Nancy. *Whitney Young Jr. and the Struggle for Civil Rights.* 1989.
Young, Whitney. *To Be Equal.* 1964.
---. *Beyond Racism: Building an Open Society.* 1969.

Websites
biography.com/people/hitney-young-jr-9539757
blackhistorynow.com/whitney-m-young-jr/
brainyquote.com/authors/whitney_m_young
britannica.com/biography/Whitney_M-Young-Jr
en.wikipedia.org/wiki/Whitney_Young
nps.gov/nr/travel/civilrights/ky2.html

Photo Credit
http://www.jfklibrary.org/Asset+Tree/Asset+Viewers/Image+Asset+Viewer.htm?guid=%7B1315203C-E131-492F-AA50-CCB787FC06C8%7D&type=Image

Chapter Seven

Muhammad Ali
Books
Bingham, Howard and Wallace, Max. *Muhammad Ali's Greatest Fight: Cassius Clay vs. the United States of America.* 2000.
Brunt, Stephen. *Facing Ali.* The Lyon Press, 2002.
Dennis, Felix and Atyeo, Don. *Muhammad Ali, The Glory Years.* Miramax Books, 2003.
Hauser, Thomas. *Muhammad Ali: His Life and Times.* Open Road Integrated Media, 2012. ISBN 978-1-4532-4119-6
Websites
brainyquote.com/authors/muhammad_ali
celebritychest5.info/10-facts-about-muhammad-ali/
en.wikipedia.org/iki/Muhammad-Ali
imdb.com/name/nm0000738
nytimes.com/2016/06/04/sports/Muhammad-ali-dies.html
thoughtco.com/muhammad-ali-1779853?print
Photo Credit
www.loc.gov

Jim Bunning
Books
Bunning, James and Bernstein, Ralph. *The Story of Jim Bunning.* Philadelphia: J. B. Lippincott, 1965.
Dolson, Frank. *Jim Bunning, Baseball and Beyond.* Philadelphia: Temple University Press, 2000.
Websites
courier-journal.com/story/news/local/2017/05/27/jim-bunning
en.wikipedia.org/wiki/Jim_Bunning
espn.com/mlb/story/_/id/19478314/hall-of-fame-pitcher-dies-age-85
govtrack.us/congress/members/jim_bunning/3000014
politico.com/story/2017/05/27/jim-bunning-dies-121196
sabr.org/bioproj/person/bcacaa59
Photo Credit
http://bioguide.congress.gov/scripts/biodisplay.pl?index=B001066

Earle Combs
Websites
baseballhall.org/hall-of-famers/combs-earle
en.wikipedia.org/wiki/Earle_Combs
psacard.com/autobiographfacts/baseball/earle-combs/271/
thenationalpastimemuseum.com/article/earle-combs
sabr.org/bioproj/person/62bcbcbd
Photo Credit
www.wikipedia.org

Denny Crum
Websites
abcnews.go.com/Sports/story?id=99809&page=1
en.wikipedia.org/wiki/Denny_Crum
famousbirthdays.com/people/denny-crum.html
imdb.com/name/nm0190036/bio
Photo Credit
Billy Reed

Paul Hornung
Websites
bleachreport.com/

articles/1213659-nfl-and-the-least-deserving-player-in-the-football-hall-of-fame-is
encyclopedia.com/people/sports-and-games/sports-biographies/paul-hornung
en.wikipedia.org/Paul_Hornung
famousbirthdays.com/people/paul-hornung.html
imdb.com/name/nm0395223/
nytimes.com/2016/07/08/sports/football/paul-hornung-sues-the-helmet-maker-riddell-over-concussions.html
vipfaq.com/Paul%20Hornung.html

Photo Credit

https://upload.wikimedia.org/wikipedia/commons/3/36/1961_Topps_40_Paul_Hornung.jpg

Pee Wee Reese

Websites

baseball-almanac.com/deaths/pee_wee_reese_obituary.shtml
britannica.com/biography/Pee-Wee-Reese
cleveland.com/Livingston/index.ssf/2016/04/jackie_robinson_pee_wee_reese.html
en.wikipedia/org/wiki/Pee_Wee_Reese
famousbirthdays.com/pee-wee-reese.html
sabr.org/bioproj/person/68671329

Photo Credit

https://en.wikipedia.org/wiki/File:1954_Bowman_Pee_Wee_Reese.jpg

Darrell Waltrip

Websites

autoweek.com/article/nascar/boogity-man-nascar-legend-
beyondtheflag.com/2016/01/16/nascar-darrell-waltrip-retire-booth/
charlotteobserver.com/sports/spt-columns-blogs/scott-fowler/article152425684.html
en.wikipedia.org/wiki/Darrell_Waltrip
foxsports.com/presspass/bios/on-air/darrell-waltrip
imdb.com/name/nm1267353/bio
motorsports.nbcsports.com/2014/03/24/darrell-and-michael-mourn-death-of-middle-brother-booby/

Photo Credit

https://completely-kentucky.fandom.com/wiki/Darrell_Waltrip?file=Darrell_Waltrip.jpg

Chapter Eight

Roy Bean

Books

McDaniel, Ruel. *Vinegaroon: The Saga of Judge Roy Bean, "Law West of the Pecos".* Kingsport, TN: Southern Publishers, 1937.
Skiles, Jack. *Judge Roy Bean County.* Texas Tech University Press. ISBN 0-89672-369-0
Sonninchsen, C. L. *Roy Bean: The Law West of Pecos.* 1943. ISBN 0-8263-0846-5

Websites

en.wikipedia.org/wiki/Roy_Bean
history.com/this-day-in-history/judge-roy-bean-dies
imdb.com/title/tt068853/
legendsofamerica.com/law-roybean/
nndb.com/people/241/000174716/
texaspecostrail.com/plan-your-adventure/historic-sites-and-cities/judge-roy-bean-visitor-center

Photo Credit

http://texashillcountry.com/judge-roy-beans-life-death/

Daniel Boone

Books

Bakeless, John. *Daniel Boone.* 1939.
Draper, Lyman C. *The Life of Daniel Boone.* Mechanicsburg. PA: Stackpole Books, 1988.
Elliott, Lawrence. *The Long Hunter: A New Life of Daniel Boone.* 1976.
Faragher, John Mack. *The Life and Legend of an American Pioneer.* New York: Holt, 1992.
Mellberg, Robert William. *Missouri Proud.* Xlibris Corporation, 2007.
Thompson, Bernice. *Famous Missourians.* Carlton Press, Inc.: New York, NY, 1992.

Websites
biography.com/people/Daniel-boone-9219543?_escaped_fragment_=
danielboone.org/
greatriverroad.com/stcharles/boonehome.html
history.com/topics/daniel-boone
notablebiographies.com/Be-Br/Boone-Daniel.html
sccmo.org/1701/The-Historic-Daniel-Boone-Home
Photo Credit
https://commons.wikimedia.org/wiki/File:Unfinished_portrait_of_Daniel_Boone_by_Chester_Harding_1820.jpg

Jim Bowie
Books
Davis, William C. *Three Roads to the Alamo: The Lives and Fortunes of David Crockett, James Bowie, and William Barret Travis.* New York: HarperCollins, 1998. ISBN 0-06-017334-3
Groneman, Bill. *Eyewitnesses to the Alamo.* Plano, TX: Republic of Texas Press, 1996. ISBN 1-55622-502-4
Hopewell, Clifford. *James Bowie Texas Fighting Man: A Biography.* Austin, TX: Eakin Press, 1994. ISBN 0-89015-881-9
Websites
dailyhistory.org/The_Mysterious_Illness_of_Jim_Bowie:-How_Did_He_Contribute_to_His_Own_Decline%31
en.wikipedia.org/wiki/James_Bowie
forttumbleweed.net/jimbowie.html
thoughtco.com/biography-of-jim-bowie-2136241
thoughtco.com.facts-about-the-battle-of-the alamo-2136256?print
tshaonline.org/handbook/online/articles/fbo45
Photo Credit
http://www.tspb.state.tx.us/SPB/Gallery/HisArt/01.htm

Kit Carson
Books
Carson, Kit. *Kit Carson's Autobiography.* Chicago: R. R. Donnelly & Sons Co., 1935.
Carter, Harvey L. *Old Kit: The Historical Christopher Carson.* Norman: University of Oklahoma Press, 1968.
Ellis, Edward Sylvester. *The Life of Kit Carson.* Lake Wales, FL: Lost Classics Book Co., 1998.
Gliester, Jan, and Kathleen Thompson. *Kit Carson.* Milwaukee: Raintree Children's Books, 1987.
Reese, Alice Anna. *Show Me Famous Missourians.* Compass Flower Press, 2014.
Thompson, Bernice. *Famous Missourians.* Carlton Press, Inc.: New York, New York, 1992.
Websites
biography.com/people/kit-carson-9239728
browsebiography.com/bio-kit-carson.html
legendsofamerica.com/nm-kitcarson.html
notablebiographies.com/Ca-Ch/Carson-Kit.html
pbs.org/weta/thewest/people/a_c/carson.html
Photo Credit
https://commons.wikimedia.org/wiki/File:Kit_Carson_photograph_restored.jpg

William J. Crowe Jr.
Websites
en.wikipedia.org/wiki/William_J._Crowe
jcs.mil/About/The-Joint-Staff/Chairman/Admiral-William-James-Crowe-Jr/
nytimes.com/2007/10/19/ashington/19crowe1.html
usna.edu/Notables/cjc-staff/1947crowe.php
Other
Stillwell, Paul. "Oral History of Admiral William J. Crowe, Jr. U. S. Navy (Retired)." Washington, D. C.,: Naval Historical Foundation, 2009.
Photo Credit
www.defenseimagery.mil

Patti and Mildred Hill

Websites

allthatsinteresting.com/happy-birthday-song-legal-history
courier-journal.com/story/news/history/river-city-retro/2015/02/27/celebrating-history-meet-hill-sisters/24143533/
en.wikipedia.org/wiki/Mildred_J._Hill
en.wikipedia.org/wiki/Patty_Hill
famouspeople.com/cat-patty-hill
musicrogirl.wordpress.com/tag/patty-hill-and-mildred-hill
songfacts.com/detail.php?id=3302
usatoday.com/story/news/nation/2013/06/29/who-wrote-the-happy-birthday-song-/2475837/

Photo Credit

https://musicrowgirl.files.wordpress.com/2015/09/29913742001_2498383756001_video-still-for-video-2496027113001.jpg

Charles Manson

Books

Atkins, Susan and Slosser, Bob. *Child of Satan, Child of God.* Plainfield, NJ: Logos International, 1977. ISBN 0-88270-276-9
Bugilosi, Vincent and Gentry, Curt. *Helter Skelter- The True Story of the Manson Murders.* W. W. Norton & Company, 1994.
Emmons, Nuel. *Manson in His Own Words.* New York: Grove Press, 1988. ISBN 0-8021-3024-0
Guinn, Jeff and Kenner, Roy. *Manson: The Unholy Trail of Charlie and the Family.* Amok Books, 2000. ISBN 1-878923-13-7
Udo, Tommy. *Charles Manson: Music, Mayhem, Murder.* Sanctuary Records, 2002. ISBN 1-86074-388-9
Watkins, Paul and Solodad, Guillermo. *My Life With Charles Manson.* Bantam, 1979. ISBN 0-553-12788-8

Websites

en.wikipedia.org/wiki/Charles_Manson

Photo Credit

https://commons.wikimedia.org/wiki/File:Manson1968.jpg

Mary Towles Sasseen

Websites

hendersonkyhistory.com/MTSasseenBio.html
historyswomen.com/more-great-women/netta-mullin/
historyswomen.com/more-great-women/marysasseen.html
mclib.net/blogs/history/?tag=mary-towles-sasseen

Photo Credit

http://hendersonkyhistory.com/MaryTowlesSasseenWilson2.jpg

About the Author

Paul William Bass was born in Independence, Missouri. He graduated from William Chrisman High School, Southwest Baptist College and Midwestern Baptist Theological Seminary. He married Jan Smashey in 1969. He served in full-time church staff positions for nineteen years in Arkansas, Alabama, and Missouri. In 1990-2007, he served at Ouachita Baptist University in Arkadelphia, Arkansas, as director of student activities and held various adjunct teaching positions. He became the intercollegiate debate coach with OBU debaters, winning three national championships. He took early retirement in 2007 and, in that year, received the Isocrates Distinguished Debate Coach Award from the International Public Debate Association. During his time in Arkansas, he served in several interim pastor positions and became a bivocational pastor at Anchor Baptist Church for twelve years.

He began his writing career in 2007 with publication of *No Little Dreams: Henry Garland Bennett, Educator and Statesman*. He received the **Henry Bennett Distinguished Fellow Award from Oklahoma State University**. In 2008, his second book in the Bennett trilogy, *Fellow Dreamers: Oklahoma, Education and the World* was published. The third book in the Bennett trilogy, *Touching the Dream: Point Four*, was published in 2009. That year he was commissioned by Oklahoma State University to write a history of their School of International Studies, entitled *Legacy, Leadership and Learning*. In 2011, he published two religious works from his pastoral experience, *In Jesus' Names* and *Minor Characters of the Bible*. In 2012, he published *Robert S. Kerr: Oklahoma's Pioneer King*. For the Kerr book, he received the **2013 Missouri Writer's Guild First Place President's Award and the 2013 Walter Williams Major Work Award**. In 2013, he published *Grace through Tolerance*. In 2014, he completed the autobiographical work *Me and Church*.

In 2015, a four-year project was published as *The History of Fort Leonard Wood, Missouri*. In May 2017, the Missouri Writers Guild awarded *The History of Fort Leonard Wood, Missouri* the **2017 First Prize Walter Williams Major Work Award**. That same year his commissioned work from Oklahoma State University, *Legacy, Leadership and Learning*, was published.

Published in the fall of 2017 was the *Pioneer Churches in Springfield, Missouri*. All profits and royalties are given to a local women's shelter and food bank. In May 2018, the Missouri Writers Guild awarded *Pioneer Churches in Springfield, Missouri* the **2018 Third Prize Walter Williams Major Work Award**. His next book was *Missouri Innovators*. It was published in the fall of 2018.

The Springfield Writer's Guild awarded the **2019** and **2020 Writer of the Year.** In 2020, he co-authored with Dr. Bob Perry, *Me and Fundamentalists*. In 2022, he co-edited with Dr. Mike Haynes, *United on Mission: The 150-Year Story of Greene County Baptist Association*. He authored the *Missouri's U.S. Senators* and *Missouri's Governors*. In addition, he authored *Called and Chosen: The History of University Heights Baptist Church, Springfield, Missouri*.

Paul and his wife, Jan, are retired and living in Willard, Missouri. His email address is bassp@obu.edu.

Index

N

O

T